"What could be more intimidating than
From Martin Luther to John Wesley, sch
its meaning for centuries. If you are looki
centered commentary on the book of I
Dr. Tony Merida has given pastors, teach   , ... a deep yet
accessible and practical introduction to the Book of Romans. I highly
recommend it!"
Dr. Winfield Bevins, Director of Church Planting, Asbury Seminary

"Tony Merida's Romans commentary is written by and for pastors who
want to preach the text with passion, insight, wisdom, and effect. He
takes you through what Paul meant and what it means for us today. This
volume is sure to be a hit with preachers who want an elder brother to
help them with their sermon prep."
Rev. Dr. Michael F. Bird, academic dean at Ridley College in
Melbourne, Australia

"No one masters the book of Romans. The book of Romans must master
us. With this spirit, Merida has written an exegetical study of Romans
that is informed and insightful, yet accessible. But, most of all, it invites
us to receive the gospel with joy that our lives may be transformed and
empowered by it."
Amber Bowen, PhD candidate, University of Aberdeen

"Tony Merida has written an excellent resource for the expositor, Bible
study leader, or the more in-depth learner. In a book full of illustrations
and loaded with practical application, Merida gives us fresh and precise
insight into the timeless letter to the Romans."
Dr. Matt Carter, lead pastor, Sagemont Church

"Tony Merida has written an exegetically careful, gospel-centered,
Spirit-illumined, Jesus-honoring commentary on Romans that will help
pastors, professors, and lay persons alike read not only this Pauline letter but the whole Bible in a more Christ-centered way. I highly recommend it!"
Matthew Y. Emerson, dean, Hobbs College of Theology and Ministry

"Dr. Tony Merida approaches the book of Romans with the skill of a
scholar, the tenderness of a pastor, and the heart of a worshiper whose
heart is made happy by the gospel of Jesus. In a day when we need the

beauty of the gospel displayed for all the nations and the practical implications of our unity in Jesus expounded and embodied in the Church, I can't think of a more timely work. This commentary will be a blessing for the pastor who longs to bring the majestic message of Romans to his flock in a theologically rich yet deeply practical way that will reach the lost and strengthen the believer."

Brian Key, pastor and residency director, Redeemer Fellowship; church residency and coaching coordinator, Grimké Seminary

"Tony Merida's *Romans* is a beautifully balanced commentary. While most commentaries are either technically sound yet unreadable, or readable with very little to offer, Merida sacrifices neither content nor accessibility. Instead, in *Romans*, Merida offers all Christians—in the pews and in the pulpit—a commentary characterized by biblical and theological rigor alongside insightful application, all while keeping Jesus at the center. In sum, Merida's commentary reflects the brilliance of Paul's own epistle: clear theology that transforms our Christian life and moves us to worship."

J. Ryan Lister, professor of theology, Western Seminary

"Tony Merida has gifted the church with an invaluable scholastic work on the book Romans. Tony's pastoral experience flavors his exegetical work, providing a theologically deep commentary that is both academic and accessible. This fresh work is rich in biblical insights and practical explanations, equally suited for the pastor and the parishioner. Tony has added to the church's treasury of commentaries on Paul's letter to the Romans."

Dr. Doug Logan Jr., president of Grimké Seminary, and Associate Director of Acts 29

"Tony Merida cares about the Bible and preaching; he cares about people and the church. This latest volume in the Christ-Centered exposition series is yet another illustration of that as Tony takes us through Romans with his eye on the big picture of the central truths of the gospel and how they build community and unity and how they motivate and mobilize us for mission. This volume will be a sure guide for preachers in their preparation and a nourishing resource for lay-people who wish to go a bit deeper. Warmly recommended."

Phillip Moore, associate director for Acts 29 & Network Director for Europe

"As a women's Bible teacher, I am grateful for this truly helpful addition to my library. This commentary allows us to mine the depths of Romans, not only for our information but also our transformation. Christ-exaltation is on every page, as Tony Merida guides us through both deep theology and everyday application. I love having a resource that I know will equip and edify readers from the pew to the pulpit!"

Jen Oshman, author of *Enough About Me*

"Romans is a big and confusing book. But it is also one of Paul's most important letters. Merida cuts through the debates and shows us the beauty of the gospel, the righteousness of God, and the centrality of Christ. This is an ideal book for pastors, small-group leaders, and student ministers. God has been, and will be, faithful to his people. Romans is not simply to be debated but let loose to change lives."

Patrick Schreiner, associate professor of New Testament and Biblical Theology, Midwestern Baptist Theological Seminary

"Tony Merida's exposition of Romans is faithful to Paul's message in the first century, but it also communicates powerfully to readers today. We are reminded by this clear and accessible commentary that the gospel is still the power that leads to salvation, and that we need to, as Luther taught us, relearn the gospel daily. Pastors, students, and all who study Romans will learn and be encouraged by this work."

Tom Schreiner, professor of New Testament Interpretation, Southern Baptist Theological Seminary

"This commentary on Romans is classic Tony Merida: a theologically rich, pastorally sensitive, and clearly communicated exposition of Scripture. This volume from Merida adds yet another excellent resource to the CCEC series."

Brandon D. Smith, assistant professor of theology and New Testament, Cedarville University

CHRIST-CENTERED

Exposition

NT / COMMENTARY FEATURING

AUTHOR Tony Merida
SERIES EDITORS David Platt, Daniel L. Akin, and Tony Merida

CHRIST-CENTERED
Exposition

EXALTING JESUS IN

ROMANS

REFERENCE
NASHVILLE, TENNESSEE

SERIES DEDICATION

Dedicated to Adrian Rogers and John Piper. They have taught us to love the gospel of Jesus Christ, to preach the Bible as the inerrant Word of God, to pastor the church for which our Savior died, and to have a passion to see all nations gladly worship the Lamb.

—David Platt, Tony Merida, and Danny Akin
March 2013

AUTHOR'S DEDICATION

To Kimberly, my beloved bride and wonderful mother of our five children: I could never thank God enough for giving me such a companion, friend, lover, and partner in the gospel.

TABLE OF CONTENTS

Romans

ACKNOWLEDGMENTS

To the elders of Imago Dei Church: it is one of the greatest privileges of my life to serve alongside you. Thank you for your faithfulness in ministry and your encouragement to me. I am also indebted to the saints at IDC whose hunger for Scripture makes the hard work of sermon preparation a joy.

SERIES INTRODUCTION

Augustine said, "Where Scripture speaks, God speaks." The editors of the Christ-Centered Exposition Commentary series believe that where God speaks, the pastor must speak. God speaks through His written Word. We must speak from that Word. We believe the Bible is God breathed, authoritative, inerrant, sufficient, understandable, necessary, and timeless. We also affirm that the Bible is a Christ-centered book; that is, it contains a unified story of redemptive history of which Jesus is the hero. Because of this Christ-centered trajectory that runs from Genesis 1 through Revelation 22, we believe the Bible has a corresponding global-missions thrust. From beginning to end, we see God's mission as one of making worshipers of Christ from every tribe and tongue worked out through this redemptive drama in Scripture. To that end we must preach the Word.

In addition to these distinct convictions, the Christ-Centered Exposition Commentary series has some distinguishing characteristics. First, this series seeks to display exegetical accuracy. What the Bible says is what we want to say. While not every volume in the series will be a verse-by-verse commentary, we nevertheless desire to handle the text carefully and explain it rightly. Those who teach and preach bear the heavy responsibility of saying what God has said in His Word and declaring what God has done in Christ. We desire to handle God's Word faithfully, knowing that we must give an account for how we have fulfilled this holy calling (Jas 3:1).

Second, the Christ-Centered Exposition Commentary series has pastors in view. While we hope others will read this series, such as parents, teachers, small-group leaders, and student ministers, we desire to provide a commentary busy pastors will use for weekly preparation of biblically faithful and gospel-saturated sermons. This series is not academic in nature. Our aim is to present a readable and pastoral style of commentaries. We believe this aim will serve the church of the Lord Jesus Christ.

Third, we want the Christ-Centered Exposition Commentary series to be known for the inclusion of helpful illustrations and theologically driven applications. Many commentaries offer no help in illustrations, and few offer any kind of help in application. Often those that do offer illustrative material and application unfortunately give little serious attention to the text. While giving ourselves primarily to explanation, we also hope to serve readers by providing inspiring and illuminating illustrations coupled with timely and timeless application.

Finally, as the name suggests, the editors seek to exalt Jesus from every book of the Bible. In saying this, we are not commending wild allegory or fanciful typology. We certainly believe we must be constrained to the meaning intended by the divine Author himself, the Holy Spirit of God. However, we also believe the Bible has a messianic focus, and our hope is that the individual authors will exalt Christ from particular texts. Luke 24:25-27,44-47 and John 5:39,46 inform both our hermeneutics and our homiletics. Not every author will do this the same way or have the same degree of Christ-centered emphasis. That is fine with us. We believe faithful exposition that is Christ centered is not monolithic. We do believe, however, that we must read the whole Bible as Christian Scripture. Therefore, our aim is both to honor the historical particularity of each biblical passage and to highlight its intrinsic connection to the Redeemer.

The editors are indebted to the contributors of each volume. The reader will detect a unique style from each writer, and we celebrate these unique gifts and traits. While distinctive in their approaches, the authors share a common characteristic in that they are pastoral theologians. They love the church, and they regularly preach and teach God's Word to God's people. Further, many of these contributors are younger voices. We think these new, fresh voices can serve the church well, especially among a rising generation that has the task of proclaiming the Word of Christ and the Christ of the Word to the lost world.

We hope and pray this series will serve the body of Christ well in these ways until our Savior returns in glory. If it does, we will have succeeded in our assignment.

David Platt
Daniel L. Akin
Tony Merida
Series Editors
February 2013

Romans

Introduction to Romans

When people read, study, and hear the book of Romans, big things happen.

Soon after surrendering my life to Jesus Christ while in college, I participated in a Bible study on Romans. It set me on fire. I have since read many commentaries on this epistle, listened to a number of sermons on it, and recently preached through it at my local church. One could certainly spend years studying it. I told our church before our last sermon on it, "We are finishing this series today, but we are not finished with Romans." You never really finish Romans. I know it is not finished with me.

Many Christian leaders in church history trace their conversion back to Romans. The great North African church leader Aurelius Augustine of Hippo (354–430) traces his conversion back to an encounter with Romans 13. He left home at age sixteen, and his life was characterized by lust, immorality, and heretical philosophy. His mother, Monica, was a Christian, but Augustine was not. She prayed for him constantly. Eventually, when Augustine was almost thirty-two years old, the light of the gospel broke through to his heart. He describes his remarkable experience in *Confessions*:

> I flung myself down beneath a fig tree and gave way to the tears which now streamed from my eyes. . . . In my misery I kept crying, "How long shall I go on saying 'tomorrow, tomorrow'? Why not now? Why not make an end of my ugly sins at this moment?" . . . All at once I heard the singsong voice of a child in a nearby house. Whether it was the voice of a boy or a girl I cannot say, but again and again it repeated the refrain "Take it and read, take it and read." At this I looked up, thinking hard whether there was any kind of game in which children used to chant words like these, but I could not remember ever hearing them before. I stemmed my flood of tears and stood up, telling myself that this could only be a divine command to open my book of Scripture and read the first passage on which my eyes should fall. . . . So I hurried

back to the place where Alypius was sitting . . . seized [the
book of Paul's epistles] and opened it, and in silence I read
the first passage on which my eyes fell: "Not in reveling and
drunkenness, not in lust and wantonness, not in quarrels and
rivalries. Rather, arm yourselves with the Lord Jesus Christ;
spend no more thought on nature and nature's appetites"
(Romans 13:13-14). I had no wish to read more and no
need to do so. For in an instant, as I came to the end of the
sentence, it was as though the light of confidence flooded
into my heart and all the darkness of doubt was dispelled.
(*Confessions*, 177–78)

Augustine was a new creation. He never turned back to his old life.

Years later Martin Luther, an eventual leader in the Protestant
Reformation, greatly wrestled with his guilt before God until he grasped
the meaning of Romans, particularly Romans 1:17. Earlier in his life
he said Romans 1:17 made him "hate God" because it speaks of God's
righteousness. Being perfectly righteous seemed like an impossible
demand. But when Luther discerned that there was a righteousness outside of himself—a righteousness that is received through faith in Christ,
not earned by religious works—everything changed. Luther said that
this passage opened the "gateway to paradise" for him. Luther's preaching, teaching, and writing changed the world as he showed others how
to enter the gateway to paradise. One such person was John Wesley, who
was apparently converted when hearing someone read Luther's preface
to his commentary on the book of Romans!

Big things happen when we understand Romans. These are but a
few testimonies. May the Lord's grace flood your heart as you read this
commentary, and may he use you as you teach the life-changing gospel.

I want to make two final introductory comments. First, my section
divisions basically reflect our sermon series at Imago Dei Church. I
often expound large passages of Scripture in my weekly preaching, and
it seems to me that studying the larger unit of thought is particularly
helpful in Romans in order to understand the flow of the arguments.
I also decided to keep it at twenty sections to make the commentary
more inviting to those who may be overly intimidated by Romans. Many
feel like Romans is too complicated to study and too difficult to preach
or teach. While it is challenging, I encourage you to dive in! I have
compressed it to try to make it inviting and to make it as close to a

semester-length study as I could. If you feel like you need a longer commentary, there are plenty out there.

Second, speaking of commentaries, I am indebted to some particular scholars. I hope I have adequately cited them. These scholars include Douglas Moo, Thomas Schreiner, Leon Morris, Michael Bird, David Peterson, F. F. Bruce, Robert Mounce, John Stott, Tim Keller, and John Piper. If you want more in-depth study of particular passages in Romans, I would direct you to their commentaries and expositions.

Tony Merida
January 1, 2020

The Gospel: The Power of God for Salvation

ROMANS 1:1-17

Main Idea: Paul magnifies the gospel, summarizing key aspects of it, expressing his eagerness to share it, and conveying his steadfast confidence in it.

I. **The Significance of Romans**
   A. Romans is a gospel-saturated letter.
   B. Romans is a community-building letter.
   C. Romans is a missional letter.
II. **A Summary of the Gospel (1:1-7)**
   A. The gospel is God's good news (1:1)
   B. . . . Promised in the Old Testament (1:2)
   C. . . . Centered on Jesus (1:3-4)
   D. . . . Designed to bring all peoples to the obedience of faith for the sake of Christ's name (1:5)
   E. . . . Transforming everyone who believes (1:6-7).
III. **A Servant of the Gospel (1:8-15)**
   A. Communion with God (1:8-10)
   B. Concern for the church (1:11-13)
   C. Commitment to preach to everyone (1:14-15)
IV. **A Steadfast Confidence in the Gospel (1:16-17)**

Paul wastes no time getting to his major theme: *the gospel*. He provides a gospel-drenched greeting and eventually arrives at his thesis in verses 16-17.

Paul's gospel focus not only prepares us for the content that follows, but it also inspires and instructs all of Christ's servants. It inspires us as we consider Paul's resolute confidence in the gospel, a confidence not weakened by the intimidating Roman Empire. We too must have an unwavering confidence in the gospel in order to make a missional impact in the world.

Paul's gospel focus is also instructive for our maturing believers. Remember, Paul is writing to Christians, yet he spends chapters unpacking the gospel. For Paul, the gospel is not just what tips a person into the kingdom, only to then leave them on their own to straighten up and fly right. Rather, the gospel shapes the very life of the believer and empowers the believer for service. Many have historically thought of Romans as only about personal salvation, but Romans is also about spiritual growth. And the way Paul goes about cultivating growth is by doing what Professor Michael Bird calls "gospelizing" (*Romans*, 32). That is, Paul wants every facet of the believer's life to be soaked in the gospel so that his or her days will reflect the realities that the gospel announces and imparts to a believer: life, hope, peace, joy, faith, obedience, righteousness, love, and more.

Our confidence in the gospel is increased when we consider who is writing this grand letter: Paul. The former persecutor of the church is now the servant of it and herald of God's grace in Christ. He is not writing as a cold academic but as one who has experienced the life-changing power of God's good news. The former persecutor writes as Christ's missionary and church planter who has been on the front lines of mission. He was a "servant of Christ Jesus" and "an apostle" who was "set apart for the gospel of God" (v. 1). Christ changed him, humbled him, sent him, and made him all about the gospel.

The Significance of Romans

Why is the book of Romans so important?

Romans Is a Gospel-Saturated Letter

The opening and closing of Romans have much in common, including the use of the word *gospel*. Eight of the eleven occurrences of *euangelion* ("gospel") and *euangelizomai* ("to evangelize") appear in these passages (Rom 1:1-17; 15:14–16:27; Moo, *Letter*, 39). The gospel thus frames the letter. Then in the body of the letter, Paul explains and defends the substance of the gospel, and he also describes how the gospel should shape Christian living and fuel Christian mission.

In today's pluralistic, relativistic, skeptical world, there is great confusion regarding the nature of God, sin, and salvation. There is also a great need for professing Christians to grow in theological discernment. Paul's letter provides answers and clarity on these big issues of life.

Romans Is a Community-Building Letter

Division is apparent among Christians and various churches in Rome, and Paul's letter addresses this disunity. He seeks to unify the believers by magnifying the reality and implications of the believers' union in Christ, thus building a countercultural community.

Paul had been a Christian preacher for about twenty years when he wrote Romans. He wrote it during a three-month stay in Corinth (Acts 20:1-5), with the help of his scribe Tertius (Rom 16:22), between AD 55 and 58 (Schreiner, *Romans*, 3). As Paul thought about his immediate trip to Jerusalem and his desire to minister in Spain, the apostle likely gave this letter to Phoebe to deliver to the church in Rome (16:1). During the time of writing Romans, Paul mentions that he is staying with Gaius (16:23), who is possibly the convert mentioned in 1 Corinthians 1:14 (ibid., 4). Paul had not yet visited Rome, and he did not found the church in Rome, but the Lord was building his church. We know that some Romans were present on the day of Pentecost discussed in Acts 2. It is possible they returned home with news of their new faith and shared it, perhaps in their own synagogues (Moo, *Letter*, 4). Further, merchants visiting Rome also would have made a gospel impact contributing to the growth of the church. What likely happened is the witness of Jewish Christians in the marketplaces and synagogues eventually impacted Gentiles, resulting in a diverse group of believers in Rome. These believers had a variety of questions about how to relate to one another, and Paul provides important instruction for how to live in harmony to the glory of God.

We know the Jews were talking about Jesus soon after Pentecost. In AD 49 Seutonius tells us that Claudius expelled the Jews from the city because they were constantly debating about one named "Chrestus" ("Christ"). This is consistent with Luke's account of Priscilla and Aquila being forced out of Italy because of Claudius's edict (Acts 18:1-2) and arriving in Corinth to meet Paul. Eventually, the Jewish Christians returned to Rome when Claudius died in AD 54 (Schreiner, *Romans*, 5). In between this time the Roman church became a mainly Gentile church, so when the Jews returned, the church became fractured along ethnic lines. You can imagine the issues. The leadership was mainly Gentile. The meetings were not in synagogues but house churches. The Jewish believers would have found many cultural practices offensive. Paul addresses these sorts of social and ethnic issues in Romans 9–11 and 14–15. Moreover, Paul's own character may have been in question, which explains why he spends so much time talking about the law and particular Jewish concepts in the book of Romans. Therefore, there was probably a Gentile majority in the church, with significant changes in leadership and practice, necessitating a community-building letter. We should be grateful for these problems because they gave Paul an occasion to create a glorious, multiethnic vision for the people of God. Bird says we should read Romans while imagining something like a group of mainly Gentile believers cramped in an apartment (called an *insula*) in an impoverished part of a Roman suburb, led by a guy named Rufus, who read the letter aloud (*Romans*, 4). As we hear Romans, we too should pray for the Lord to help us love our (diverse) brothers and sisters better.

Romans Is a Missional Letter

One of the purposes behind Romans is this: Paul is seeking support for his mission to Spain. This becomes clear in 15:24-29. Paul wants to unify the Christians in Rome so they may be a home base for his mission to Spain. Further, the missional spirit of Romans is sensed throughout the entire letter as Paul talks about the power of the gospel, the necessity of preaching it, and his focus on the nations.

This letter was written for ordinary Christians, as Romans 16 shows us. Paul was not writing for trained scholars but for ordinary people who had been changed by the gospel. These are the people God uses to build his church and advance the gospel among the nations.

A Summary of the Gospel
ROMANS 1:1-7

Paul's opening underlines several key components of the gospel message. We may summarize his description this way: *The gospel is God's good news, promised in the Old Testament, centered on Jesus, designed to bring all peoples to the obedience of faith for the sake of Christ's name, transforming everyone who believes.*

The Gospel Is God's Good News (1:1)

It is the "gospel of God"—that is, God's own good news. It is from God (cf. 1 Cor 2:1) and reveals the nature and work of God. Leon Morris says, "God is the most important word in this epistle. Romans is a book about God. No topic is treated with anything like the frequency of God. Everything Paul touches in this letter he relates to God" (*Epistle*, 40). In Romans, Paul unpacks much about God's righteousness, among other attributes.

The word *euangelion* ("gospel"/ "good news") was a common term used in emperor worship during Paul's day. Good events related to the emperor were declared as good news for the people. Paul wants to be clear what good news he is talking about! It is God's good news for the world concerning his Son, Jesus. Do not forget that God is the source of the gospel. People did not make it up. It originates with God. We must not adjust it or edit it but proclaim it.

. . . Promised in the Old Testament (1:2)

Contrary to popular opinion, the Old Testament and the New Testament do not feature two different Gods! There is continuity between the Testaments. The Old Testament is the foundation for the gospel. Although God revealed the gospel to the apostles, it did not come to them as something entirely new, for it was already promised in the "Scriptures" (cf. 1 Cor 15:3-8). The gospel is not a Johnny-come-lately story. Gospel promises had been written down for hundreds of years, and Christ fulfilled these hopes. This is why Christians have a thick Bible and not just a pocket New Testament! The Scriptures are like a treasure map that leads to Jesus, the promised Messiah. The categories and themes of prophet, priest, king, mediator, temple, sacrifice, the second Adam, the promise to Abraham, the Son of David, the Son of Man, the Son of God, the Servant of the Lord, the Messiah, the King, the Redeemer, the Savior—all of these and more are fulfilled in Jesus. The first gospel promise appears in Genesis 3:15, and the whole sweep of the Old Testament is moving to the One who will crush the head of the serpent. Our God is a promise-keeping God. There is not a promise of God that he will not fulfill.

Notice also the phrase, "through his prophets in the Holy Scriptures" (v. 2). See the act of divine inspiration here. God spoke through the prophets, and it ended in a book! God speaks, and we have a book that is holy. This should cause us to love the Bible. God is speaking in the Scriptures. He meets us in his Word.

. . . Centered on Jesus (1:3-4)

The Bible is from God and about Jesus. The gospel is not preached if Christ is not preached. The good news is supremely about what Christ has done for sinners. If someone asks, "What's the gospel about?" you can answer, "It's about Jesus." Paul launches into the person and work of Jesus in the greeting. These verses may have been part of an early creed. Regarding Christ's person, Paul says that Jesus was the "descendent of David according to the flesh" (v. 3); that is, he is the promised Messiah. (See 2 Sam 7; Isa 11:1-5,10; Jer 23:5-6; Ezek 34:23-24; Matt 1:1; 20:30-31; Luke 1:27,32; Acts 2:30; 13:22-23; 2 Tim 2:8; Rev 5:5; 22:16.) Paul then speaks of Christ's deity (v. 4). Regarding Christ's work, the implication between verses 3 and 4 is that this Messiah died. He could not rise if he did not die. This was devastating for many people who had no category for a suffering and crucified Messiah. But this was part of God's great plan.

But Jesus's work did not end with his death, for he was vindicated as the Son of God at his resurrection. By saying that Jesus was "appointed" to be the Son of God, Paul is not implying that Jesus became the "Son of God" only at the resurrection. Paul is simply drawing attention to the next phase of Jesus's redeeming work. He is emphasizing Jesus's exaltation and coronation, and he probably is alluding to Psalm 2:7—which speaks of the coronation of the Davidic, messianic King. In other words, in Jesus's earthly life he was the Son of David in weakness (hungry, tired, etc.), but after the resurrection he was weak no more! He was/is the risen and reigning and glorified King! So Paul is contrasting humility with exaltation. Jesus's invisible reign now will one day be a visible, climactic reign.

This resurrection event also ushered in a new era, the age of the Spirit. The phrase "according to the Spirit of holiness" is probably a reference to the power of the Holy Spirit as the agent of the resurrection. There are many links between the Holy Spirit and the resurrection. Later Paul writes, "the Spirit of him who raised Jesus from the dead" dwells in us (Rom 8:11). And we will be raised by the Spirit of God as well. This means that if you die before you finish reading this commentary, and you are in Christ Jesus, you can go with the assurance that you will be raised from the dead! (And immediately you will know more about Jesus than I am trying to teach you in this little book!)

Therefore, from the beginning of Romans, we see how important the resurrection is. Paul opens the letter with an empty tomb! How can anyone beat sin and death? You can't unless you are united to Jesus. You have a greater chance of beating basketball giant Lebron James in a one-on-one match than beating death! Only in Christ, and Christ alone, do we have the sweetest of victories.

. . . Designed to Bring All Peoples to the Obedience of Faith for the Sake of Christ's Name (1:5)

In verse 5 we see the purpose of the gospel (the nations' obedience) and its ultimate goal (Christ's glory). Paul's mission was to take the gospel to all people groups. These opening verses in Romans, as well as Romans 16:26, highlight the global nature of the gospel.

Paul's longing is that the nations may have an obedience that flows from faith. That is what "the obedience of faith" (v. 5) means—a faith that leads to obedience. Faith is the root; obedience the fruit. Saving faith is an obedient faith. We trust in Jesus, and now by the Spirit we live our lives in obedience to Christ.

The ultimate goal of gospel ministry is then stated: "for the sake of his name." "His" refers back to Jesus in verses 3-4. The goal is that Jesus would be honored and praised as he deserves.

. . . Transforming Everyone Who Believes (1:6-7)

Having mentioned that grand scope of the gospel, Paul tells the Romans where they fit in. They are among the Jews and Gentiles who are part of this redemptive plan. The gospel radically transforms those who believe.

Paul tells us that when you become a Christian, you get a new identity. The gospel changes who we are and what we stand for: holiness. He says we are "called by Jesus" (v. 6). We are his. We are not enslaved to sin but are children of God (Rom 8). Further, we are also "loved by God" (v. 7). This is a remarkable statement of transformation in view of the opening three chapters of Romans that describe our sinful nature. We do not deserve God's love, and yet those in Christ are God's beloved children because of Christ's saving work on our behalf.

Paul adds to the list that Christians are "called as saints." Jesus is the true Israel, and in him we are made part of the people of God. We are holy ones—not in ourselves but because we are in the Holy One. A saint is not one who has done something extraordinary but one who is in the One who is truly extraordinary. As saints, our responsibility is to now walk in this new identity and status by pursuing practical holiness.

A Servant of the Gospel
ROMANS 1:8-15

In these verses we read of Paul's thanksgiving/prayer report concerning his apostolic visit to Rome, a visit he is eager to make because he longs to preach the gospel there and share in the saints' fellowship. Before diving deeper into his theology, Paul gives the Romans (and us) a look into his heart and life. We see what motivated and sustained him in ministry. We learn about his prayer life, his love for the church, and his obligation to world evangelism. Consider the personal language of Paul:

- "whom I serve with my spirit" (v. 9),
- "my prayers" (v. 10),
- "I want very much to see you" (v. 11),
- "I often planned to come to you" (v. 13),
- "I am obligated" (v. 14), and
- "I am eager" (v. 15).

The apostle's ministry motivations and intentions are thus presented to us.

Remember: he has not been to Rome, but he is planning a visit. So he is building rapport. He is cultivating a partnership and friendship. He opens up his heart so that they may know him. You can learn a lot about a person by reading his books. But if you were able to travel with missionary heroes, spend time with godly wives or mothers or singles, or hang out with faithful pastors, that would certainly have a tremendous impact on you (cf. Phil 3:17).

Notice also Paul's heart for something in particular—the gospel. Paul is a man consumed with the good news. We see it in the phrases "telling the good news about his Son" (v. 9) and "eager to preach the gospel" (v. 15).

Therefore, by exposing his heart to us and by exalting the gospel message for us, Paul shows us that he has both a shepherd's heart and a missionary's heart. He loves the saints, and he loves the lost. His passion and priority are a pattern for all who seek to be servants of the gospel in either an official or lay capacity.

Communion with God (1:8-10)

Paul begins by thanking God and speaking of his personal prayer life. Paul opens with the word *first* (v. 8), but he never really gets to *second*! So he is expressing a priority rather than a list. His first priority is to give thanks to God for the church. His thanksgiving flows from his humility before God. Proud people do not give thanks. Humble, grace-filled people say thanks frequently. Paul fills the opening of his letters with thanksgiving to God. We would do well to begin our days with thanksgiving to God and to pepper thanksgiving to God into our everyday conversations with one another.

Paul directs his thanks to "my God" (v. 8). The Christian faith is personal. It is not cold and detached. His prayer is made "through Jesus Christ" (v. 8). He again draws attention to the Savior, who provides the way for us to have a personal relationship with God. Then Paul gets specific: "because the news of your faith is being reported in all the world" (v. 8). There were Christians in Rome whose faith was proclaimed in regions outside of Rome. They were part of a worldwide communion of saints.

Next we see Paul's passion displayed. In verse 9 we first notice a God-centered passion. He says that God can vouch for the truthfulness of his claims ("my witness") and that the apostle serves (or worships) God in "telling the good news about his Son." His ministry of the gospel has a vertical dimension. He performs worshipful service to God, not begrudging service to God. This is an important reminder to all believers.

In verse 10 Paul mentions a more people-centered passion. He says he never ceases to mention the Romans in his prayers. Paul has been away from the Roman saints physically, but his heart has not been away from them spiritually. The apostle regularly mentioned his constant prayers for the church (cf. 1 Cor 1:4; Eph 1:16; Phil 1:3; Col 1:3; 1 Thess 1:2).

Paul wants to go to Rome, but he knows if he cannot be there, he can still pray for the church—and that those prayers matter. He does not say, "I can't get to Rome, so maybe I will do something for you once I arrive." We should see here that our prayers for the saints around the world really matter.

In the second part of verse 10, Paul expresses his desire to visit Rome. It was the capital of the Roman Empire and therefore the most strategic city for Christian mission, but the great apostle had not reached it yet. So he says, "If it is somehow in God's will, I may now at last succeed in coming to you." In other words, getting to Rome was at the top of his priority list. In verse 13 he says that he has been "prevented" from visiting. His failure to minister in Rome was not due to lack of desire but other issues, like being busy with preaching the gospel from Jerusalem around to Illyricum (Rom 15:17-23). We know from the rest of Scripture that Paul has been tending to church problems from Antioch, Galatia, Corinth, and Thessalonica. He has also had a few stints in prison, a few beatings, and oh yeah, he's been writing part of the Bible! That is a full life!

Paul's reference to "God's will" (v. 10) shows how he trusts God's sovereign plans. Paul is not paralyzed by God's sovereignty. He expresses his desire and then leaves it to God. He seems to imply that some obstacles have been removed, but we know from Acts that more trouble awaited Paul. This letter reached the Christians at Rome about three years before he got there. He would eventually make it to Rome but only after being mobbed, arrested, imprisoned, and having survived a shipwreck! Moreover, he entered Rome as a prisoner (Acts 27–28). We too never know what awaits us.

So, this is the first passion we see that drove this servant: communion with God. Does it drive you? Do you have a vibrant prayer life filled with thanksgiving, intercession, and submission to God's will?

Concern for the Church (1:11-13)

Paul then says why he wants to make it to Rome (vv. 11-12). He wants to bless the church through his gifts of leadership and teaching. (Paul writes more about the use of one's gifts in 12:3-8.)

Paul also recognized his own need for encouragement. He thus mentions mutual encouragement (v. 12; see also 15:2,19). Paul—like all Christians—needed encouragement.

Learn from this example. You need other believers, and other believers need you. Sometimes people ask, "Why do I need the church?" That question often comes out of pride and self-absorption. Here are two reasons you need the church: you need to be built up, and other believers need you. Regarding the latter, you should remember that your spiritual gifts are not for you but for the good of other believers.

Commitment to Preach the Gospel to Everyone (1:14-15)

A third motivation is found in these verses. After mentioning his inability to get to Rome previously (v. 13a), he says that he longs to visit Rome in order to "have a fruitful ministry among [them], just as [he has] had among the rest of the Gentiles" (v. 13b). Here is another example of the missional thrust of Romans. Paul's ministry included Jews and Gentiles, or "everyone" (v. 16). This "fruitful ministry" or "harvest" (ESV) probably refers to more Gentile converts, but it may also include the general strengthening of the Roman Christians.

Paul continues by further expressing his heart for every kind of person (v. 14). Rome was filled with all kinds of people: Greeks, Barbarians, civilized, brutish, wise, and unlearned. Paul says that he is under obligation to preach to all of them. Tim Keller describes this gospel obligation:

> It is illustrative to think about how I can be in debt to you. First, you may have lent me $100—and I am in debt to you until I pay it back. But second, someone else may have given me $100 to pass on to you—and I am in debt to you until I hand it on. It is in this second sense that Paul is "obligated" to everyone, everywhere. God has shared the gospel with him. But God has also commissioned him to declare it to others. So Paul owes people the gospel. (*Romans 1–7*, 17)

Do you sense that same obligation? We owe people the gospel. We must tell others about it. From the scholars at your local universities to refugees trying to learn English, and everyone in between, from the children to the elderly, from your neighborhood to the nations.

In verse 15 Paul expresses his longing to preach to both the believer and the unbeliever. Schreiner says, "Both initial evangelism and the strengthening of believers is in Paul's mind" (*Romans*, 54). The gospel is for both evangelism of unbelievers and edification of believers. Obviously unbelievers need the gospel, for as Romans 1:18–3:20 will explain, they are guilty before a holy God, and only through Jesus can they be saved. But believers also need the gospel. We need a better understanding of various doctrines, we need to apply them to our lives, and we need to be reminded of our fundamental identity as well as the hope that is ours in Christ.

A Steadfast Confidence in the Gospel
ROMANS 1:16-17

Paul arrives at his thesis: *The gospel is the saving power of God in which the righteousness of God is revealed* (Schreiner, *Romans*, 59). This is the "nerve center" of the letter (Bird, *Romans*, 40), a central claim or proposition Paul will explain and defend. One may look at Romans through this lens of "righteousness."

- 1:18–3:20—We see that no one is righteous.
- 3:21–5:21—We see that by faith in Christ one is declared righteous.
- 6:1–8:39—We see that Christians are now "slaves to righteousness."
- 9:1–11:36—We see Paul's defense of God's righteousness.
- 12:1–15:13—We see what a righteous life looks like in the church and in the world.

So Romans tells unrighteous people how to be positionally righteous and then how to live out practical righteousness. It comes through faith in Jesus, the righteous One.

Paul says that he is "not ashamed of the gospel." This is an indirect way of saying "I am proud of the gospel" (Bird, *Romans*, 40). Some thought he should be ashamed of the gospel. Paul says to the Corinthians that this message is "foolish" to some people, for it's a stumbling block to the Jews and foolishness to the Gentiles (1 Cor 1:23). What is so foolish about the gospel? Everything, if you do not have eyes to see! Here are a few truths people find foolish:

- There is one triune God—not many gods or an impersonal consciousness at the heart of the universe—and this God created the world.
- Humans have wicked hearts and are radically sinful.
- The single most important weekend in the history of the world is that of Jesus's crucifixion and resurrection.
- Jesus atoned for our sins on the cross; he did not merely give an example of sacrifice to follow.
- God raised Jesus bodily, not just spiritually.
- Jesus is Lord over all things.
- Jesus is the only way to salvation; there are not many ways.
- Being born again is a real experience, and the Holy Spirit really indwells believers.
- The church is made up of the redeemed who make known the manifold wisdom of God; it's not some religious society of backwards people with Victorian morals.

- At the return of Jesus, everyone will bow and confess that he is Lord—every Jew, Muslim, Hindu, atheist, Scientologist, Baptist, etc.
- There will be a final judgment, and Jesus will separate the "sheep" and the "goats"; one group will perish, and the other will have a glorious inheritance (paraphrased from Bird, *Romans*, 48).

Many mock such affirmations. They say, "You should be embarrassed by such beliefs." Perhaps most Romans said something like what we hear today: "We are too sophisticated to believe that archaic stuff." Paul says, "I'm not ashamed."

We really only have two options: abandon the gospel out of embarrassment or embrace the shame. I say we stand with Paul. We must not be ashamed when we are shamed. Jesus warned his disciples not to be ashamed of him and his words (Mark 8:38), and we must heed this same warning.

Paul tells us some important truths about this gospel of which he is so proud. First, it is God's power for salvation (v. 16). The very message that people consider foolish actually contains the power of God for salvation (cf. 1 Cor 1:17-18). If you try to clean the gospel up, you lose it. It cannot be domesticated. It is a message about a bloody Savior and an empty tomb.

The gospel is not simply *about* the power of God (though it is), but it *contains* the power of God—in the sense that God actualizes his saving work through it. Bird says,

> The gospel is a speech-act, in that it not only announces the
> way of salvation, but actualizes the salvation in those who hear
> it with faith. . . . The gospel manifests God's death-defeating,
> curse-reversing, evil-vanquishing, devil-crushing, sin-cleansing,
> life-giving, love-forming, people-uniting, super-*über*-mega-grace
> power that results in salvation. (*Romans*, 48)

Our confidence is not in our ability. Our confidence is in God's work and God's gospel!

Paul's mention of "salvation" (v. 16) is fairly broad and denotes a *rescue*. Salvation has both an "already" and a "not yet" dimension to it, as we shall see (e.g., 5:1,9; 8:1,18,23,30,33; 10:10). We have true salvation now, but we await the glorious fulfillment of certain saving benefits. Indeed, our salvation is a glorious salvation. We are saved *from* something terrible and *for* something glorious!

Regarding the people in need of the gospel, Paul says that the gospel is for "everyone who believes, first to the Jew, and also to the Greek" (v. 16). The priority of the Jews here reflects a historical reality. God chose Israel; however, it was not just for Israel's sake but so that they would be "a light to the nations" (Isa 42:6; 49:6). A transformed Israel would help transform the world. But both Jew and non-Jew have the same need: salvation through Jesus.

Paul goes on to say that the gospel reveals God's righteousness (v. 17). The phrase "righteousness of God" here has led to great debates. I am going to cut to the chase and say that I think Paul has two things in mind: God's righteous activity and human receptivity. Regarding God's activity, he has in mind the idea that God demonstrates his righteous character in his saving actions. Regarding human receptivity, he means that God bestows a righteous status on unrighteous people. John Stott summarizes: "The righteousness of God is God's righteous initiative in putting sinners right with himself, by bestowing on them a righteousness which is not their own, but his" (*Message*, 64). Later, in Romans 3:21-26, Paul unpacks how we receive this new status by faith in Christ (cf. 2 Cor 5:21). The righteousness God requires from us is the righteousness God has provided for us in Jesus.

Paul adds in verse 17 that the gospel is received by faith. He uses a peculiar construction: "from faith to faith" or "from faith for faith." Does he mean (1) from God's faithfulness to human faith, (2) from Jewish faith to Gentile faith, (3) from Christ's faithful life to our faith, or (4) faith from start to finish (Bird, *Romans*, 44)? Usually, Paul uses the term "faith" to talk about the instrument by which we receive the saving benefits of Jesus's death and resurrection. If that is the case here, Paul is saying that salvation is by faith from beginning to end or "start to finish" (NLT). Real faith results in "obedience" (v. 5), but the whole Christian life is a life of faith from start to finish.

Paul concludes this section with a quote from Habakkuk 2:4 to underscore that this emphasis on faith is consistent with the rest of Scripture. Interestingly, Paul quotes from the Old Testament in Romans more than in all his other letters combined. There are at least sixty-one direct quotations from fourteen different books (Akin, "The Epistle to Romans"). And there are many more echoes of the Old Testament. Psalms and Isaiah are the most frequently quoted. Paul's point here is that faith is the way in which one stands right before God. The whole Bible is teaching us this.

Romans 1:1-17 is filled with gospel gold! If you are not a Christian, then realize you cannot earn righteousness; it is received by faith in Christ. Embrace the Savior! If you are a believer, then allow this opening section to clarify your understanding of the gospel, to impact your motivations for ministering the gospel, and to inspire greater confidence in the gospel.

Reflect and Discuss

1. Why is the book of Romans important for you, your church, and the world?
2. What do you find to be most interesting about the background of the book of Romans?
3. Why is it significant that Paul summarizes the gospel using the Old Testament as a foundation?
4. What does Romans 1:1-7 teach us about the person and work of Christ?
5. Is your life characterized by thankfulness? Whatever your answer, take a moment to express thanks to God.
6. What does Romans 1:8-15 teach us about our relationships to one another in the body of Christ?
7. What do we learn about evangelism in verses 14-17?
8. Why might someone be ashamed of the gospel today?
9. Why is it essential to have an unshakable confidence in the gospel?
10. Explain the importance of God's righteousness as presented in the book of Romans.

Why We Need the Gospel: God's Righteous Judgment

ROMANS 1:18–2:29

Main Idea: Paul describes the nature of human sin and its consequences, showing us our great need for the gospel.

I. **Judgment and the Gentile (1:18-32)**
  A. God's wrath (1:18)
  B. The reasons for God's wrath (1:19-32)
    1. The movement to idolatry
    2. The madness of idolatry
    3. The misery of idolatry
    4. The moral rebellion of idolatry
II. **Judgment and the Jew (2:1-29)**
  A. Truths about God's judgment (2:1-16)
  B. Jewish hypocrisy (2:17-29)

Sinclair Ferguson reports the following story. A few years ago, a campus ministry group in one of the larger universities in the United Kingdom was seeking to reach students with the truth of the gospel. So they printed out the words of Romans 1:18-32 in a contemporary format with no verse numbers. They did not specify the source. It was simply written as if these words were composed in the twenty-first century. Soon after the document was distributed, the leaders were called to go before the university authorities. The students were told in no uncertain terms that they would be censored for their offensiveness. And the authorities demanded that the students produce the author of this offensive piece of writing (Ferguson, "When God Gives Up")!

Indeed, the early chapters in Romans are clear and offensive to many people, but we must grapple with them, as this is God's Word. Paul is not trying to give us a nice little back rub here! He is telling everyone about the nature of sin and its consequences. He spends a lot of time talking about human depravity and God's righteous judgment, but this is a gift. Until we know we need the gospel, we will not cry out in repentance toward God and in faith in the Lord Jesus.

The message is clear: *none are righteous.* In Romans 1:18-32 Paul has mainly the Gentiles in mind. He indicts them for rejecting God's glory. In Romans 2:1–3:8 Paul has the Jews primarily in mind. His argument is like that of Amos 1–2, with an element of surprise, first declaring the sin of the Gentiles before turning to the sin of the Jews (Schreiner, *Romans,* 102). Paul may have even adapted a basic sermon that he would have used in the Jewish synagogues (ibid.). Paul concludes the section in 3:9-20 by proclaiming that "no one is righteous" (3:10).

After what Paul said in Romans 1:16-17, you might expect him to explain how the righteousness of God comes to us, but we do not get there until Romans 3:21! Instead, we read of our great need for the gift of Christ's righteousness. Before Paul gets to the good news in 3:21, he gives us this bad news in 1:18–3:20. His words address everyone: the smug self-righteous person, the wild unrighteous person, and everyone in between.

Judgment and the Gentile
ROMANS 1:18-32

Verse 18 is the heading not only over 1:18-32 but actually over 1:18–3:20. All people outside of Christ stand condemned under the righteous wrath of God (Moo, *Letter,* 97).

Observe a few aspects of the structure of 1:18-32. Notice how frequently connecting words like "for" and "therefore" appear. These words show how the subject material is tied together as a unit. In verse 18 Paul shows us God's wrath against sin, and then he gives the basis for it (vv. 19-32). Consider also the "exchanges" in the text: verses 22-23, 25-26, and 28 (implied). As a result of these corrupt decisions, Paul gives us God's response: "God delivered them over." He states it three times (vv. 24,26,28).

God's Wrath (1:18)

Many have a hard time with the concept of God's wrath. We must remember that God's wrath is not a wild, emotional outburst. God is "slow to anger," but he does not wink at sin. God's wrath is a righteous wrath. God's anger is a holy anger. We should tremble at God's wrath, and we should be thankful for the Savior.

Paul says this wrath "is revealed" (v. 18). Usually when we think about God's wrath, we think about his past or future judgments. While both are realities, Paul here is speaking about a present reality. God's wrath is *being* revealed. Although God will inflict his wrath on the last day, once and for all, there is an anticipatory working of God's wrath in the events of history (Moo, *Letter*, 101). Notice the repeated phrase, "God delivered them over." God hands people over to their sin and its consequences; this judgment is a foretaste of ultimate judgment to come. In other words, sin leads to misery, not fulfillment, and it is a foretaste of eternal misery. The Greek verb for "deliver over" has its roots in the Old Testament. God handed over Israel's enemies so that they would be defeated (e.g., Josh 6:2). At other times, God handed over Israel to their enemies as an act of judgment (e.g., Judg 2:14). For some, this experience may lead to an awakening, a prodigal-son experience, but sadly, some never turn to God in repentance.

Wrath is being revealed against "godlessness and unrighteousness." These are not to be understood as two separate causes for his wrath but two ideas that speak of the same problem—that is, an attack on the majesty of God. Sin, as D. A. Carson puts it, involves "the de-godding of God" ("What Is the Gospel?").

God's wrath is being revealed "from heaven." This phrase emphasizes God's majesty and his all-seeing eye. All that does not submit under heaven and is not in Christ is under God's wrath.

Paul says in their unrighteousness they "suppress the truth." That is, they fail to respond to God's revelation. This idea serves as a transition into the next section.

The Reasons for God's Wrath (1:19-32)

Paul says that the whole array of sins that characterizes humanity has its roots in the soil of idolatry. Sin problems are worship problems. In verses 19-21 he speaks of the movement to idolatry. In verses 22-23 he speaks of the madness of idolatry. In verses 24-25 he speaks of the misery of idolatry. He concludes the section in verses 26-32 by speaking of the moral rebellion that follows idolatry.

Regarding **the movement to idolatry**, he supports his claim that everyone has suppressed the truth (v. 18) by pointing out that the whole world has natural revelation of God (v. 19), but apart from divine grace they do not respond rightly to it.

In verses 19-20 Paul teaches that the world knows there is a God. How so? He says first that *you have a revelation of God's character around you* (vv. 19-20). God's "eternal power," his "invisible attributes," and his "divine nature" have been revealed in creation (v. 20). God's existence has been plain in creation throughout history. So, people have a sense of God as they observe his creation and his works in history. Everything is stamped "Made by God" (see Ps 19). Consequently, Paul says, "People are without excuse" (v. 20), meaning everyone is accountable to this revelation of God. They have understood something about God but, by rejecting him, are without excuse.

These verses show us why we must take the gospel to the nations. People who have never heard the gospel are in need of *specific* revelation, that is, the knowledge of the specifics of the gospel, which are not plain in creation! You cannot get from the sunsets (general revelation) to substitutionary atonement (specific revelation) without a specific explanation of the gospel.

Paul adds that God's existence is also displayed in this way: *you have an awareness of the presence of God invading you* (v. 19). The words "evident among them" or "plain to them" (ESV) can be translated "within them" (NASB). The knowledge is plain *to* them because it is plain *in* them. The revelation around them produces this result. There is a sense of God in the conscience of an image bearer of God.

But what do rebellious people do? They respond wrongly (v. 21). Paul builds on verse 19. What do the unrighteous do with the revelation of God? Suppress it. Hold it down. Reject it. Although they "knew God," they did not "glorify him" or "show gratitude" (v. 21). They do not honor him. Instead of responding positively to the light, sinners' "thinking became worthless" and their "senseless hearts were darkened" (v. 21). The word *heart* denotes the center of the person. The person who suppresses the truth is marked by intellectual futility and spiritual darkness. He needs the light of the gospel to overcome this darkness.

Regarding **the madness of idolatry**, Paul says these rejecters of the divine claim to be "wise" but are in reality "fools" (v. 22). Their foolishness is displayed not just by refusing to give thanks to God (v. 21) but also by worshiping pitiful substitutes, including images, birds, animals, and creeping things (v. 23; see also Ps 106:20). In our sinfulness, we can worship all manner of things.

But what does this idolatry produce? It leads to **the misery of idolatry**. Paul says, "Therefore God delivered them over in the desires of their hearts to sexual impurity, so that their bodies were degraded among themselves" (v. 24). God leaves the idolater with his or her acts of impurity and dishonor. It does not bring satisfaction but misery. Idolatry leaves us restless and unfulfilled.

Paul adds, "They exchanged the truth of God for a lie, and worshiped and served what has been created instead of the Creator, who is praised forever. Amen" (v. 25). This is what sin involves: turning from that which will ultimately satisfy you—namely, the Creator and Redeemer, who is blessed forever—to something that will only leave you more miserable—namely, a created thing.

We should remember that humans are worshipers. The question is not, Do you worship?, but Whom or what do you worship? Idolatry involves looking to something other than God to give you what only he can give you (to paraphrase Tim Keller). Those things we seek in idols involve joy, security, provision, peace, freedom, satisfaction, fulfillment, love, and beauty. But only in the God who made us do we have these things. Idols can involve money, sex, approval, achievement, power, family, and a host of other things that can actually be good things when viewed rightly. We should be thankful for this portion of Romans because Paul shows us that real life begins by worshiping the Creator God, not created things.

Idolatry has practical implications. It leads to **the moral rebellion of idolatry** (vv. 26-32). This rebellion can be expressed in several ways, including exchanging "natural sexual relations" for "unnatural" relations (v. 26). Paul singles out homosexuality first with women and then among men (v. 27). While many in our culture find these verses offensive and unacceptable, Paul makes clear that these actions are sinful and shameful.

What Paul means by "natural" is just that: these other relations are contrary to natural law. In other words, homosexuality is contrary to God's divine design. To go against nature is therefore to go against God. And God's design is *a good design*. This is not a fluid cultural matter; it is an unchanging creation matter. It is timeless. God is infinitely good and wise, and his designs are best and for our good, for our flourishing. Homosexual activity is contrary to God's will, it is a violation of the created order, and it is another example in this text demonstrating a departure from a true knowledge of God and the worship of God.

In verse 27 Paul says that men sexually pursuing other men is a departure from nature. He uses strong language to characterize it: "inflamed in their lust for one another" (v. 27). These lusts are then expressed in "shameless acts." Such activity necessitates the judgment of God, as Paul says that these individuals "received in their own persons the appropriate penalty of their error" (v. 27). It is a judgment that is already occurring. These individuals are restless and discontented because they are not finding their rest in God. They face all manner of consequences for going their own rebellious, self-centered way. And it warns of an eternal judgment that will come unless the individual repents and trusts in Christ.

The reasons for homosexual attraction are complex and include biology and biography as well as spiritual brokenness, and we must always minister to people graciously and humbly, but Paul is clear that acting on such attraction offends God. The good news is there is mercy, forgiveness, and transformation for all those who will turn to Christ. Paul told the Corinthians,

> *Don't you know that the unrighteous will not inherit God's kingdom?*
> *Do not be deceived: No sexually immoral people, idolaters, adulterers,*
> *or males who have sex with males, no thieves, greedy people,*
> *drunkards, verbally abusive people, or swindlers will inherit God's*
> *kingdom. And some of you used to be like this. But you were washed,*
> *you were sanctified, you were justified in the name of the Lord Jesus*
> *Christ and by the Spirit of our God.* (1 Cor 6:9-11)

I love the phrase "some of you used to be like this" in this context. That is the story of sinners (who are capable of all manner of sin) who have been transformed by the saving grace of God. Those who have been transformed by God's grace will still have to fight sin in this life. It will be a hard fight, one that will require a lot of grace and a lot of love and support and prayers from the Christian community, but that is how we all fight temptation, regardless of what sin it lures us toward. But this is discipleship—denying self, taking up a cross, and following Jesus.

In verses 28-32 Paul gives more examples of disobedient behavior flowing from a failure to rightly acknowledge God. In verse 28 he says that fallen people on their own do not rightly acknowledge God, so God delivered them over to a "corrupt mind." The previous delivering over was to sexual sin (vv. 26-27); here they are handed over to a worthless mind. What everyone needs is what we will read about in Romans 12:2—a renewed mind. Only a work of the Spirit can overcome our blindness and twisted thinking. Praise God, we who were given to a worthless mind have been transformed and are being renewed daily through the Word by the Spirit.

In verses 29-31 we read a vice list. This is a long list of sins that are common in this sinful world, and they were also common in Paul's day among philosophers. Such lists appear throughout the New Testament. We may put the sins in four groups:

- "unrighteousness, evil, greed, and wickedness";
- "envy, murder, quarrels, deceit, and malice";
- "gossips, slanderers, God-haters, arrogant, proud, boastful, inventors of evil, disobedient to parents";
- "senseless, untrustworthy, unloving, and unmerciful."

This list demonstrates how a corrupt mind produces all kinds of social evils. It demonstrates how one's corrupt mind affects others.

In verse 32 Paul notes that those who engage in such activity know what they are doing is wrong. People in general have some awareness of wrongdoing and that they deserve judgment. Then Paul adds that they are doubly accountable because they not only do such things but also "applaud" others who practice them. They call light darkness and darkness light (Isa 5:20). This surely comes from an unsettled conscience. When your conscience is killing you, you are tempted to justify your actions in order to silence it; one way to do that is by applauding the behavior and recruiting others to participate in it. Sinners often think there is safety in numbers.

Romans shows us that the only way to deal with a shredded conscience is to experience the transforming grace of Jesus, who can give you peace and a whole new identity through faith in him (Rom 5:1). This has been made possible because someone else was "handed over": Christ. "[God] did not even spare his own Son but gave him up for us all. How will he not also with him grant us everything?" (8:32). God delivered over his beloved Son, Jesus, for sinners, so that all who look to him can be forgiven and have new life. Romans 1:18–3:20 shows us why we need the gospel, and the book of Romans leaves us praising God for this gospel!

Judgment and the Jew
ROMANS 2:1-29

In this next section, connected by "Therefore" (2:1), Paul primarily has the Jewish person in mind, though much of 2:1-16 applies to everyone. Leon Morris says,

Jews would have agreed heartily with all that Paul has had
to say about the Gentile world. They were always ready to
condemn the Gentiles, but they saw themselves as on a much
higher plane. (*Epistle*, 107)

We are reminded in these two chapters that one can be lost in unrighteousness or self-righteousness.

It is good to keep these two chapters together because religious,
self-righteous hypocrites (who are not true Christians) tend to heap
condemnation on those who practice the sins in Romans 1:18-32, but
they often fail to consider their own sinfulness before the Holy One.
Jesus has come not for the "righteous"—that is, for those who *think* they
are righteous—but for "sinners," those willing to *admit* their need for
him (Mark 2:17). Both groups, the irreligious and the religious, must
repent and turn to Christ for salvation.

Paul says to the Jewish hypocrite, "Every one of you who judges is
without excuse" (2:1a). Notice the connection to the Gentiles being
"without excuse" (1:20). Paul says, "For when you judge another, you
condemn yourself, since you, the judge, do the same things" (2:1b).
Though the outward manifestations may be different, the Jews practice
the same kinds of evils they criticize in the Gentiles, and they also stand
indefensible before God.

Truths about God's Judgment (2:2-16)

We may summarize Paul's teaching on God's judgment with eleven
truths (building on Ferguson's expositions in Romans 2). Each point is
intended to humble the self-righteous that they may cry out to God and
say, "God, have mercy on me, a sinner!" (Luke 18:9-14).

First, God's judgment reflects the reality of the situation (2:2). Paul says
that God's judgment is "based on the truth." God's judgment is not
based on external appearances or some other standard. God's judgment is always just.

Second, God's judgment allows for no exceptions (2:3). The apostle adds,
"Do you think—anyone of you who judges those who do such things
yet do the same—that you will escape God's judgment?" Human nature
gravitates to this defense: "I'm the exception," and that was certainly
the tendency of the Jews, who had been given certain privileges. Paul
says, No! God does not grade on a curve if you are a religious person
instead of irreligious, if you are part of one particular party instead of
another, or if you are of one particular ethnicity rather than another.

There are no exceptions regarding the reality and standards of God's righteous judgment. As long as you think you are an exception to God's judgment, you will never repent and turn to Jesus—why would you need to (Ferguson, "Without Excuse")?

Third, God's judgment means you should not presume on his kindness but turn to him in repentance (2:4). God's kindness is meant to lead a person to life-changing repentance. However, many presume on God's kindness, never repenting yet believing that God will simply say on the last day, "Oh, y'all come on in." Others base their assurance on some emotional experience in the past or some religious ritual, but they have never been made a new creation in Christ Jesus. Paul does not want us to presume on God's grace because he wants to see people saved (see Titus 3:4-7). In God's kindness he makes us aware of our sin, and our responsibility is to then turn to him in repentance and faith. Do not presume on God's kindness but receive his transforming grace through genuine repentance.

Fourth, God's judgment will result in God's just wrath on the unrepentant (2:5). Paul says if you go on in unrepentance, living as if you have no need to repent, then you are "storing up wrath for yourself in the day of wrath, when God's righteous judgment is revealed." Time is running short, and soon it will be too late to repent. For those who have presumed on God's grace but have never truly been converted by God's grace, Jesus will say to them, "I never knew you" (Matt 7:23).

Fifth, God's judgment is based on what we have really been, sought, and done (2:6-10). Paul continues, "He will repay each one according to his works" (v. 6), thus echoing the Old Testament (Ps 62:12; Prov 24:12). He contrasts two different types of motives and lifestyles, leading to two different results:

> *eternal life to those who by persistence in doing good seek glory, honor, and immortality; but wrath and anger to those who are self-seeking and disobey the truth while obeying unrighteousness.* (vv. 7-8)

The first group seeks the things of God and the glory of God, and the second group seeks only self. Paul reiterates this basic contrast of motive and behavior by saying,

> *There will be affliction and distress for every human being who does evil, first to the Jew, and also to the Greek; but glory, honor, and peace for everyone who does what is good, first to the Jew, and also to the Greek.* (vv. 9-10)

So, our identity, our beliefs, and our motives lead to particular deeds. Christians are justified by grace alone, but this grace is a transforming grace that leads to deeds. Good works done by us are the outworking of Christ's work for us. Our works, particularly those intended to glorify God, demonstrate that we belong to Christ Jesus. Therefore, the always relevant question is, Are you living for God's glory?

Sixth, God's judgment has eternal consequences (2:7-8). One group will receive "eternal life" and the other will experience "wrath and anger." Paul began this long section by introducing the concept of God's wrath (1:18) and here continues to support it. Paul emphasizes this concept not because he takes delight in the thought of people being under God's wrath but because he wants to see them saved from it. The reality of God's eternal judgment should cause people to ask, "Where will I spend eternity?" and thus flee to Christ for refuge.

Seventh, God's judgment is pronounced individually (2:6-10). Do not miss what Paul says in these verses: we must each give an account to God. He says, "each one" (v. 6), "every human being" (v. 9), and "everyone" (v. 10) stands individually before God. You will not get a free pass yourself because your mother or father or sister or brother was a believer in Christ. You must believe in Christ personally to escape God's judgment.

Eighth, God's judgment is without partiality (2:11). Paul plainly makes the point, and he directs it to the Jewish individual who thinks he or she is an exception because of Israel's special privileges. God will judge evenhandedly, regardless of one's ethnicity and background. Paul clearly recognizes that Israel has certain privileges (3:12; 9:4-5), but those privileges come with responsibilities. Having privileges is one thing, but responding rightly to them is another. Having privileges does not keep you away from God's impartial judgment. The gospel is for both Jew and Gentile because both stand under the impartial judgment of God.

Ninth, God's judgment is for everyone regardless of how they have received the law, either on tablets or on the heart (2:12-15). Paul says whether one sins "without the law" (Gentiles) or one sins "under the law" (Jews), both are condemned (v. 12) apart from Christ. To the Jew, he says what counts is not having the law but being "doers of the law" (v. 13), meaning that what matters is not merely possessing the law but responding rightly to that law. Then he says that the Gentiles have the law in a certain sense (vv. 14-15), meaning that the Commandments God gave on tablets display the basic instincts God has written on the human heart at creation

(Ferguson, "Reality Check"). This does not mean that one's conscience always serves as a perfect moral compass but that the existence of the testimony of the conscience is sufficient to render a person accountable to God.

What Paul means when he says that the Gentiles sometimes "do what the law demands" and that their thoughts "accuse" them or sometimes "excuse" them is debated. Paul could mean that by God's common grace, a Gentile may occasionally live a virtuous life, though not one sufficient for salvation. Others say Paul could have a Christian Gentile in mind, who by the Spirit now lives a new life (cf. Jer 31:33). I think the former is in view. At any rate, the overall point is clear regarding judgment: neither the Jew nor the Gentile can escape.

Tenth, God's judgment reaches to the secrets of our hearts (2:16). Paul says, "God judges what people have kept secret" (cf. Heb 4:12). God's judgment goes all the way to our innermost being.

Finally, God's judgment is in the hands of the Lord Jesus Christ (2:16). The apostle concludes this heavy section by saying that this judgment is "according to my gospel"—that is, judgment is an important aspect of the gospel—and that it is "through Christ Jesus." God has appointed this judgment to Christ, which we read elsewhere (cf. John 5:22,27; Acts 17:31; 2 Cor 5:10).

Look over the list. Do you see why we need the gospel? We need a gospel that is *powerful* and *saving*, and Paul said in his thesis that this is the kind of gospel we have (Rom 1:16)!

Jewish Hypocrisy
ROMANS 2:17-29

Paul focuses more on the Jews' privileged position, showing that mere possession of the law and circumcision cannot shield them from judgment (Schreiner, *Romans*, 127). The Jews gloried in the *covenant*, the *law*, and *circumcision* routinely. These were the "three pillars of Judaism" of sorts. Some Jews wanted to hide behind these things. But Paul says there is nowhere to hide from the judgment of God except in Christ Jesus. These pillars are useless if no obedience springs from faith.

As we read about what Paul says to the Jews, please know that there is not an ounce of anti-Semitism here. If anyone loved the Jews, it was Paul (cf. Rom 9:1-5), and out of love he speaks the truth to them.

These verses are applicable for everyone, not just the Jew, in that it is possible to be deeply religious yet not be converted. It is possible to be an unconverted irreligious person or an unconverted religious person. *You do not practice what you preach from the law of God (2:17-22).* Paul begins a dialogue with a (hypothetical) Jewish instructor. He says to him, "You call yourself a Jew" (v. 17), a name originally associated with the region of Judah that refers to those belonging to the people of Israel. The name suggested a special status. He continues, saying, "[You] rely on the law," meaning you trust in your possession of the law. He adds, "[You] boast in God," which is not wrong, but when it creates pride and superiority instead of humility, then it is less about God and more about self-boasting. Further, Paul says the Jewish instructor knows God's will (v. 18a). The Jews had the written Word of God, a tremendous privilege. Further, "[You] approve the things that are superior" (v. 18b). They were able to apply the law, making moral judgments. Additionally, Paul says, the Jew is "instructed from the law" (v. 18c). This is how they could know God's will and approve what is best. In the synagogues and from childhood and in other contexts, they would have been instructed.

Paul adds to these privileges a statement about the Jewish instructor's ability to guide those in darkness, to instruct the ignorant, and to teach the immature with the law (v. 19). Having been taught, Jews were to teach others. This was part of the Jewish mission—to be a light to the nations (Isa 42:6; 49:6). The Torah was to be a beacon of justice in an unjust world. Israel was to show the world what God was like.

The problem, of course, was that the Jew needed a new spiritual heart, just as a non-Jew needs a new heart. Today a person can strut around with a Greek or Hebrew Bible he can quote, but not be converted. It is indeed a privilege to have and be instructed in the Word of God. But there is a world of difference between the possession of privileges and the possession of saving faith.

Paul poses a set of questions to the privileged Jew regarding how well he has lived up to these privileges. He asks, "Don't you teach yourself?" (v. 21). Implication? Your life indicates that you do not sit under your own preaching. Three particular sins are then mentioned: (1) you preach against stealing, yet you steal (v. 21b); (2) you preach against adultery, yet you commit adultery (v. 22a); (3) you preach against idolatry, yet you benefit from the idols you detested (v. 22b). Does this mean every Jew committed these sins? Of course not. Not every Jew robbed temples! These are colorful examples of lawbreaking. Paul is saying something that is true generally: all Jews are guilty before God. They have not kept the law of God fully. The Gentiles have not kept the law of God written on the heart, and the Jews have not kept the law written on tablets.

You dishonor the name of God (2:23-24). Next we see the shameful effects of hypocrisy. In verse 23 Paul says that by not practicing what you preach, you "dishonor God" (23; cf. 1:21). In verse 24 Paul seems to combine Isaiah 52:5 and Ezekiel 36:22. In both texts God's name had been dishonored because the people had not been faithful, and they were consequently conquered by foreign powers. What honors God and attracts the nations is faith-fueled obedience to God.

You need to be transformed inwardly by the Spirit of God (2:25-29). The Jews have the Torah but have not kept it. Now Paul says they have circumcision but have not experienced circumcision of the heart. Circumcision was a sign pointing to God's covenant with Israel (Gen 17:9-14), but it was not a magic charm. It did not provide protection from God's wrath. Some Jews had apparently developed a superstitious attitude about this, believing that circumcision prevented one from descending to Gehenna.

The sign of circumcision was meant to point to an inner reality. This is made plain throughout the New Testament (e.g., Gal 6:15). While baptism and circumcision are different, they share a connection. Baptism is to be a sign of an inward reality, but the sign is worthless without the reality—new life in Christ. So Paul tells the Jews in Rome that circumcision is no substitute for the obedience of faith.

In verses 25-26 he says that circumcision has value if you keep the law. Paul validates the divine origin of circumcision but clarifies that it has with it a requirement to obey the law. Circumcision is a sign of the covenant, and the covenant involved a commitment to obedience. If you are circumcised and you break the law, it is as if you have not been circumcised (25b). On the other hand, if you have not been circumcised but keep the law, it is as if you have been circumcised. Again, what matters is not possession of the law or the external act of circumcision but obedience that springs from faith.

In verse 27 he adds a shocking thought: the obedient Gentiles will sit in judgment over the disobedient Jews. The Jews thought they were sitting in judgment, but Paul flips it on them (cf. Matt 12:41-42).

Paul then gets right to the heart of the matter. He tells us who the true people of God are. True Jewishness is not something outward and visible but inward and invisible (v. 28). One can be a Jew ethnically but not spiritually (cp. 9:6). Paul paves the way for a later discussion in chapter 9, where he will distinguish between Israel according to the flesh and Israel according to the promise (9:8). By speaking of the obedience of the Gentiles, Paul introduces a concept he will elaborate on more fully—he is provoking the Jews to holy jealousy (11:11).

Paul's statement about true circumcision being a matter "of the heart—by the Spirit" (2:29) is not new to him. It occurs regularly in the Old Testament. God tells his people to circumcise their hearts (Deut 10:16) and also promised a new heart. In the new covenant era the Holy Spirit will make this a reality in believers (Ezek 36:25-27; cf. Rom 7:5-6), as Paul says, "By the Spirit, not the letter," meaning the Spirit will do something the law could not do: make us new! The phrase "That person's praise is not from people but from God" (v. 29) means God will approve the person with the new heart. Paul probably has something at the end in mind. On the final day, God will honor those who are truly his people.

Therefore, outward conformity cannot save. The Spirit of God must transform one inwardly. This can happen through the gospel, which is powerful enough to save both the Jew and the Gentile (1:16).

Reflect and Discuss

1. Why would people today find Romans 1:18-32 deeply offensive? Should you avoid teaching it? If not, how do you think this material should be presented?
2. What does Paul say about people knowing of the existence of God in 1:18-23?
3. How does Paul connect idolatry to immorality (1:18-32)?
4. What does Paul mean by "God delivered them over" (1:18-32)?
5. Why do both the self-righteous moralist and the unrighteous hedonist need the gospel?
6. What points about God's judgment do you find most striking? Why?
7. What does Paul say about the law of God on tablets and the law written on hearts?
8. Why do religious people need to give careful attention to Romans 2:17-29?
9. Explain Paul's emphasis on internal transformation as opposed to external circumcision in 2:25-29.
10. What should all this teaching about the reality of God's judgment cause us to do?

Why We Need the Gospel: No One Is Righteous

ROMANS 3:1-20

Main Idea: Paul describes how no one is righteous before God, thus showing us our desperate need for salvation in Christ Jesus.

I. **In the Classroom with Paul (3:1-8)**
   A. What advantage does the Jew have (3:1-2)?
   B. Does Jewish unfaithfulness nullify God's faithfulness (3:3-4)?
   C. Are we doing God a favor by sinning (3:5-8)?
II. **In the Courtroom with Paul (3:9-20)**
   A. The accusation (3:9)
   B. The evidence (3:10-18)
      1. The character of the accused (3:10-12)
      2. The conversation of the accused (3:13-14)
      3. The conduct of the accused (3:15-81)
   C. The verdict (3:19-20)

I love being a pastor, but one of the things I dislike about my role is having people feel like they should change their normal behavior around me. I cannot tell you how many times I have been in the middle of a conversation with a stranger when he or she asks the inevitable, "What do you do for a living?" I always hesitate to answer because I know shock or negativity may follow. Sometimes when I say, "I'm a pastor," the stranger will say, "Oh I'm sorry, I didn't mean to cuss" (or say something else that was inappropriate). One night I was watching a New Orleans Saints football game, and I had been interacting with the fans next to me, who were not using many church words. Eventually, after finding out I was a pastor, one of the guys said, "Please, don't think too badly of me. I'm a good guy." I gently responded to this particular guy, "Hey, I appreciate it, but you aren't accountable to me; you are accountable to God." It made for an awkward moment, but I hope he remembers this statement.

Paul shows us in Romans 3 that the whole world is accountable to God, who sees all and knows all. We see here what is wrong with the human race and why we desperately need the Savior.

Paul's teaching skills are on display in verses 1-8. He paints a hypothetical picture of someone interrupting his teaching with objections, so he answers the imaginary objector's questions.

Paul's lawyer skills are then on display in verses 9-20. He seeks to bring a verdict of "guilty" on all of humanity. As a theological-prophetic lawyer, Paul is remarkably convincing. Paul is not a shady lawyer. He is a theologically precise lawyer with a big heart for people. His goal is for people to see their sin so that they will see their need for Christ. John Piper says of Romans 3:9-20,

> This is not a popular message. Understandably. It is no more popular than the doctor's words: "Your tumor is malignant." But it is vastly more hopeful. "Your tumor is malignant," may or may not be hopeful news, because the doctor may or may not have a cure for your cancer. But "you are under the power of sin and a child of wrath" always has a cure. That is what the book of Romans and what Christianity and the Bible are all about. (Piper, "All Jews and Gentiles Are under Sin")

So let's read of our dreadful condition, and then let's turn to the glorious cure.

In the Classroom with Paul
ROMANS 3:1-8

Paul anticipates objections and questions like a good teacher. The questions are essentially about the character of God—his faithfulness and righteousness. Paul is defending God's character. He answers four questions, but I will combine questions three and four.

What Advantage Does the Jew Have? (3:1-2)

Short answer: Israel was entrusted with the promises of God.

Based on what Paul said at the end of chapter 2, the question is natural: What is the point in being a Jew? Are there any advantages? Yes and no. The yes comes here in verse 2: "They were entrusted with the very words of God." The no comes in verse 9: "Are we any better off? Not at all! For we have already charged that both Jews and Greeks are all under sin."

Regarding the yes, the Jew should consider that it is a glorious privilege to have the Scriptures (cf. Rom 9:4-5). The Jews received God's specific revelation. They had the promises of God—promises made to the patriarchs, promises made regarding God's character, and promises made about the coming Messiah. This possession did not mean, however, that they were actually saved. They were not saved simply by being Jewish (some people seem to believe this today). Many Jews have failed to believe in the Messiah. So the privilege of having God's Word does not take you very far if you do not believe in the promised One, Jesus. The Savior rebuked the religious leaders for not believing in him, the one to whom the Scriptures testify:

> *You pore over the Scriptures because you think you have eternal life in them, and yet they testify about me. But you are not willing to come to me so that you may have life.* (John 5:39-40)

Does Jewish Unfaithfulness Nullify God's Faithfulness? (3:3-4)

Short answer: Of course not! Paul introduces a concern here that he will address more fully in Romans 9, where he defends the idea that God's Word has not failed (9:6).

God promised to be faithful to Abraham's descendants, but Paul says the Jew is guilty. Does the Jews' lack of faithfulness to God's promises make God unfaithful? Paul gives an emphatic negative: "Absolutely not!" (3:4). Paul cannot imagine the idea of God being unfaithful. God's faithfulness is not contingent on Israel's response (Bird, *Romans*, 93). Paul rejects the idea that for God to be faithful he must accept Israel whether they are right or wrong. (Later, in Romans 11, Paul will elaborate more fully God's plan for Israel in the future.)

Paul then adds a proverbial statement: "Let God be true, even though everyone is a liar" (v. 4). If every human being who ever lived declared that God is faithless, God would be found true and every man who testified against him would be found a liar. There is an allusion here to Psalm 116:11. God will win the verdict when the world goes on trial. He is true. He is faithful. Even though the world is full of liars, God never lies. He is always true.

We should take great comfort in the fact that God is faithful. Take comfort in the fact that he is true and his word is entirely trustworthy.

Paul goes on to cite Psalm 51: "That you may be justified in your words and triumph when you judge" (Rom 3:4). Paul adds a note from the Jews' great king David, who agrees with the apostle. After David sinned against God in the Bathsheba incident, he was willing to be judged, and God proved right in judging him. David says God's judgment was "blameless" (Ps 51:4). Our covenant-keeping God is faithful and just in his judgment.

Are We Doing God a Favor by Sinning? (3:5-8)

Short answer: no! (See Piper, "Let God be True.") This is an outrageous line of thinking. Addressing an imaginary objector who asks this question, Paul gives two examples, the first regarding *unrighteousness* and the second regarding *lying*. Concerning the first scenario he asks, "If by committing an act of *unrighteousness,* God's *righteousness* shines, then how is it right for God to be angry with me?" (vv. 5-6, paraphrase). The second scenario is painted similarly: "If *lying* makes God's *truth* look glorious, then why am I still condemned for it?" (vv. 7-8, paraphrase).

The answer to the first scenario comes in verse 5: "Is God unrighteous to inflict wrath?" Answer: "Absolutely not!" The notion that unrighteous conduct could ever serve a good purpose of enhancing God's righteous character is strictly a "human argument" (v. 5). It arises from "a corrupt mind" (1:28). Reasoning in this way required the denial of a basic truth the Jews believed—that God will judge the world in perfect righteousness (v. 6; cf. Gen 18:25; Ps 96:13; Joel 3:12). If punishment on God's part implied injustice at all, he could not serve as the final judge of all humans.

Paul then repudiates the other scenario: lying for the purpose of magnifying God's truthfulness (v. 8). God is not pleased when you lie. He is not grateful that you lied in order to magnify his truthfulness.

Verses 5-8 bear similarity to the question Paul poses in Romans 6: "Should we continue in sin so that grace may multiply?" (6:1). His answer there is: "Absolutely not!" (6:2).

Attempting to show God's glory by sinning is outrageous and can never be justified. We must not do evil that good may come of it. We must remember that God is the just Judge. He hates evil, and we must too. We must not put the Lord to the test. You are never doing God a favor by sinning!

Paul rounds out this section with a clear response (3:8). It is appropriate to condemn those who argue in this way.

People are not only sinful in behavior but also twisted in their reasoning. There is a warning here to all who want to play games with the Bible or come up with wild philosophical objections to hide from the reality of God's holiness. Do not do that! See the plain teaching of Scripture and respond in humble repentance and faith.

In the Courtroom with Paul

ROMANS 3:9-20

After answering these questions, Paul concluded the section of Romans 1:18–3:20, proclaiming that the whole world is under the judgment of God. In verse 9 he levels an accusation; in verses 10-18 he gives the evidence; and in verses 19-20 he pronounces the verdict.

The Accusation (3:9)

In verse 2 Paul said the Jews had an advantage because they had been entrusted with God's oracles. But they are not in a better position when it comes to their status apart from Christ. Are they any better off than the Gentiles spiritually? Answer: "Not at all!" (v. 9).

Are the Jews privileged? Yes. Are they without accountability before God? No. Paul adds, "For we have already charged that both Jews and Greeks are all under sin" (v. 9). It turns out that their advantages are not that advantageous (Bird, *Romans*, 97). When it comes to judgment, they are in the same position as the Gentiles. Both are "under sin" (cf. 6:6,14-15,20; 7:14).

The Evidence (3:10-18)

To support this argument that all are guilty, Paul rattles off a list of passages, with a heavy emphasis on the Psalms. There is so much gospel in the Psalms! These allusions are taken from the Jewish Scriptures, so the Jews could not refute Paul's argument. The big theme here is the universality of sin. No one is righteous, no one good, no one acceptable to God. The whole world needs the gospel!

Before we look at these verses, remember that Paul is not denying what we call "common grace." Unrepentant people can do remarkable things as image bearers of God. However, no one is perfectly good and never sins. No one is acceptable to God based on works. Without common grace, there would be total anarchy in the world.

If you wanted to tally up everything on this sin list, it comes to something like fourteen total charges to prove that unrepentant humanity is guilty before God. Tim Keller points out seven effects of sin in the list, saying that sin has affected (1) *our legal standing* ("No one is righteous"); (2) *our minds* ("no one . . . understands"); (3) *our motives* ("no one . . . seeks God"); (4) *our wills* ("all have turned away"); (5) *our tongues* ("their throat is an open grave"); (6) *our relationships* ("swift to shed blood"); and (7) *our relationship to God* ("no fear of God before their eyes"; *Romans 1–7*, 67–68). This is indeed a helpful way to consider the sinfulness of sin.

To look at it in an even more simplified way, I want to arrange them in three categories: (1) the *character* of the accused (vv. 10-12), (2) the *conversation* of the accused (vv. 13-14), and (3) the *conduct* of the accused (vv. 15-18). Each highlights various aspects of human sinfulness. However we group or number the statements, we see that sin affects every part of us—mind, emotions, conscience, behavior, and speech.

The Character of the Accused (3:10-12). The accused are noted first as being *unrighteous.* Paul quotes what appears to be Ecclesiastes: "There is no one righteous, not even one" (v. 10). "There is certainly no one righteous on the earth who does good and never sins" (Eccl 7:20). Because righteousness is such an important concept in Romans, it is not surprising that "unrighteousness" tops the list here.

Next, Paul adds *ignorance* to the list (v. 11a; cf. Pss 14:2; 53:2). It is God by his Spirit who graciously opens up our spiritual eyes to understand. Unrepentant people can be very intelligent, but that's different from having the knowledge of God.

Humanity is also marked by *godlessness.* Paul says, "There is no one who seeks God" (v. 11; cf. Pss 14:2; 53:2). Humanity rebels against God (cf. Rom 1:18). This is restated in verse 18: "There is no fear of God before their eyes." When people renounce God, they plunge into all manner of evil. God in his grace does seek sinners, though they do not seek him. C. S. Lewis said, "Amiable agnostics will talk cheerfully about 'man's search for God.' To me, as I then was, they might as well have talked about the mouse's search for the cat" (*Surprised by Joy,* 227). If you are currently seeking God, realize you are doing so by his grace.

Next we read of *waywardness.* Paul says, "All have turned away" (v. 12; cf. Pss 14:3; 53:3; Isa 53:6). If a person is spiritually ignorant and does not seek God, then naturally he will go his own way. "I did it my way" is not just the line to a famous song but the way of life for everyone (Bird, *Romans,* 103). In our own sinfulness and selfishness, we choose the wrong way.

The terrible profile continues as Paul says that in our sinfulness we are also *worthless*. He says, "All alike have become worthless" (v. 12; cf. Pss 14:3; 53:3). Again, this is not a denial of the things humanity can do by God's common grace, but it does mean that apart from Jesus we cannot bear fruit (John 15:1-8). At the final judgment, all that is done apart from Jesus will be seen for what it is. One of the reasons we should follow Jesus is that we want to give our lives to that which truly matters.

The last comment summarizes the character of sinful humanity: "There is no one who does what is good, not even one" (v. 12; cf. Pss 14:1,3; 53:1,3). Jesus told the rich young ruler this same thing (Mark 10:18). Sure, in God's common grace unbelievers may contribute to society and create some amazing things. But when it comes to standing before God, no one measures up. No one is so good that they do not need the saving grace of Jesus.

Look at this list and notice the universality of sin. Note how often Paul uses the words *all* and *no one*. The entire human race needs divine grace.

The Conversation of the Accused (3:13-14). Paul now shifts to talk about how our sin is expressed through our speech. Recall Jesus's words: "The mouth speaks from the overflow of the heart" (Matt 12:34). Our words reveal the condition of our hearts. Numerous proverbs talk about the destructive nature of the tongue (e.g., Prov 10:31-32; 18:21).

Paul says of sinful humanity that *their throats are open graves,* full of corruption and infection (v. 13a; cf. Ps 5:9). We cover up graves out of respect. We try to keep people from seeing the decay and corruption there. Paul says the unregenerate opens his mouth and testifies to spiritual death.

The apostle adds that *their tongues practice deceit* instead of being dedicated to the truth (v. 13b; cf. Ps 5:9). Lying and other forms of deceit are regular practices of the unrepentant. The movie starring Jim Carey, *Liar Liar,* made the point in a comedic way: our sinful hearts gravitate to lying. Lying and deceit have killed millions and damaged reputations for centuries. Jezebel's lies had Naboth killed (1 Kgs 21). Potiphar's wife's lies damaged Joseph's reputation and brought him much suffering (Gen 39).

Next, Paul says *their lips spread poison like snakes* (v. 13c; Ps 140:3). Jesus and John the Baptist called the religious teachers "vipers" (Matt 23:33; Luke 3:7).

Further, he says *their mouths are filled with cursing and bitterness* (v. 14; Ps 10:7). They lash out with hostility expressed against an enemy. Throughout the ages, humanity has used its mouth to spout out bitterness.

An analysis of human speech vividly illustrates the doctrine of sin. If you are a Christian, even though you have been declared righteous and are being sanctified now, you will still deal with the residue of the old self. Guard your words carefully. This is a spiritual battle (see Eph 4:25-32). And if you do sin with your lips against a brother or sister, then apologize humbly and seek reconciliation.

The Conduct of the Accused (3:15-18). This third category of sin involves one's "feet," or way of life. Paul says of sinful humanity that *their feet are swift to shed blood* (v. 15; cf. Prov 1:16; Isa 59:7). The violence in man's heart is expressed through violent and murderous actions. Millions of image bearers have literally been murdered throughout history. After we read of sin entering the world in Genesis 3, we immediately read of a son killing his brother (Gen 4). Without the restraining influences of things like laws, family, government, and prisons, there would be more murder.

Paul adds that *their paths are full of ruin and wretchedness and they have not known the path of peace* (vv. 16-17). Sin always leaves a trail of pain, despair, and heartache. It leaves you in ruin and wretchedness, and it causes misery for others. It leads to restlessness, not peace. A life of righteousness through Christ leads to peace.

It is important to pause and reflect on the effects of sin here. Our world tries to sell sin as something that's fun. Adult video stores or clubs may take the name "Sinsational" as if to say sin is fun (Bird, *Romans,* 104). But sin actually leads to misery and death.

Paul finishes the list by saying, *there is no fear of God before their eyes* (v. 18; Ps 36:1). They do not tremble in God's presence. This absence of the fear of the Lord leads to sin, folly, and rebellion. The book of Proverbs illustrates this with a variety of examples.

As you look over the list, what Paul is saying is clear. The evidence is overwhelming. No one has perfect righteousness outside of Christ, no matter how moral or religious one may think he or she is.

This black backdrop of sin is important because soon Paul will show us the beautiful diamond of the gospel. Against this dark backdrop we behold the beauty and wonder of what God has done for sinners.

I heard a story of a man carrying a leather case. The case looked like a camera case, only it contained a Bible, not a camera. Some kids, thinking he was holding a camera, came up and asked him to take a picture of them. So he pulled out the Bible and read Romans 3 to them! He said, "This is a picture of your spiritual condition." People today would be offended by this man's action, but I submit to you that the whole world needs to know Romans 3:10-18 so that they will understand their need for the Savior and trust him for the forgiveness of sin and eternal life. You and I will meet people who are intelligent, athletic, and beautiful. These traits are obvious externally, and they are things we can rightly admire. But they do not convey the whole story about a person. Romans 3 tells us that while you may be smart, gifted, and attractive, you are still marked by sin and in need of saving grace in Christ.

The Verdict (3:19-20)

Paul now brings his argument that began in 1:18 to a close. He concludes with an undeniable verdict of "guilty." Every unbeliever, whether Jew or Gentile, is under God's holy law and is accountable to him.

The response to this verdict is *silence* (v. 19). Every mouth is shut. No one has an argument. Everyone is accountable. The verdict is clear: we are guilty. The idolatrous, ungodly Gentiles are "without excuse" (1:20). All Jews, the critical moralists and religious legalists, also have no excuse (2:1). In the presence of God, there is no defense apart from Christ.

Notice Paul's reference to the "law" in these last two verses. Having declared that all are under sin (3:9) and having proved this assertion with a number of Old Testament texts (vv. 10-18), Paul adds that the law is saying the same thing about humanity (vv. 19-20). The phrase "those who are subject to the law" has particular relevance for the Jew. Paul says, in effect, "I'm not asking you to judge yourself based on some other religious writings. Your own writings say this! Own what the law says! You must accept the verdict."

In verse 20 Paul ends with a clarifying purpose of the law that transitions into the next section (vv. 21-26). He says,

> For no one will be justified in his sight by the works of the law, because the knowledge of sin comes through the law. (v. 20)

He seems to anticipate the argument that some people might actually live out the law perfectly. But Paul declares what we find him saying a lot in Galatians: no human being will be justified (declared righteous) by works of the law—that is, deeds done in obedience to the law. The problem is that sinful man is utterly incapable of keeping God's law perfectly. No one has the ability, or even the desire within oneself, to obey God perfectly.

Yet humans tend to believe in works-based righteousness. It is like the default mode of the heart. People think they can somehow merit or earn salvation. This belief is expressed in a number of different ways. People will do all kinds of things to feel good about themselves. Both religious people and irreligious people will do all sorts of works in an attempt to remove guilt. But it will not work.

It is important to underscore what Paul says here about one of the primary purposes of the law. He says through the law we become conscious of sin (v. 20b). The law wants you to know that you are guilty. The law tells you of your unrighteousness. Your righteousness can never be earned. When you add to this the words of Jesus—where he goes beneath the law to talk of our motives and attitudes, not merely our actions (e.g., Matt 5–7)—then we see our need for forgiveness even more.

As we come to the end of verse 20, we could present a question now to Paul: Is there any hope for humanity? We might expect him to say no, if we had no more words in the Bible other than Romans 1:18–3:20. But the answer is actually yes! All you have to do is read the next paragraph (3:21-26). The law tells us that no one is righteous. The gospel tells us of a righteousness from God that is received, not earned—through faith in Christ Jesus.

The next paragraph points to the hinge of history. If we may peek into it, we find some of the sweetest words in Romans—and indeed the whole Bible: "But now" (v. 21). The good news for sinners is that God has intervened to rescue sinful humanity. In Romans 1:18–3:20 we are naked and bare before God with no words. In Romans 3:21-26 we are clothed in the perfect, spotless, righteous garments of Christ!

Therefore, Romans is teaching that sin is much worse than most people believe, but the salvation provided by Jesus is more amazing than most people ever stop to consider. Sin is worse. Salvation is greater.

If you are not a Christian, then please consider the message of Romans. See the verdict pronounced here, but also see the provision made for you. Turn away from self and your sin, and trust in Jesus Christ for the forgiveness of sins. Turn to the all-sufficient Savior who will save you, for there is only one who kept the law perfectly: Jesus. Consider that list of passages in verses 10-18 and compare these sinful actions to the life of Jesus. The Savior never turned aside. He never uttered a sinful word. His feet were never swift to shed blood, though he gave his own blood that sinners like us may be saved. He made it possible for us to know everlasting joy and peace, not ruin and wretchedness.

If you come to him, you are free. You are right with God. You do not have to live trying to prove yourself to God and others. You get to live a life of obedience *because* you are loved and accepted, not to *earn* love and acceptance.

Christian, be thankful for the Savior who came to seek and to save the lost (Luke 19:10). Pour your heart out in gratitude to the God who sought you when you matched the description of Romans 3:9-20. Reflecting on this passage, Tim Keller helps us feel the wonder of God's saving grace:

> When we consider our own path to finding God, we need to realize that we did not seek him out; he drew us to him. We decided to put our faith in him only because he had decided to give us faith. What difference does this make? You *rejoice* to see that God is not trying to hide from you, that all the things you know about him he has chosen to reveal to you. You are *humbled* by the truth that there is nothing better or cleverer in you which means you sought God; that you have nothing that you weren't given (1 Corinthians 4:7). You are *comforted* and *confident* "that he who began a good work in you will carry it on to completion until the day of Christ Jesus" (Philippians 1:6). And you praise God with *greater gratitude*, because you know that everything about your salvation comes from him, from first to last. Salvation did not begin with you deciding to seek God, but with him choosing to seek you. You know that everything you have and are is by sheer grace. You sing:
>
> > 'Tis not that I did choose thee, for, Lord, that could not be;
> > This heart would still refuse thee, hadst thou not chosen me. . . .
> > My heart owns none before thee, for thy rich grace I thirst;
> > This knowing, if I love thee, thou must have loved me first.
> > (*Romans 1–7*, 70–71; emphasis added; song by Josiah Conder, italicized in original)

May God's saving grace cause us to rejoice, may it make us humble, may it comfort us, may it give us confidence, and may it deepen our gratitude. And out of that, let's tell it to the whole world who needs to hear that Jesus Christ came into the world to seek and to save Romans 3:9-20 kind of people. The next passage proclaims this good news loud and clear.

Reflect and Discuss

1. How is Romans 3:1-20 connected to 1:18-32?
2. What do the questions presented in 3:1-8 teach us about sinful humanity?
3. What do the questions presented in 3:1-8 teach us about God's faithfulness?
4. How are the Jews privileged? How are they also no better off than the Gentiles?
5. What are the three categories of accusations in 3:9-20, according to this commentary?
6. Consider Paul's Old Testament references in 3:9-18. Which reference is most striking to you?
7. Go back and read the chapters from which each Old Testament reference is found. What additional insights do you glean by reading those entire chapters?
8. What does Paul's emphasis on sins of the tongue say to us about this particular example of human sinfulness?
9. What is one purpose of the law, according to Romans 3:20?
10. How does Romans 1:18–3:20 prepare us for 3:21-26?

The Glory of Christ's Salvation

ROMANS 3:21-31

Main Idea: Right standing with God can only come through faith in Jesus's atoning work.

I. **Intervention (3:21a)**
II. **Justification (3:21-24a)**
III. **Redemption (3:24b)**
IV. **Propitiation (3:25a)**
V. **Demonstration (3:25b-26)**
VI. **Implications (3:27-31)**

Have you ever been to a Brazilian steak house? Recently the pastors and elders at Imago Dei Church took a group of our aspiring pastors to one. After we took our trip around the salad bar, it was game on. Each of us received a little card, red on one side and green on the other. Red means, "I'm full. No thanks." Green side up means, "Keep the meat coming!" The waitstaff approach green card holders asking, "Filet?" "Sirloin?" "Lamb leg?" "Sausage?" We had a remarkable dining experience!

This passage reminds me of going to a Brazilian steak house. With phrase after phrase of gospel goodness, Paul just keeps putting more theological meat on our plates.

We find here some of the most important truths in the Bible concerning the nature of salvation. In Romans 1:18–3:20 we saw that we are great sinners. Now, in 3:21-26, we learn of the greatness of Christ's saving work on behalf of sinners. In 1:18–3:20 the universal human problem is exposed: sin. In 3:21-26 the universal human problem is solved—in Christ Jesus.

Romans is one of the most important books in the Bible for understanding the gospel. Verses 21-26 may be the most important in the book of Romans (Schreiner, "The Saving and Judging Righteousness of God"). What we are studying is more important than the latest news story. It is more important than the latest sporting event. It is more important than how much money you make and how well you look externally.

Consider what a few scholars have said about this passage. Reformation leader Martin Luther said that it is "the chief point, and the very central place of the Epistle, and of the whole Bible" (in Morris, *Epistle*, 218). Morris says it "is possibly the most important single paragraph ever written" (*Epistle*, 173). New Testament scholar C. E. B. Cranfield rightly calls this passage "the center and heart" of the whole letter (in Longenecker, *Romans*, 391). Mike Bird calls it "the epicenter of [Paul's] gospel" (*Romans*, 110).

It is a theological feast. We see the mega themes of the saving righteousness of God: justification, redemption, propitiation, grace, faith, and more. Morris points out that there is wonderful imagery present here as Paul speaks of salvation as *justification* (using law court imagery), salvation as *redemption* (using the imagery of the marketplace; I would add of the exodus event also), and salvation as *propitiation* (using the image of a sacrifice that averts wrath; *Epistle*, 173). We will explore each of these concepts along with the other themes present here.

In short, we learn a lot about what makes the gospel such good news. Let's consider Jesus's atoning work on behalf of sinners under six headings.

Intervention

ROMANS 3:21A

Paul begins with the two sweet words, "But now" (v. 21a). After describing humanity's dreadful condition, Paul gives us glorious hope. God has done something on behalf of sinners. He has intervened to rescue us from the wrath to come (cf. 1 Cor 15:20; Eph 2:13; Col 1:22).

Verse 21 is not just a literary shift in the letter; it also signifies a historical shift in salvation history (Moo, *Letter*, 126). God's saving power has invaded the world in the coming of the Messiah. This is good news! The life, death, resurrection, and ascension of Jesus changed everything. The whole world stands in the dock waiting for God's judgment, but now Christ has appeared, and his arrival is the ultimate game changer.

These two words ("But now") denote God's gracious intervention. Imagine playing a basketball game at a city park. Your team is horrible. You just keep getting beat. Then someone says, "Hey, Anthony Davis just showed up." After some discussion he gets placed on your team. Your team was awful, "but now" you have hope. But now you have victory. With the coming of the all-star Davis, your situation has been reversed.

In an infinitely greater and more important way, Jesus has changed our situation. We were losers, lost and without hope, but now Christ Jesus has done what we could not do for ourselves. Through our union with him, we will not perish but will have victory over death. God's intervention in Jesus Christ gives hope to sinful humanity.

Justification

ROMANS 3:21-24A

Once again the important theme of *righteousness* appears in Romans. The Greek root behind *righteousness* and *justification* is found throughout Romans. It dominates this particular passage (notice how frequently these words appear in vv. 21-31).

How can one be right with God? That is the question answered here. By faith in Christ, we are put in the right before God; we are justified. We are given a righteousness we cannot earn (cf. Phil 3:9).

Wayne Grudem defines *justification* this way: "Justification is an instantaneous legal act of God in which he (1) thinks of our sins as forgiven and Christ's righteousness as belonging to us, and (2) declares us to be righteous in his sight" (*Systematic Theology*, 723). So God is our judge. We all sit before him, and he declares only those in Christ to be in the right (cf. Rom 4:22). If you put your faith in Jesus, God declares that you are forgiven, acquitted, and put into a right relationship with God based on what Christ has done for us through his sinless life and his death and resurrection (Bird, *Romans*, 115; cf. 2 Cor 5:21). Justified people have a new status, a new identity, a new family, and a new hope of enjoying a new creation.

In verse 21 Paul says, "The righteousness of God has been revealed," that is, in Jesus. In verse 22 he says that "righteousness" has been given to us; that is, God has provided a righteousness for sinners through their faith in Christ. In verses 25-26 he goes on to say that the cross shows God's righteous character (as we will examine later). The character of God is righteous, and our salvation is about being declared righteous before him.

Job asked the question, "How can a person be justified before God?" (Job 9:2). The two answers given throughout history are these: (1) human achievement or (2) divine accomplishment. The gospel is what God has accomplished for us in Christ Jesus; it is not about how we can achieve right standing before God on our own.

Here is good news. In Jesus, God gives us a righteousness that we do not have and we cannot earn—it is "apart from the law" (v. 21). This saving righteousness is received by faith.

Why do we need God's saving righteousness? Paul tells us: "For all have sinned and fall short of the glory of God" (v. 23). Paul reminds us of the previous section in Romans (1:18–3:20). Every single person, Jew and Gentile alike, has fallen short of God's glory. Compared to other people, you may feel fairly good about yourself. But in light of God's glorious character, our sin is exposed. We are miserably short of God's standard. Paul says this is true of everyone; "There is no distinction" (3:22). We are not just a little naughty. We are not just a little bit mischievous. We have fallen way short of the glory of God. This is why we need God's saving righteousness.

Paul's phrase "apart from the law" (v. 21) or "apart from the works of the law" (v. 28) shows us that right standing before God cannot be earned by doing good works, by following either Jewish laws or some other standard of laws. Following the rules cannot save you. The spirit of legalism crushes people; it does not liberate them. It is a false gospel. By saying this, Paul is not disrespecting the Mosaic law. This passage displays its importance. The law shows us our need for the Savior. No one can obey the law perfectly. This is not a new idea. Paul will show from the life of Abraham in chapter 4 that justification/salvation has always been by faith apart from works of the law.

This passage also teaches us the important truth that salvation is received by *faith* in Christ alone—the Christ who was perfectly faithful and righteous. Notice the repetition in verse 22: "to all who believe." Morris points out that verse 22 contains the first time in Romans that *faith* is expressly linked to Christ (*Epistle*, 175). The call to believe is repeated throughout the paragraph (vv. 25-28,30). Paul is not speaking of a generic faith but faith with a particular object, faith in a particular person: Christ. Throughout Romans faith in Christ appears repeatedly. We are not put in the right before God by working for God but by trusting in the Savior.

In verse 28 Paul reiterates this point: "A person is justified by faith apart from the works of the law." Obedience to the precepts of the law cannot save a person. Following religious systems cannot save you. Following any set of religious rules as a means of gaining salvation is not the gospel. Yet many today still preach a "Jesus + something else" gospel. Mike Bird states this point provocatively:

In my short time, as a follower of Jesus, I've had people tell
me that in order to be saved, I need to speak in tongues,
partake of some sacrament, only read the King James Bible,
subscribe to a certain confession, believe in this diagram of
the end times, jump through a dozen other hoops that seem
to serve the purpose of validating the rantings of some lunatic
with an opinion and a desperate desire to force it on others.
Fortunately for me, I was well discipled by Christian leaders
and attended churches where the pastors were committed
to biblical preaching, so I never got suckered into the "Jesus
plus" stairway to salvation. But sadly many do. (*Romans*, 128)

Praise God we have been saved not on the basis of our works but on the
basis of Christ's work for us!

Paul's reference to "the Law and the Prophets" refers to the Old
Testament (v. 21; cf. Luke 5:17; 24:27). The Old Testament teaches us
about the saving righteousness of God. The gospel is no afterthought.
The cross was not plan B but always plan A (Moo, *Letter*, 126). So the Old
Testament and the New Testament teach the same message of salvation,
not two different messages of salvation. Paul uses Abraham as a model in
chapter 4, and he has already quoted Habakkuk in 1:17. These are but
two examples of the continuity between the Old Testament and the New
Testament. The Old Testament speaks of the saving righteousness of God
in Christ: the Messiah would come. A messianic wind blows throughout
the pages of the God-breathed Scriptures. And some texts are so obviously messianic—found in verses, visions, promises, experiences, and
victories—that they are like flashing lights pointing to an emergency exit
(Bird, *Romans*, 112; see Gen 3:15; 12–15; 49:10; Lev 17:11; Deut 18:15;
2 Sam 7:11-14; Isa 11:1-16; 52:13–53:12; Jer 31; Ezek 34).

Further, Paul teaches that our justification comes "by his grace as a
gift" (v. 24 ESV). It is given freely, and we receive it in the same way we
receive a gift. We cannot win God's grace by meticulous Torah observance or by religious deeds (Bird, *Romans*, 116). "God helps those who
help themselves" is a popular concept, but it is not the gospel. It is not
in the Bible. God is not a self-help guru who is helping us improve ourselves a bit (ibid.). God is the gracious Savior who saves those who cannot save themselves.

Salvation is not about trying harder or doing more. It is about receiving God's grace and being transformed. Justification, the act whereby

God declares us righteous in Christ, is rooted in God's undeserved favor bestowed on sinners. It is all of grace (see Eph 2:8-9).

Redemption
ROMANS 3:24B

The next metaphor of salvation Paul mentions is "redemption" (v. 24b). There are numerous references to redemption in Paul's writings (see Rom 8:23; 1 Cor 1:30; 6:20; Eph 1:7,14; 4:30; Col 1:14; 1 Tim 2:6; Titus 2:14), as well as in the rest of the New Testament (see Matt 20:28; Mark 10:45; Luke 21:28; Heb 9:15; 1 Pet 1:18). Morris notes that this picture has its origin in the release of prisoners of war on payment of a price, and it included the freeing of slaves through a payment (*Epistle*, 179). In a similar way, apart from Christ we are captives (cf. Rom 7:14), but we can be free through the payment of a price. In the death of Jesus, our price was paid. Paul says our salvation comes "through the redemption that is in Christ Jesus" (v. 24). Our freedom is tied to the work of Christ. Jesus's death has infinite value because he is of infinite worth! The all-sufficient Savior, the spotless Lamb of God, paid the price so that we could go free! As a result, we are no longer slaves but sons and daughters of God (Gal 4:4-7).

In the Old Testament the dominant image of redemption is the exodus event. Liberation from Egypt and the blood of the Passover Lamb immediately come to mind. The exodus event involved these basic components: (1) the need for redemption, (2) the price of redemption, (3) the glory of the Redeemer, and (4) the familial nature of redemption (Lau and Goswell, *Unceasing Kindness*, 119). These components are important to understand in order to rightly appreciate the Christian's greater exodus through Christ. N. T. Wright says,

> In the classic biblical picture, all together are enslaved, like Israel in Egypt. What God did for Israel then, he does for the whole world now, in Jesus: he provides "redemption." . . .
>
> [T]he death of Jesus is indeed the New Exodus, the moment when the slaves are freed. . . . God has supplied what the world needs, namely, release from slavery. (*Romans, Part 1*, 54–55)

We *need* redemption because we are weak and helpless. In the exodus, the people of Israel were enslaved to Egypt. Not only were they under political slavery, economic slavery, and social slavery, but they were also under spiritual slavery—for God desired to deliver them so that "they [could] worship [him]" (Exod 9:1). In the New Testament our need is magnified. We are dead in sin and in need of new life (Eph 2:1-3). We are under God's wrath (Rom 1:18-32; Eph 2:3). We are slaves to sin (Rom 5:12; 6:16-20,23). We are in the kingdom of darkness, in need of transference into the kingdom of light (Col 1:13-14).

Regarding the *price* of redemption, the sacrificial lamb and the deliverance from Egypt are bound together. This lamb would save Israel's firstborn, but the Egyptian firstborns would not be spared because they were not under the blood of the lamb. In the New Testament this theme escalates. Paul says we were "bought at a price" (1 Cor 6:20; 7:23). We have freedom from bondage through the death of Jesus, the Passover Lamb (1 Cor 5:7). Atoning blood was shed to purchase our freedom, as Paul goes on to say in our text (v. 25). Jesus's death is the ransom paid for us (Mark 10:45). Peter says we have been redeemed, not with silver or gold but with the precious blood of Christ (1 Pet 1:18-19). We could cite more references, until we arrive at Revelation, where Jesus is worshiped as the Lamb who was slain for sinners from every tribe and tongue (Rev 5:9).

Regarding the *glory* of the Redeemer, God's redemption throughout the Old Testament is expressed through his *willingness* and his *ability* to redeem; his *character* and his *power* are magnified in his work of redemption. God was willing to hear the cries of Israel and able to deliver them from the world's superpower, Egypt. After freeing his people, the Lord then issued instructions so that his people would reflect his character. They were to show grace to the sojourner because they were once strangers in the land of Egypt before the Lord brought them out (cf. Lev 19:33-34; Deut 10:19). God's heart for redemption was to be expressed through his people, who were to care for the widow, the orphan, and the stranger. Further, they were not to enslave one another, since they used to be slaves in Egypt. The releases described in Leviticus 25 are like micro-exoduses.

The glory of Christ our Redeemer is evidenced in both his *willingness* to redeem and in his *ability* to do it. His willingness is described in various places, like Philippians 2:5-11. His love and grace are demonstrated in his life and his death for sinners (cf. Rom 5:8). And how can his death atone for so many? Because of his own immeasurable worth, his death has immeasurable value.

Finally, when we think about redemption, we need to remember that redemption is tied to *family*. In the exodus God's redemption is explained with familial language. God is the ultimate *go'el* (Redeemer) who rescues his people. He calls Israel his "son" (Exod 4:23). God told Moses of the purpose or goal of his redeeming work: "I will take you as my people, and I will be your God. You will know that I am the LORD your God" (Exod 6:7). Thus, redemption and covenant relationship are tied together. In the New Testament the relationship between redemption and familial intimacy can be found in various places. The redeemed are the adopted (cf. Rom 8:12-30; Gal 4:4-7; Eph 1:3-14). They become brothers and sisters in the household of God.

Propitiation
ROMANS 3:25A

Paul continues by telling us that our salvation was paid for by Christ's propitiatory sacrifice. He says that God put Christ forward as "a propitiation" (v. 25a ESV) or "the mercy seat" (CSB) by his blood. Christ was put forward publicly. His death was not hidden away in a corner. And his death was sacrificial.

The sacrifice of Jesus involved more than just physical sacrifice. The idea of propitiation involves appeasing the righteous wrath of God. The Son bore the penalty from God and paid the price that sinners owed to God. His death involved penal substitution. He took our penalty. Jesus satisfied the just demands of the law, bore the Father's wrath against sin, and reconciled believers to the Father.

There is a lot of debate around this Greek word *hilastērion*. Some translate it as "propitiation" (ESV) or "sacrifice of atonement" (NIV). Others translate it as "expiation" (RSV). *Expiation* means the cleansing, or the wiping away, of sin. It emphasizes how our sins are erased. Jesus does cleanse us from sin. But is that the best rendering of this word?

It seems that the idea *propitiation* is better, even though many do not like the idea of Jesus appeasing his Father's wrath. This is what the word means in ordinary Greek—it was the "mercy seat," which was the Old Testament means of propitiation (Exod 25:21-22). And this is the context of Romans (beginning with Rom 1:18). Jesus appeased or satisfied God's wrath. God has righteous anger against us because of our sin, and his wrath must be appeased or satisfied. If someone does not take our punishment, we are still under God's wrath (cf. John 3:36). Those who reject Christ are targets of God's wrath.

So wrath and propitiation go together. We have offended the King of the universe, and he will punish sin. The good news is that Jesus satisfied the Father's righteous wrath on our behalf. The Son of God died to save us from the wrath of God.

To be clear, the picture is not of the Father as an angry old man and Jesus as a nice and mild man who offers to satisfy the rage of his crazy dad. There is unity in the action and purpose in this work. The Father puts the Son forward, and the Son willingly obeys the Father. Love and justice motivated the cross event. We should remember both of these attributes when considering the cross. What motivated the atonement? Both love and justice.

What is the result of embracing the biblical teaching of the propitiation? It is this: we have peace with God (Rom 5:1). We are no longer enemies of God. We are reconciled to God (5:6-11). The wrath of God has been turned away so that we may be reconciled to the Father and brought into his family.

While Christ as our substitute is not a popular idea, the reality is, if you reject the atonement, you are rejecting the greatest news in the world. For here is the good news, Christian: you never have to live a day in fear of the Father's wrath. His Fatherly discipline is transformative but not punitive. Jesus bore your punishment already. We are the Father's kids. He loves us. On our worst days we can run into his presence, and he will not tell us "Get out" but "Welcome." Praise God for the cross!

Demonstration
ROMANS 3:25B-26

So, in salvation, God declares unrighteous people righteous through faith in Christ's atoning work. This salvation not only involves a *declaration* of righteousness; it also involves a *demonstration* of God's righteousness. Twice we read of this demonstration of God's character (vv. 25b-26). Later Paul says the cross demonstrates God's love (5:8), but here he emphasizes that the cross displays God's righteousness. Through the work of Christ on the cross, God has vindicated his own righteous character and at the same time bestowed a righteous status on sinners.

Paul adds that God, in his divine forbearance, "passed over the sins previously committed" (v. 25b). How could God possibly tolerate the sins people committed before the cross of Christ (cf. Acts 17:30)? At one level we should remember that God actually did punish before the cross. Just read the Old Testament stories (e.g., see the flood, the tower of Babel matter, the consequences of the various rebellions of Israel). However, God did not exact the *full penalty* for sinning against his glorious character.

God, then, was showing mercy and patience with a view toward showing his righteousness in the future at the cross. God did not overlook sin because he is fickle or forgetful but because he is kind and patient, desiring people to repent (Rom 2:4) and because he planned to act in the cross.

So, the problem being addressed is this: How can a holy God accept sinful men and women without violating his justice? And that problem is resolved in the cross. At the cross God both upholds his just character and accepts sinners as righteous before him. As Paul says, he "would be just and justify" (v. 26). His righteousness is vindicated, and believing sinners are justified. Tim Keller comments that Paul explains that the cross shows us that

> God is *both* the Judge, who cares enough about the world to set standards and hold us accountable to them; *and* the Justifier, who has done everything necessary to forgive and restore us. He is a Father worth having, and he is a Father we can have. The cross is where, graciously and liberatingly, we see that he is "just and the one who justifies those who have faith in Jesus." (*Romans 1–7*, 85; emphasis in original)

The glory of this salvation shows us the wonder of God's love and justice, and it shows us that Jesus occupies a unique position, being the only one who could both save sinners and satisfy God's wrath. He represents us as he takes our punishment, and he represents God in giving us perfect righteousness.

Paul has been presenting a tension thus far—the good news of salvation (1:1) and God's intention of punishing both Jews and Gentiles for their guilt (1:18–3:20). How will this happen? How can God justify the ungodly and also punish? How can God be the impartial cosmic Judge and be faithful to his promises to save through the Messiah? Answer: God is both the Judge and the Deliverer. He pardons and he punishes. Both can be seen at the cross.

Implications
ROMANS 3:27-31

Like a good preacher, Paul moves from explanation to implications. Having viewed the gospel from various angles, Paul now addresses our hearts and our relationships in light of these gospel truths. In verse 27 we see the exclusion of boasting (humility), and in verses 28-31 we see the idea of this same message of salvation being for both Jew and Gentile (unity).

So, first, the good news should humble us. Paul says, "Boasting? It is excluded" (v. 27). If Romans 3:21-26 is true, and it is, how could anyone boast? All reason for boasting is destroyed. Did you earn this salvation? No! Did you work for it? No! Are you righteous by yourself? No!

Ministers often speak of the "five *solas*" of the reformation: grace alone, through faith alone, in Christ alone, based on Scripture alone, for the glory of God alone. This passage (vv. 21-31) has all of these components, with verse 27 falling in the "glory of God alone" category.

One of the signs that you grasp the gospel is that you give praise to God. You become a humbly grateful person. You recognize that the greatest thing in the world you have has been given to you by grace. You did not earn it; it came through the "law of faith" (v. 27b), that is, the "principle of faith," not through works done in obedience to the law. It is by grace through faith; therefore, the giver of this salvation gets the glory.

Second, the good news is the basis for our Christian unity (vv. 28-31). All humans, Jew and Gentile alike, are saved the same way, before the same God, and are therefore united in the gospel. If the Jews could attain salvation in some special way, there would be separation, but they cannot. The cross, then, destroys discrimination.

In verse 30 Paul says that God will justify both by faith. This is why ethnic hostility is so out of step with the gospel. The ground is level at the cross. The gospel changes everything—not just our vertical relationship with God but also our horizontal relationships with others. The gospel is the heavy artillery that destroys the barrier between us and God, and it destroys the barrier between ethnicities. Jesus Christ unites the ethnicities by his cross work. His forgiveness enables us to forgive and love. His grace enables us to be "gracists," not racists.

In verse 31 Paul says, "We uphold the law" but not as a means of justification. Paul is saying that the cross, which makes salvation possible, not only does not nullify the law but confirms it. The cross confirms the law because it sends us to Jesus for salvation. It confirms the law in that we see the penalty for lawbreaking paid. It also opposes antinomianism (salvation without any expectation of obedience), for the Spirit now empowers us to obey God as justified people.

If you are not a Christian, then see your need, and trust in Christ alone for salvation. There is a solution to your greatest problem: Christ in the place of sinners.

Christian, rest in this grace. Rejoice in the work of Christ. Retell this good news to the world. Allow this good news to humble you and unite you to other believers.

Reflect and Discuss

1. Why is this passage so important to the story line of Scripture in general, and to the book of Romans in particular?
2. Why is the phrase "but now" so significant (3:21a)?
3. Read back through this passage and note how often the words *righteousness* or *just* or *justification* appear. How does this passage and this concept relate to Romans 1:18–3:20?
4. How is this passage teaching *divine accomplishment* instead of *human achievement* in salvation?
5. How does the concept of redemption in the exodus event help us understand our redemption in Christ?
6. Why do people have a hard time with the idea of "propitiation"? Have you encountered negativity when talking to people about Jesus satisfying the Father's wrath? How might you respond clearly and winsomely to this objection?
7. How is God's righteous character displayed at the cross?
8. Why does the gospel crush human pride?
9. Why should the gospel unify diverse believers?
10. Take a moment to thank God for your salvation; ask him to give you opportunities to share this gospel with others.

Faith Alone

ROMANS 4

Main Idea: Paul illustrates the doctrine of justification by faith alone by reflecting on the story of Abraham.

I. **Believing: Abraham, Counted Righteous by Faith Alone (4:1-8)**
II. **Belonging: Abraham, the Father of All Who Believe (4:9-17)**
   A. Not justified by circumcision (4:9-12)
   B. Not justified by the law (4:13-17)
III. **Believing: Abraham and Us (4:18-25)**
   A. The marks of Abraham's faith (4:18-22)
   B. The Messiah and resurrection faith (4:23-25)
   C. Practical reflections

This text is about *believing* and *belonging*. Paul has been arguing that we are saved by faith in Christ alone (3:21-26). Now he supports this doctrine with the story of Abraham. Additionally, from the story of Abraham, Paul also teaches that all true believers in Christ—whether Jew or Gentile—*belong* to Abraham's family.

Perhaps you heard this song growing up: "Father Abraham had many sons. Many sons had father Abraham. I am one of them and so are you. So let's all praise the Lord." (I grew up on '80s hair bands and various hip-hop artists, but I later learned this little church tune!) Scholar Michael Bird says this children's song is a good summary of this text. By faith in Christ alone, we are not only counted righteous (4:23), but we are also made part of the family of God. Bird says,

> [F]aith is not just what I assent to; it is also about whom I belong to. Faith is about family, a Christ-shaped, Spirit-filled, and God-centered family. . . .
> Faith is not a privatized affair but is a genuinely family event. God does not save us and then assign us a number until it is time to go to heaven one individual at a time. Rather, God saves us and puts us into his family for the purpose of sharing in the family business of worship and mission. . . .

Our sense of identity, purpose, security, and worth is bound up with belonging. The church is the place where that identity, purpose, security and sense of worth are formed. It is this sense of belonging that enables us to flourish as individuals and even as whole communities. (*Romans*, 159)

Belonging to a community is a basic human desire, and in the gospel that need is met. Believing means belonging, and in this experience we grow and flourish.

The glory of this family is that it is so diverse. Christians do not belong to a look-alike club but to a diverse, global family. The family of Abraham is like a great bowl of gumbo; in it, all types of believers are united in one Lord.

Recently, I was in Seattle talking to a pastor friend. He was telling me about the church's small-group ministry. One of his groups consists of a leader of a multinational technology company but also includes a single mom with a checkered history, some couples with diverse backgrounds, a few new believers, and a few college students. It was a joy to sit and reflect on how these diverse people came together each week to study, ask questions, pray, share life, and serve the local community. That hints at what the gospel does. To be a believer means you are now a "belonger."

In Romans 4 Paul uses Abraham to support his argument for justification by faith, particularly what the Scripture says about him in Genesis 15:6: "Abram believed the LORD, and he credited it to him as righteousness" (see Rom 4:3,9,22; cf. Gal 3:16; Jas 2:23). Paul establishes that the Scriptures have always taught salvation by faith alone. He shows the Jewish folks that Abraham's faith story proves this argument. He will argue that Abraham is a prototypical Christian.

Paul also describes what salvation does not consist of. A person is not justified by works, circumcision, or law keeping. One is saved by faith alone. Stop and scan Romans 4. Paul often speaks of "believing," "faith," being "counted righteous," and "justification." The message is clear: by faith alone one is justified, that is, counted righteous in Christ.

Now scan the page to see the emphasis on *belonging*. The inclusion of the Gentiles is emphasized: Abraham is "our forefather according to the flesh" (4:1); Abraham is the father of both Jews and Gentiles (vv. 9-12); he is "the father of all who believe" (v. 11); and he is "the father of many nations" (v. 17).

So, let's keep these two themes in mind as we consider the doctrine of salvation by faith alone. We will look at the chapter in three parts.

Believing: Abraham, Counted Righteous by Faith Alone

ROMANS 4:1-8

Paul begins this section by arguing that Abraham was counted righteous by faith alone and not by works. Abraham is introduced in verse 1. To say Abraham was a big deal to the Jews (see John 8:53) would be a bigger understatement than to say quarterback Tom Brady has been a "big deal" in the NFL.

A common Jewish misunderstanding was that Abraham was justified by *works* of righteousness. As one Jewish source, Jubilees 23:10, says, "Abraham was perfect in all his dealings with the Lord and gained favor by his righteousness throughout his life" (for quotes on Abraham in the Jewish tradition see Bird, *Romans*, 143). And another Jewish source says, "Was not Abraham found faithful when tested, and it was reckoned to him as righteousness?" (1 Macc 2:52 NRSV).

Paul argues against this common idea. He says that Abraham was not justified by works. Paul draws attention to God declaring him righteous in Genesis 15.

It is important to have a sketch of Abraham's story in our minds. First, God called Abram to leave the country of Ur (in modern Iraq), promised to show him another land, and promised to bless all the peoples on earth through him (Gen 11:27–12:1). Second, God identified this other land as Canaan. Then he declared that though Abram and Sarai were unable to have children, Abram's descendants would be as numerous as the stars in the sky (Gen 13:14; 14:16; 15:5). (This is before the medical advances of our day!) By believing this last promise, Abram was justified (Gen 15:6). Third, when Abram and Sarai were old, God confirmed his promise of a son, changed Abram's name to Abraham to signify that he would be "the father of many nations," and gave him circumcision as the sign of his covenant (Gen 17).

In Romans 4:2-3 Paul expounds on Abraham as being justified by faith, not by works. Paul does a bit of expository preaching from Genesis 15:6. He argues that Abraham could boast if his right standing had to do with his works, but he was in fact not righteous based on his works. From God's perspective ("not before God" v. 2), he could not boast because he was not and could not be justified by works. In verse 3 Paul quotes Genesis 15:6 to prove it. This is a foundational verse (see also Gal 3:6). Abraham was a pagan, but God in his grace appeared to him; Abraham believed, and he was counted righteous. The word *credited* (Gk *logizomai*) appears five times in six verses (vv. 3-8). It is an accounting term. By God's grace, God would account to him a righteousness that he did not have on his own. God granted him the status of "righteous" when he believed.

Verse 3 is instructive in another sense. Paul asks the question, "What does the Scripture say?" This and his answer remind us of a number of things regarding the doctrine of Scripture. He reminds us, first of all, that the Old Testament is Holy Scripture. It is God's Word. Second, he reminds us that the Bible is a unified book. Paul can use Abraham as an example for believers in his time. Third, he reminds us that Scripture is our authority. We must always start here on all matters of faith and practice: "What does Scripture say?" In this case Paul explains that Scripture says Abraham was counted righteous, not by his works but by faith!

In verses 4-5 Paul provides a general application of Abraham's righteous status for everyone to consider. He contends that God gives believers what they did not, and cannot, earn.

Paul's point is clear. When a person works and his employer pays him a wage, it is not considered a gift but a payment of obligation. If the employee does not get paid, the employer is being unjust. One expects to get paid when working a job. But salvation is not based on this work-reward payment system. It is a gift of God's grace. We cannot earn it; we can only receive it by faith.

In verse 5 Paul takes it a step further. He says that not only did we not earn righteousness, but the gift of righteousness has been given to those who are actually "ungodly." God justifies the wicked out of his mercy and grace. What is also striking here is that Paul puts Abraham, the father of all of God's children, in the category of the *ungodly*. This reminder is actually good news for sinners. J. I. Packer says,

> Nobody can produce new evidence of your depravity that will make God change his mind. God justified you (so to speak) with his eyes open. He knew the worst about you at the time when he accepted you for Jesus's sake; and the verdict which he passed then was, and is, final. (*Knowing God*, 273)

He knows it all, but he declares believers righteous!

So, the idea of justification by faith is not that some people just need God to make up for that little bit they cannot do on their own. It is not that some just need a little help, but God has to work extra hard on other sinners! No, it is not that Jesus paid 20 percent of it for me and 80 percent for her. The gospel is that Jesus paid it all! The phrase "his faith is credited for righteousness" (v. 5) underscores the basic concept of "faith alone." Faith unites us to Jesus, and in being united to him we receive his righteousness. We cannot earn it.

Paul ratchets up his exposition by bringing in another key Old Testament figure, David (vv. 6-8). He argues that David confirms the reality of salvation by faith alone. Drawing on Psalm 32, Paul asserts that David's story also confirms justification by faith, not by works. By adding David's story, Paul demonstrates that salvation by faith alone runs across redemptive history. Abraham serves as proof from one portion of Scripture (which many refer to as *the Law*); David's psalms serve as proof from another part of Scripture (*the Writings*).

In Psalm 32 David says that people to whom God credits righteousness apart from works are "blessed" (Rom 4:7). The key point David makes is that people who are blessed have not earned this blessing but have received it. It is a gift to have one's sins covered. What a thought! God does not hold our sins against us! God's gracious gift of forgiveness of sins should regularly put us on our faces in awe or leave us beside ourselves with joy.

David's psalm emphasizes the *pardon* element of justification. Up to this point in Romans, the dominant idea has been having the righteousness of God credited to us. But here the focus is on our need to "get unrighteousness off of us." In justification both are essential: unrighteousness gets removed, and righteousness is received. Believer, you are forgiven *and* covered. Your sins are not counted against you, and Christ's righteousness has been credited to you. And you did not earn this standing before God. It is the bestowal of divine grace received by faith alone.

Belonging: Abraham, the Father of All Who Believe
ROMANS 4:9-17

Now we move from the emphasis on our vertical relationship to God to our horizontal relationship with other brothers and sisters—brothers and sisters of all ethnicities. Paul makes two points in verses 9-17:

- *Not Justified by Circumcision.* Because justification is by faith alone, *not religious ceremony* (i.e., *circumcision*), believing Gentiles are part of the family (vv. 9-12).
- *Not Justified by the Law.* Because justification is by faith alone, *not by the law*, believing Gentiles are part of the family (vv. 13-17).

Not Justified by Circumcision (4:9-12)

Paul draws our attention first to the chronology of events in the life of Abraham to show that the Gentiles can be included in the people of God. He reminds us that the blessing of acceptance before God cannot be restricted to Jewish believers (the circumcised) because Abraham was counted righteous *before* he was circumcised (vv. 9-10). Abraham was declared righteous in Genesis 15:6. Circumcision was introduced in Genesis 17. The declaration of "righteous" came some ten to fifteen years before circumcision (or twenty-nine years, according to some traditions; Moo, *Romans*, 152). The order is important: justification *then* circumcision. Abraham was justified while he was *uncircumcised.*

In verse 11 Paul makes an additional point, explaining the meaning of circumcision. Drawing on Genesis 17:11, he states that circumcision was a *sign* and a *seal* of Abraham's righteousness. Circumcision was an external mark. What mattered was the inner reality. Therefore, circumcision was not the basis for Abraham's right standing before God. It was important but not the basis. It was a sign of what was already true.

The word *basis* is important in this entire discussion about justification. Unbelievers may do some good things in life, people may do some religious things in life, but those things will never be the basis for justification. Indeed, the world is a better place when people go about doing good things, but those things are never the basis for right standing before God. Our right standing with God only comes by grace alone through faith alone.

Paul goes on to highlight the significance of this argument for Gentiles. He argues that believing Gentiles can call Abraham their spiritual father. Believing Gentiles are part of the family of God too. The Gentiles do not need to be circumcised to be included in the family (cf. Acts 15). Abraham was justified when he was uncircumcised, and the same can be true for all the uncircumcised. The Gentiles do not need to become Jewish in order to become Christians. In Romans 9 Paul will add some thoughts about God's promises to the patriarchs and the outworking of

God's purposes for the Jews. For now, we must see that unity should exist among different ethnicities because we are here by grace alone through faith alone, not on the basis of works or religious ceremony.

Not Justified by the Law (4:13-17)

Paul continues the argument, claiming that because justification is by faith alone, *not by the law,* believing Gentiles are part of the family. In verse 13 he says that inheriting the world depends on faith, not the law. In Genesis the promise of Canaan included north, south, east, and west of where Abraham was standing (Gen 13:12-17). But here Paul says that the promise involved being an heir of the world. How did this land become the world? First, it has to do with the global reach of the promise—all the families of the earth will be blessed through him. Second, it has to do with the Messiah—through Abraham's ultimate off-spring, Christ, believers will "inherit the earth" (Matt 5:5; 1 Cor 3:21-23). Christ, the ultimate offspring, will rule over the world in the future, and we will reign with him. Third, it has to do with the culmination of the land promise to Abraham. Canaan was a type of the new creation to come. Often in prophecy there is escalation; the fulfillment is greater than what was originally given.

This promise to be an heir of the world is based on God's gracious promise received by faith. It was not based on adherence to the law but on faith. Elsewhere Paul says that the law was given 430 years after this promise (Gal 3:17). The same truth is implicit here, just not developed and explained (Stott, *Message*, 131).

The phrase in verse 14, "those who are of the law," refers to those who base their standing with God on their doing of the Mosaic law. If people could inherit the blessing by keeping the law, faith and promise would be worthless. So *grace, faith,* and *promise* are interlocking concepts; *law, transgression,* and *wrath* belong to another system (ibid.). In verse 15 Paul says, "The law produces wrath." Specific laws make us aware of our sin, and the result of that sin is punishment/wrath.

Stop and consider that we are given two options for our eternal destiny: (1) inherit the world through Christ by faith, or (2) inherit wrath by trying to earn salvation by the law. God didn't say to Abraham, "Obey this law, and I will bless you forever." He said, "Believe this, and I will bless you forever." God is saying to the world now, "Believe on Christ and you will be saved and blessed forever." Salvation is by way of God's gracious promise, not our good performance. This promise is held out to every tribe, tongue, and people.

In verses 16-17 Paul brings together grace and faith, continuing with the same logic. The point is simple: God is gracious, and salvation is a gift of his grace. In God's grace he makes promises, which we receive by faith. This salvation or promise is one from which both Jew and Gentile can benefit. The gospel of grace through faith unites believers. Thus, Scripture is fulfilled (Gen 17:5): "I have made you the father of many nations" (Rom 4:17). Through Christ, Abraham's greatest offspring, all believers are part of Abraham's spiritual family. Only justification by grace alone through faith alone could make this a reality.

Let's not miss the implications of what Paul is saying. Justification by faith is not just a doctrine for individual salvation (though it is). It is also a doctrine for the community of faith. Believing leads to belonging. The church is the community of the justified.

In verse 17 Paul shifts to analyze the *nature* of Abraham's faith. Paul says that Abraham is a model for us, as he believed in God who "gives life to the dead and calls things into existence that do not exist." In light of verses 18-20, the reference of bringing life out of the dead refers to the "dead womb of Sarah" (Moo, *Romans*, 159). God created a nation from this frail, elderly man and woman. The writer of Hebrews says,

> *By faith even Sarah herself, when she was unable to have children, received power to conceive offspring, even though she was past the age, since she considered that the one who had promised was faithful. Therefore, from one man—in fact, from one as good as dead—came offspring as numerous as the stars of the sky and as innumerable as the grains of sand along the seashore.* (Heb 11:11-12)

God not only literally created the world out of nothing; he also figuratively gave Abraham and Sarah a child "out of nothing." He formed a people out of nothing! And he continues to bring spiritual life out of nothing. We believers belong to this people!

Believing: Abraham and Us
ROMANS 4:18-25

Abraham and Sarah's faith in God for a child foreshadows *resurrection faith*. Isaac's birth may be seen as a preview of things to come in the resurrection of Jesus. After talking about the character of Abraham's faith (vv. 18-22), Paul ends the chapter by bringing together those two foundational beliefs: the resurrection and justification by faith (vv. 23-25).

The Marks of Abraham's Faith (4:18-22)

Abraham's faith is exemplary in several ways. As we read what Paul says, we should reflect on our own lives. Assess your own faith in God and seek to grow in faith as you consider Abraham's example.

First, he believed God even though the situation seemed hopeless (v. 18). From a worldly perspective, there was no grounds for Abraham's confidence. But true faith is linked with hope, a settled confidence in the promises of God. Morris says, "But Abraham was not without God and therefore he was not without hope" (*Epistle*, 210). In contrast, unbelievers are "without hope and without God in the world" (Eph 2:12). Saving faith is hope-filled faith. Abraham believed God could do the humanly impossible, and God fulfilled his promise to Abraham, making him the father of many nations.

Second, Abraham's faith did not weaken or waver (v. 19). It is one thing for a person to start out with faith in God, but many expressions of faith fizzle out like a dud firecracker. Paul tells us that Abraham's faith remained steadfast even though he and his wife were nearly dead. He never drifted into unbelief in the promises of God. Abraham grew strong in faith by the grace of God.

Third, Abraham "gave glory to God" (v. 20). This point is not made in the Genesis narrative, but Paul draws it from the story in general. When we trust in God, we are glorifying him as the one who keeps his promises. We glorify his truthfulness, his faithfulness, and his covenantal love. We recognize that he is the sovereign ruler of all things. Faith and the glory of God go together, just as faith and hope go together. In contrast, unbelievers exchange the glory of God for idols (1:22-23). Faith-filled saints believe in God and live to the glory of God.

Fourth, Abraham believed that God was able to fulfill his promises (v. 21). True faith rests in God's ability. At first, it seemed that Abraham questioned God's ability to fulfill his promise (Gen 17:17-18). But even though Abraham laughed at the possibility, he was eventually "fully convinced" or "persuaded" (NIV). He was a human being like us, so faith was not automatic. Though he initially found it hard to believe, he became convinced of God's ability to fulfill his promise (Gen 17:21-27).

Finally, Abraham's faith illustrates how God counts people righteous through faith alone. Paul now bookends the section (see v. 3; Gen 15:6) by saying, "Therefore, it was credited to him for righteousness" (v. 22). God justifies a people for himself by grace through faith, as the story of Abraham illustrates.

Let's live by faith in our all-powerful, life-giving, barrenness-overcoming, miracle-working, death-defeating God of redemptive history! We are not being called simply to admire Abraham here; we are being called to believe in the life-giving God of Abraham. What makes trusting someone difficult? Is it not that you find them *unreliable?* This whole chapter is telling us that God is totally trustworthy and reliable. Faith involves trusting in God's divine faithfulness. We begin the Christian life by faith and continue by faith. God always keeps his promises! Therefore, trust him wholeheartedly for his glory.

The Messiah and Resurrection Faith (4:23-25)

Paul now applies the faith of Abraham to his present audience—those living in the new covenant like us. Abraham's story was written for our instruction (Rom 15:4). Paul essentially says what was true of Abraham is also true for believers in Christ (Bird, *Romans*, 151). Abraham was counted righteous by faith alone, so believers in Jesus are counted righteous by faith alone. However, the focus of the faith gets more specific. Saving faith is belief in "him who raised Jesus our Lord from the dead" (v. 24). Throughout the New Testament, saving faith has its object in the resurrected Messiah, or it is not true faith (see Rom 10:9-10; 1 Cor 15:3-5; 2 Cor 5:15; 1 Thess 4:14).

The tense here is also important. Paul says, "It will be credited" (v. 24). It is a present reality for believers, but it also awaits a future fulfillment in the resurrection of the body (Rom 3:22-24; 5:1,9; 8:30,33; 10:10). Morris says,

> The future points to the eschatological aspect of justification.
> In one sense believers are justified now; they have received
> right standing with God and this is their present possession.
> From another point of view the consummation waits till
> Judgment Day and thus may be referred to as still future.
> (*Epistle*, 214)

Like several doctrines of salvation found in Romans, there is here an already/not yet dimension to recognize and celebrate.

In verse 25 Paul finishes his marvelous exposition of Abraham. Here Paul says that the cross and resurrection are the result of the Father's initiative (Stott, *Message*, 135). Jesus the Messiah, the Suffering Servant of Isaiah, was "delivered up for our trespasses." He was our substitute, dying in the place of sinners (cf. 8:32). But three days later the Father raised him up, and Jesus stepped out into the sunlight as the vindicated and victorious Son of God, "raised for our justification." His resurrection demonstrated that the Father accepted the Son's sacrifice. The Son completed his work, and as a result believers are counted righteous. Through Jesus's cross and resurrection work, we are forgiven and justified. Thus, the events of Easter stand at the center of our faith.

Practical Reflections

Allow me to gather several applications for believers based on this chapter.

First, let us never get over the good news of justification by faith. Praise God, Jesus died and was raised for our justification; we are forgiven and counted righteous! Marvel at this grace!

Second, let us never get over the fact that we are part of the people of God. By faith in our resurrected Messiah, we are not only justified personally, but we are also incorporated into the people of God. Believing in the Messiah leads to belonging to the Messiah's people.

Third, let us allow the doctrine of justification by faith to shape our lives and the lives of our churches. Why does Paul spend so much time on the doctrine of justification by faith? He obviously wants the Romans to know it and believe it. But I think he has more in mind than personal salvation. Paul also wants the Romans to be *shaped* by the doctrine of justification by faith alone. He wants the doctrine of justification by faith to affect their whole lives. To quote Bird, Paul is "gospelizing" this church. He is teaching individual salvation to be sure, but he is also stressing that the community of faith is the community of the justified.

What should this believing community look like? *We should be a humble people* (vv. 1-5). Since justification undercuts boasting, then the church should be filled with grateful servants, dying to ego and self-exaltation, who make Christ alone their boast.

We should also be a happy people because justification by faith brings the richest of blessings (vv. 6-8). This word *blessed* is a rich term that carries the idea of joy, happiness, fulfillment, and satisfaction. That is precisely what the gospel produces in us. May our communities of faith be known for having cheerful Christians who are dazzled by grace!

We should also be an obedient people because justification by faith clarifies the proper place of works and obedience (4:9-11a). We should not dismiss works as unimportant. Keep Romans 1:5 in view—"the obedience of faith" or the obedience that springs from faith. Justification by faith shows us the proper place of works: justification first, *then* works. Works are *not the basis* for justification, but they are the fruit of it. Ephesians 2:8-10 gives us that order. James also argues for a faith that functions (Jas 2:14-26). As has often been said, "We are justified by faith alone, but the faith that saves is never alone"—that is, it also results in good works.

We should also be a missional people because justification by faith opens the way for the nations to be part of God's family (vv. 11b-12). The Great Commission does not start in Matthew 28. From the beginning, God has had a plan for the nations to be blessed through the Messiah. Justification by faith is therefore a missionary doctrine. It says there is one way of salvation, and that one way is available to the nations. Our global engagement does not consist of telling people to conform to American culture or Jewish culture or any other culture but to believe the gospel and live it out in one's own culture.

Finally, *we should be a hope-filled, faith-filled people* because justification by faith reminds us of God's power, grace, and faithfulness. Our God keeps his promises. He fulfilled his promise to Abraham, and he will fulfill all his promises to us, including the promise of inheriting the earth (vv. 13-17).

Reflect and Discuss

1. Take a moment to read back through Romans 3:21–4:25 in order to see how Paul uses Abraham as an example of justification by faith.
2. Why does Paul use Abraham as an example of saving faith? What does Paul say about Abraham's faith in relation to circumcision?
3. How do you see the themes of *believing* and *belonging* worked out in this chapter?
4. How can God declare the ungodly to be righteous? How is this message different from other world religions?
5. How is Abraham the father of many nations?
6. What does it mean to "inherit the world" (4:13)?

7. What do you find most challenging about Abraham's life of faith (4:18-21)?
8. What does Paul say about God in this chapter that makes God so trustworthy?
9. Why are verses 24-25 such a good summary of the gospel?
10. What effects should the doctrine of justification by faith have on the people of God?

The Blessings of Justification by Faith

ROMANS 5:1-11

Main Idea: Paul rejoices in the good news as he highlights six spiritual blessings that come to those who have been counted righteous through faith in Christ Jesus.

I. We Have Peace with God (5:1).
II. We Stand in Grace (5:2a).
III. We Rejoice in Hope (5:2b-4).
IV. We Know a Love like No Other Love (5:5-8).
V. We Have Assurance of Final Salvation (5:9-10).
VI. We Exult in God Himself (5:11).

Learning the lingo is a necessary aspect of joining a particular community. Every group or tribe has its own vocabulary. If you are not familiar with certain phrases, you will be out of the loop. In business we hear phrases like "due diligence" and "sweat equity." The police force has many codes (code 8, code 11, etc.). The military has a host of acronyms. Politics also has its own lexicon: right wing, left wing, POTUS, SCOTUS, and filibuster. Sports have all kinds of unique phrases. In baseball one can hear announcers talk about a "duck snort," the "bullpen," "cheese," "dinger," a "frozen rope," and many other strange expressions. And, of course, teenagers have their own jargon, which, at the time of this writing, includes PAP (post a picture), IDEK (I don't even know), BAE (before anyone else), dime (a 10 on a scale of 1–10); tope (a blend of "totally" and "dope," with "dope" meaning "seriously great").

Language serves to convey information, and specific jargon creates community among particular groups. Here in Romans, Paul is using the grammar of the gospel to convey the best news in the world and to unite diverse believers. We see many gospel words like *justification, condemnation, propitiation,* and *reconciliation.* Grasping concepts like resurrection, grace, the love of God, substitution, the work of the Holy Spirit, faith, sin, judgment, hope, and repentance transforms our lives, shapes our worldview, and builds community.

In Romans 5:1-11 we see a whole slew of gospel terms (just scan the page). In some ways this is a summary of where we have been and serves as a preview of what is to come. Specifically, Romans 5:1-11 teaches us about the *blessings of being justified by faith alone*; that is, the blessing of being "declared righteous" (5:1).

Having stated the need to be justified by faith (1:18–3:20) and having stated the way of justification (3:21–4:25), Paul now revels in the glories of it (5:1-11). Paul's style shifts from argumentation to adoration. Notice the repetition of the term "boast" in verses 2, 3, and 11 ("rejoice" in ESV; "exult" in NASB). The overall tone of the text is celebratory, triumphant, and jubilant. Martin Luther commented, "In the whole Bible there is hardly another chapter which can equal this triumphant text" (*Romans*, 88). If we may adjust Kool and the Gang's old-school lyrics, Paul is saying, "Celebrate good news, c'mon!" This celebration climaxes in verse 11, where Paul says we rejoice/exult/boast *in God* himself.

In other words, Paul is helping us *enjoy God* here. There is a difference in saying "I'm a Christian" and actually enjoying God. It is one thing to be legally married, but it is another thing to enjoy your spouse—to have a great meal together, to laugh together, play together, and enjoy a date night together. It is one thing to have children, but it is another thing to have them greet you at the door, to enjoy a fun vacation with them, or to have them text you something sweet. Romans 5 is a wonderful gift for rekindling the Christian's enjoyment of God. Do you love him? Do you exult in him? Do you adore him? Paul is radiating a contagious Christian joy and excitement because of what God has done for us in Christ. And we should join him in this gospel celebration. Let's consider six blessings of justification by faith that should cause joy to arise in our hearts.

We Have Peace with God
ROMANS 5:1

Paul begins with the word "Therefore," a significant term used throughout Romans, guiding us through some major movements in the letter. We find a therefore of (1) *condemnation* (Rom 3:20 NIV), (2) *justification* (5:1,12), (3) *no condemnation* (8:1), and *dedication/transformation* (12:1). Here in Romans 5:1 Paul is recapping previous material and launching into implications.

In Romans 4:23-25 Paul taught that our justification is rooted in the cross and resurrection of Jesus. Christ Jesus was "raised for our justification" (4:25). The events of Easter are central in human history, and they have abiding significance. Those who believe in the work of Christ are counted righteous (4:22). Being counted righteous leads to the celebration we see in 5:1-11.

"Peace with God" is the first blessing mentioned. Being declared righteous leads to peace. There is a *peace now*, as a result of our reconciliation with the Father, but also a *not-yet peace* that the believer anticipates in future glory.

True believers are able to say, "It is well with my soul." Regardless of what might be going on all around us, the believer can experience the peace *of* God because he or she has peace *with* God. The unregenerate person's life is marked by *restlessness* because he or she has no peace with God. But the gospel brings new believers rest of soul because they are at peace with God (cf. Matt 10:28).

The idea of reconciliation with God recurs later in this passage (5:10-11). Before becoming Christians, we were enemies of God. There was hostility. But Christ has killed the hostility by being crushed in our place. He took our place, bearing our penalty, thus granting us forgiveness and right standing with God.

Modern people love the idea of peace. Often those outside the faith hear believers talking about peace, and they consider it to be some kind of therapeutic feeling of peace. But our peace is different from stretching exercises, deep-breathing activities, the smell of essential oils, calm walks beside creeks, or peaceful bike rides in the woods. Christian peace is rooted in something objective: the cross and resurrection of Jesus. Certain experiences can give one a sense of peace, but the ultimate peace is not found in the gifts of creation but in the Creator himself, who has reconciled us to himself through Christ Jesus. Sin has created the problem of alienation from God, and there is only one cure: Christ Jesus.

It is impossible to know the peace *of* God if you do not have peace *with* God. Paul is speaking of an objective peace that comes from our being counted righteous. Jesus is the fulfillment of the promised peace that would come through the Davidic king (see Isa 9:6-7; Ezek 34:23-31; 37:24-28; Mic 5:4-5). Jesus Christ has won the war, abolished the hostility, and brought us peace.

There are times in which believers do not experience the peace of God, even though we do have peace with God. We should have experiential peace, but we often do not live in it because of spiritual warfare and trouble around us. We need to read through God's Word until it gets through us (Col 3:15-16). We need to "pray until we've prayed," as the old divines used to say (Phil 4:6-7). We need to join biblical communities, where brothers and sisters can gospelize us (2 Cor 7:5-7).

We Stand in Grace
ROMANS 5:2A

With the blessing of peace with God, something negative has been removed: hostility. But there is more! Here in verse 2 Paul says that something gloriously positive has been provided: we also have a warm relationship to God (Keller, *Romans 1–7*, 110). "Grace" here refers to ongoing favor with God that we possess because of our new relationship with God. We now live in the realm of God's grace and power.

We not only get into relationship with God by grace, but we also live out this relationship in day-to-day life by grace. We never put grace behind us. We "stand" in it. We live in it.

Because of our new standing with God, we have a new access to God. We do not just have periodic access to the King; we live in the palace as children of the King! The gospel gives you a new identity, which is why you have this access into this grace (Eph 2:11-22; Heb 4:14-16). Tim Keller quipped, "The only person who dares wake up a king at 3:00 AM for a glass of water is a child [of the King]. We have that kind of access" (Twitter, 2/23/15). Similarly, Mike Bird says, "It is a grace that means we always have a VIP pass into the hallways of heavenly power" (*Romans*, 163).

What a privilege to stand in grace and not be under the judgment of God! What a privilege to know God as Father, who stands ready to hear our cries. Becoming a Christian involves entering a world of the Father's grace. We have access. We can go to him anytime. He hears us. He loves us. Every day his Word tells us, "My child, remember whose you are." We should remind ourselves daily of what we deserve (judgment) but what we have received instead (grace). That should prompt praise and communion with God. We can go to our Father all the time with our worries, problems, concerns, and fears and present them to him, knowing that he not only hears us but also welcomes us.

We Rejoice in Hope

ROMANS 5:2B-4

Paul adds to the list of blessings of the justified. Notice the word "hope" in 2b and at the end of verse 4. Also notice the repetition of "boast" or "rejoice" (vv. 2b,3). Hope and rejoicing should mark the Christian. So Paul has three tenses of salvation in verses 1-4 (Keller, *Romans 1–7*, 111). In Christ we have been freed from our past and already have peace with God (v. 1); in Christ we stand in grace now in the present moment (v. 2a); and in Christ we look forward to the hope of glory (vv. 2b-4).

Our hope is an undeserved hope. Based on our immorality and idolatry (1:18–3:20), we do not deserve to enjoy God's grace and God's glory, but through Christ these blessings are ours (8:18-39). We who scorned God's glory (1:21-23) now share in God's glory! What was lost in Adam will be restored, and an even greater glory than Adam enjoyed will be ours.

In the New Testament, hope is not wishful thinking, like "I hope the Lions win the Super Bowl." The believer's hope is assured. It is tied to what has happened in the past. Those whom God justified "he also glorified" (8:30).

What does this future *glory* involve? It will involve conformity to Christ, for John says we will see him and be like him (1 John 3:2). It will involve total peace. Righteousness will reign forever in a place with no sin and death (2 Pet 3:13). It will involve thrilling beauty, as the glory of God will cover the earth "as the water covers the sea" (Hab 2:14). It will be a place of perfect harmony and love. Christ prayed that his followers would see this glory (John 17:24). He wants us to see glory and wants to deliver us from this body of death. What a Savior! What undeserved hope!

Paul tells the Colossians that this hope is actually inside the Christian already, using that memorable phrase, "Christ in you, the hope of glory" (Col 1:27). The Christian may look unimpressive externally. We are kind of like Cameron Indoor Stadium, where the legendary college basketball team, the Duke Blue Devils, play: unimpressive on the outside, but on the inside, filled with glory.

This eschatological hope should energize our lives. A new job can give one a sense of excitement about the future. Looking forward to a week at the beach with your spouse may inspire you to endure the challenging days leading up to it. But nothing is greater to fuel fruitfulness and happiness than this hope Paul describes.

Paul will tease this doctrine out more fully in Romans 8. It is crucial to have the right expectations of the Christian life: suffering now, glory later. If you do not understand this, you will not understand Christianity, and you will get mad at God. Suffering is normal in a fallen world (John 16:33). How do we endure the suffering? We remember the glory. It is so easy to lose sight of this future when you are in the midst of suffering. I love the story I heard about a college baseball player, whose team won the College World Series (LSU, if I remember correctly). Following the game, he decided to get a bottle full of the dirt at home plate. The next season he took it with him to every game. When times got difficult, he would whip out that bottle and say, "Guys, get a whiff of Rosenblatt Stadium [former home of the NCAA College World Series]. That's where we are going." Dear Christian, we need to get a whiff of glory every day as we open God's Holy Word. It reminds us where we are going. We have suffering now, but glory awaits us.

Paul says that we "rejoice in our afflictions" (Rom 5:3a). Paul is not saying we should enjoy pain. He is saying you can rejoice in the midst of it. We can do this not only because we know glory awaits us in the future but also because we know that our sufferings are producing *maturity* in the present (vv. 3b-4). The believer knows that this suffering is doing something beneficial in our lives. Suffering builds a saint's character and creates in him or her a longing for glory.

Consider three applications from verses 3-4. These are basic discipleship principles new believers need to know and seasoned saints should never forget.

First, God's priority is not to take away all of your problems; it's to make you like Jesus. The Christian message is not, "Come to Jesus, and all of your problems will be solved." Rather, the saint's testimony is, "These afflictions are making me more like Jesus." Just look at Paul, a good Christian example. His life was filled with suffering, not devoid of it (2 Cor 6:4-10). Through these trials he was made more like Jesus (Phil 3:10-11). Suffering refines us and makes us more like Jesus. It weans us off the pleasures of this world and reminds us of ultimate realties.

Second, God's purposes can be trusted. God is working all things together for our good as he conforms us to the image of his Son (Rom 8:28-30). While we may not always understand the purposes of God, saints can trust in the purposes of God. The Father may prune us that we bear more fruit, but not a single cut from this pruning knife is purposeless (John 15:1-2). The Father may discipline us that we may be more obedient, but that discipline is done in love and for our good (Heb 12:10).

Third, God's pattern can be anticipated: afflictions—endurance—character—hope. Suffering is a great seminary (Ps 119:71). It builds "endurance" and "proven character." Elsewhere we read that our trials mature us (Jas 1:2-4).

Afflictions train us to endure under various pressures and hardships. Suffering makes us stronger and able to persevere through the next trials. It develops "proven character" in that we become the kind of Christians who have been tested and found approved (Phil 2:22). When I was in high school, our baseball team would travel down to Florida during spring break to play a bunch of different teams. Being from Kentucky, our season was just beginning (and most of us had been playing basketball for months), but many of the Florida players could play baseball year-round. Since the teams were better in Florida, we got beat a lot that week. But when we came home, we had fewer nerves at the plate because we had just faced incredible pitching and strong teams. We had more poise as a result of that week of grueling games. We could play well back home because we had been tested and challenged. Likewise, trials and suffering build our character and give us confidence in God as we endure more trials to come.

But how does suffering produce hope? One way is this: enduring in faith reassures you that you really do belong to Jesus. It assures you that your faith is real (cf. Mark 4:17). The person with real faith then can anticipate the glory to come not as a pipe dream but as a certainty. And this assured saint knows that God is using these things to make him/her like Jesus.

We Know a Love like No Other Love
ROMANS 5:5-8

In verse 5 Paul goes on to tell us that the Holy Spirit, the one who enables us to endure suffering with faith and faithfulness, assures us of God's love on an *experiential* level. Then in verses 6-8 he says that the cross of Jesus assures us of God's love on a historical, objective level. In all four verses we should note the Trinitarian love of God. The Holy Spirit floods our hearts with God's love, and the cross of Jesus Christ in human history has once and for all demonstrated God's love for us.

Paul's point about the Holy Spirit is spectacular (v. 5). The Holy Spirit floods our hearts with the indescribable love of God (cf. 8:14-17). This is a dynamic experience. When people put their faith in Jesus, the

Spirit of God comes to dwell inside of them. The indwelling Spirit is a gift. Here we see that the Spirit is the gift of love. God's love for us has streamed like a cloudburst into our hearts, and we then pour forth love for others. We who have received love from God now have great love for God and for others. John Owen said, "We are never nearer Christ than when we find ourselves lost in a holy amazement at His unspeakable love" (*Hebrews*, 549). The Spirit creates this holy amazement.

Regarding the cross (vv. 6-8), we see that God's love does not float apart from historical anchor, but it is tied to the objective work of Christ on the cross (Schreiner, *Romans*, 259). Some have seen Paul as a writer of *arguments*, while John is the writer of *love*. I think this view does not represent Paul fairly. After all, we find Paul speaking of God's love regularly. Leon Morris says Paul uses the word *love* 75 of the 116 times it is used in the New Testament (*Epistle*, 221). Here, having stated that the cross of Jesus is indeed a display of God's *righteousness* (3:21-25), Paul now declares that divine *love* was also displayed at the cross. Our God is not distant or remote but full of love and personally involved in our redemption. Paul underlines two truths regarding the greatness of God's love displayed at the cross.

First, the greatness of God's love is displayed in the cost of it (5:8). God gave his own beloved Son for sinners (John 3:16; Rom 8:32). Genuine love is always sacrificial, and this was the preeminent sacrifice. God's love was not a sentimental kind of love. God did not merely say he loved sinners; he acted on their behalf by putting forward Christ in their place. And Jesus willingly gave himself up, paying a price we will never fully comprehend. He would leave heaven for earth; he would live a sinless life; he would be betrayed; he would be abandoned; he would be tortured; and he would endure the Father's wrath in place of those who deserved it. Let's never lose sight of the cost of our salvation. And let's also remember that Christ's love is not only the reason we are saved but also the example of love we are to follow as we seek to love others (cf. Eph 4:32–5:2; 5:25).

Second, the greatness of God's love is displayed in our unworthiness of it (5:6-8). We were unable to save ourselves. We were "helpless" when, "at the right time, Christ died for the ungodly" (v. 6). Not only were we "ungodly," but verse 8 says we were "sinners" and verses 9-10 remind us that we were "enemies." God's love is uncommon, for Christ did not die for a "good person" (v. 7). Maybe one would take a bullet for a national hero, but what about for a serial killer? Christ died for his enemies, for people who did not deserve to be saved. Sinners, who have been justified by grace alone through faith alone in Christ alone, know a love like no other love.

We Have Assurance of Final Salvation
ROMANS 5:9-10

In verses 9-10 Paul declares that we are saved—now and forever. Here again, salvation has both an "already" and a "not yet" aspect. Paul also highlights a negative and a positive aspect of this glorious salvation.

Negatively, believers have no fear of future wrath (v. 9). Christ has taken our place, and we do not have to fear the judgment. We will be saved from future wrath—let that sink in (cf. Rom 8:1).

If profound gratitude does not arise in our hearts when we ponder that no future wrath awaits us, then it is probably because we have forgotten what we deserve. Instead of deserved wrath, we are standing in grace! This should prompt praise, joy, and holy awe.

A few weeks ago, a well-known pastor friend came for a visit. We had a delightful chat, getting caught up with each other. As I was backing out of my driveway to take him back to his hotel, I said something like, "Hey man, thanks for reaching out. This was good for my soul. Text or call me if you need anything, ever."

He said, "Yeah man. Likewise." Then he said, "We should be in hell, bro."

His sobering words really struck me. I thought, *This escalated quickly!* I was just saying, "Text me," and he said, "We should be in hell, bro." But he was right. And in that simple statement of where we would be without Christ, he was reminding me that he and I do not deserve God's grace. We do not deserve to be saved or to have a ministry. We are infinitely better off than we deserve! I determined to start my days with this reminder: "I am not in hell today." That perspective will put things in proper view.

Believers do not have wrath remaining on them or awaiting them. We are standing in God's amazing grace and anticipating glory to come. Therefore, let's serve our Lord with gladness and praise him wholeheartedly.

Positively, Paul also says believers are reconciled to God now and forever (v. 10). "Saved by his life" seems to refer to Christ's resurrection and ongoing intercession (Schreiner, *Romans*, 264). Through his resurrected life we are saved today, tomorrow, and forever. Not only did he come back to life after being our sacrifice, but he came back to life in order to be our high priest. We are not just celebrating the astonishing fact that Jesus came back to life ("Oh wow, that's cool!"), but we are celebrating that he lives and reigns forever! And he will never die! We are saved by the *living* Lord of glory. He is alive forever, and all who are in him will also live forever. We share his life now; we will share his life through the resurrection later.

How do we know this for sure? Look at Paul's simple logic, with the phrase "how much more." It flows from present to the future, and from difficult to easy (Bird, *Romans*, 166; Morris, *Epistle*, 225). If God has already done the difficult thing (justifying us through the blood of Jesus and reconciling us to himself while we were enemies), can we not trust him to do the comparatively easy thing of completing the task (saving us from upcoming wrath since we are now his people)? Of course we can! He has justified us through the blood of Jesus while we were sinners; he will certainly save his justified people from wrath.

So rejoice in this assurance, believer. The work of Christ in the past brings us ongoing security in the present and assures us of the glory to come. We do not fear wrath, but rather we enjoy sweet fellowship with God because of the reconciling work of Jesus.

We Exult in God Himself
ROMANS 5:11

Paul has given us many reasons to rejoice, but now he reaches the apex of his celebration. Schreiner comments, "The capstone of the believer's experience is boasting and exulting in God himself" (*Romans*, 265).

Paul says we "rejoice in God." Believers do not look at God as some means to an end. We see him as glorious. We see him as beautiful. He is the end for which we have been created, to glorify him and enjoy him forever. So are you enjoying him? Tim Keller offers the following signs of rejoicing in God:

1. Your mind is deeply satisfied with the doctrine of justification by faith. You rejoice in it by studying it and speaking about it to others.

2. You only think of your past in terms of it. You don't say: *What a mess I made of it there!* Instead you say: *Me, a Christian! Despite my deep flaws, despite my record! Yet it is absolutely true!*

3. When you discover in yourself a new character flaw, . . . the discovery does not make you doubt God's love. Rather it makes you feel closer to him, and his grace for you becomes more precious in your sight.

4. When your conscience accuses you and says: *How could God love you after what you've done?* you don't try to answer with reference to your performance.

5. When you face criticism, you don't say *This is totally unfair.* You rejoice gently inside with thoughts like, *Well, I'm really a much worse sinner than they know but. . . . Well may the Accuser roar, of sins that I have done: I know them all, and thousands more: Jehovah knoweth none.*

6. When you face death, you do it with serenity because you are going to a friend. (Keller, *Romans 1–7*, 120–21; emphasis in original)

Dear saint, let's rejoice in our gracious God!

This holy enjoyment comes "through our Lord Jesus Christ." Christ has not only saved us from future wrath; he has also brought us present joy.

Genuine faith leads to a deep love for God. A Christian has been awakened to the beauty of God. A Christian boasts in God, the one who has reconciled him or her to himself through Jesus. Hostility has been replaced with warmth. He or she has the intimacy of communion with our Father, through the cross work of Jesus.

Mike Bird rightly says of this passage, "Salvation for Paul is so rich and so amazing that it requires a full quiver of metaphors to come even close to grasping it" (*Romans*, 167). Indeed, for the rest of our lives, we will be learning more about the richness of our salvation in Christ. We have looked at some glorious truths here in Romans 5:1-11. Being declared righteous by faith in Christ means having peace with God, standing in grace, rejoicing in hope, knowing a love like no other, being assured of final salvation, and exulting in God himself, who is our treasure. Sweeter words and more satisfying news do not exist. And to think that we are but scratching the surface of the bottomless depths of the gospel!

The love of God is greater far
Than tongue or pen can ever tell;
It goes beyond the highest star,
And reaches to the lowest hell;

The guilty pair, bowed down with care,
God gave His Son to win;
His erring child He reconciled,
And pardoned from his sin.

O love of God, how rich and pure!
How measureless and strong!
It shall forevermore endure—
The saints' and angels' song!
—Frederick Lehman (1917)

Reflect and Discuss

1. How is Romans 4:23-25 tied to 5:1-11?
2. What does it mean to have "peace with God"? How is this peace different from the way people talk about peace today?
3. What does it mean to stand in grace? How should this reality inspire our prayer lives?
4. Why is it important for believers to meditate on future glory?
5. Based on verses 3-4, how should we view our afflictions in this life?
6. Based on verses 5-8, explain how we know the love of God.
7. Compare the motivations for Christ going to the cross in Romans 3:25-26 and in 5:8.
8. Explain why the believer has assurance of salvation based on this passage.
9. What does it mean to "rejoice in God"? Which point in Tim Keller's list of "signs of rejoicing in God" do you find most difficult? Why?
10. Look back over Romans 5:1-11 and consider all the blessings of justification by faith. Spend some time thanking God for this glorious salvation.

Christ's Triumph over Sin and Death

ROMANS 5:12-21

Main Idea: Paul explains the believer's salvation in view of the grand story of redemption.

I. **The Conflict (5:12-14)**
II. **The Contrasts (5:15-19)**
   A. Trespass and gift (5:15)
   B. Condemnation and justification (5:16)
   C. Death and life (5:17)
   D. Disobedience and obedience (5:18-19)
III. **The Conclusion: Christ Has Overcome! (5:20-21)**

I am not a big *Star Wars* fan (to the dismay of many of my friends), but I do appreciate many of its themes. Mike Bird points out that one of the major story lines in *Star Wars* illustrates something of this text, which focuses on the disobedience of Adam and the obedience of Christ, or as Paul says elsewhere, the "first man Adam" and the "last Adam" (1 Cor 15:45). *Star Wars* features a tale of two Skywalkers (Bird, *Romans*, 188). The first Skywalker (*Anakin* Skywalker) faced the temptation to give in to "the dark side" of the Force. And he did give in to it. Death, destruction, and chaos followed. In *contrast*, the second Skywalker (*Luke* Skywalker) faced the same temptation. But Luke was faithful and obedient to the Jedi vocation (ibid.). Consequently, hope, life, and the triumph of good followed. In fact, Luke was able to redeem the first Skywalker, his evil father Anakin. Filmmaker George Lucas said that the entire *Star Wars* saga—or at least the first two trilogies—was concerned with the redemption of Anakin Skywalker (ibid.).

Similarly, you could say that the entire story line of the Bible is about the redemption of Adam by the last Adam, Christ Jesus. Whereas *Star Wars* is fiction (and obviously derived from a competing worldview), Romans 5 is teaching us about the true story of the whole world. Our passage begins with the first man, Adam, and moves to the work of Christ, and it includes the future reign of Christ; we go from creation to new creation. Having focused in on our personal salvation in

Romans 5:1-11, Paul switches to a wide-angle lens and puts our salvation within the grand story of redemption.

This is a most relevant text because it speaks to every human who has ever lived. And it is a wonderfully encouraging text because it points us to Christ's triumph over sin and death and reminds believers of our security in him. Schreiner states,

> Adam and Christ are the two most influential individuals in human history, and believers can take confidence because they belong to one who has overturned all that Adam introduced into the world. (*Romans*, 282)

Adam and Christ are not merely two historical figures; they are also two representative figures. Adam is the head of a race of sinners: all of us. Christ is the head of a new race of redeemed people: all those who trust in him. In some ways, Romans 5 is an explanation of 1 Corinthians 15:22: "For just as in Adam all die, so also in Christ all will be made alive." (Paul draws out more contrasts in 1 Cor 15:45-49.)

So, what is the overarching application of all this? Everyone is either in Adam or in Christ. These are the only two options. Note the repetition of the word "one" throughout Romans 5:12-19. It is used twelve times. Paul is emphasizing our identification with Adam and/or with Christ.

In Christ, sons of Adam can be redeemed, restored, and renewed, and they will one day gain the paradise God destined them to dwell in for all eternity. There is a lot of emphasis on Adam's fall, sin, and death, but we must not miss Paul's overriding concern here: to share the good news of Christ's triumph. The major emphasis is not on Adam's failure (Paul is assuming people know about that) but on Christ's triumph over sin and death.

The Conflict
ROMANS 5:12-14

Paul begins with another "Therefore" statement (v. 12). He is picking up with the previous discourse in 5:1-11, where he explained believers' peace with God through Christ and their standing in grace and future glory (vv. 1-5). Paul also described how God has reconciled believers to himself through Christ (vv. 6-11). Verses 12-21 deal with the same ideas, only here Paul tells us about the enemies that threaten these blessings: sin and death.

Sin and death have brought the great conflict. Because of sin, people are alienated from God. *Peace* and *access* (vv. 1-2a) were lost because of sin. *Future glory* (v. 3) was lost because of sin and death. *Trials* (v. 4) exist because of sin and death. *Reconciliation* (vv. 6-11) needs to happen because sin and death have put us at odds with God. The good news of Romans 5:12-21 is that peace can be restored through Christ. The glory that Adam lost will be restored even greater through Christ. And in Christ, believers are reconciled to God.

A close look at verse 12 shows us the basic truth that Adam's fall introduced sin and death into the world. The Genesis narrative makes this point plain. Sin was not merely breaking a rule or taking a bit of fruit. It was *treason*. It was *idolatry*. It was a *failure to love God as he loved us*. It involved the attempt to dethrone God. The effects of this rebellion were and are devastating. So, notice this three-stage chain reaction in verse 12: (1) sin entered the world through Adam; (2) death entered the world through sin; and (3) death spread to all humans because all sinned (Keller, *Romans 1–7*, 124). We then see the entrance of sin, the entrance of death, and the spread of universal death because of sin (ibid.). Adam was to rule the world for God and subdue creation. But when he sinned, he suffered alienation from God, corruption, and death. He passed on that same alienation, corruption, and death to his descendants.

Paul does not dive into all the theological and philosophical questions often raised about original sin. He simply focuses on the consequences of sin—condemnation and death. Doug Moo says, "The universal consequences of Adam's sin are the *assumption* in Paul's argument; the power of Christ's act to cancel those consequences is the *goal*" (*Letter*, 315; emphasis added).

In verse 12 Paul makes an important universal statement—"because all sinned"; that is, humanity sinned in this one past action (Keller, *Romans 1–7*, 124). We not only sin *like* Adam, but we sin because we are all *in* Adam (ibid., 125). Because all sinned there is "condemnation for everyone" (v. 18). Apart from Christ we are under condemnation. Paul has already made this point (1:18-19; 3:9,23). We enter a world alienated from God so we commit sin and we die. The effects of Adam's sin are *universal*.

In verses 13-14 Paul speaks of sin and death even apart from the law. He thus reinforces his point about the universality of death. Many Jews believed there could be no death or sin apart from the law (Moo, *Letter*, 330). When there was no law, did the people before the law avoid sin? Of course not! Paul says, "In fact, sin was in the world before the law" (v. 13a). The next phrase is not as straightforward: "but sin is not charged to a person's account when there is no law" (v. 13b). I take this to mean that there was sin in the world before the law was given, even though it was not technically specified as a violation of a revealed commandment.

Paul continues, "Nevertheless, death reigned from Adam to Moses, even over those who did not sin in the likeness of Adam's transgression. He is a type of the Coming One" (v. 14). So the people between Adam and Moses (those who did not have the law or disobey specifically revealed commandments as Adam did) are still held responsible for sin. We know they are accountable because they lived under the reign of death. Death provides the evidence of this fact. The law helped later identify the specificity of sin, but sin and death existed before the law. (This is consistent with what we saw in Romans 2: there is real guilt for those who do not have the revealed law, as God's law is written on the human heart; see 2:12-15; Keller, *Romans 1–7*, 125.)

G. K. Chesterton famously quipped that *original sin* is the only doctrine that is empirically verifiable! Just go on a bowling lock-in with a bunch of middle-school boys, talk to a police officer, or even better, ask someone who lives with you about your sin and failures! Parents know you do not have to teach a child to say, "Mine!" I currently have five teenagers in my house, and they continue to express the same tendency (as do their parents). Whenever people tell me they want to be in a profession that "works with people," I always question them: "Are you sure about that?"

Our basic human experience tells us something is wrong with the world. Even those who have a secular worldview know this to be true, though they may not like the word *sin*. Schreiner cites researcher Burton White (who has engaged in a lot of empirical research on children for decades) in *The New First Three Years of Life: The Completely Revised and Updated Edition of the Parenting Classic* to illustrate this point:

> From fifteen to sixteen months on, as his self-awareness becomes more substantial, something in his nature we don't fully understand, will lead him to deliberately try each of these forbidden activities, specifically to see what will be allowed and what won't. In other words, he will begin systematically to

challenge the authority of the adult he lives with. Resistance
to simple requests becomes very common at this time, and if
there is more than one child around, this can be a low point in
the parenting experience. (Schreiner, "Grace That Conquers")

Did you catch that phrase "something in his nature, which we don't
fully understand"? Well, we do understand it because God has revealed
it to us in the Scriptures. We are children of Adam. And that is why we
experience such "low points"!

The good news is that Christ has come to overcome the effects of
sin. That last phrase in verse 14, Adam as "a type of the Coming One,"
is the subject of the following verses. A *type* is a person, place, or event
that foreshadows or symbolizes another. Adam points forward to Christ.
In Christ we can overcome condemnation and death.

Before moving to the contrasts of Adam and Christ, it is worth under-
scoring this idea of federal headship, representation, or solidarity that
is being taught here. Those in highly individualistic cultures may have a
hard time accepting that they sinned in Adam. We can understand that if
we do something personally wrong, we should face the consequences of
it. But the thought that we should suffer for the consequences of someone else's actions is a bit strange to us. However, many illustrations of
representation are familiar to us. Take the Olympics. The athletes are not
competing simply as individuals but as representatives of their countries.
And when our country's athlete wins a medal, it is common to hear something like, "We won a gold medal last night." However, one representative won the medal, not the rest of us who were eating popcorn while
watching it. Adam was our first representative, and when he sinned, we all
sinned. The effects of his sin did not merely affect him but all of humanity. The sin we now commit is because of Adam's sin. But this is not the
end of the story; Adam as our representative is bad news, but Christ as our
representative is glorious news! We are either in Adam or in Christ, and
now Paul tell us something of the differences between these two heads.

The Contrasts
ROMANS 5:15-19

Note the phrases "much more" in verses 15 and 17 and "[just] as . . .
so also" in verses 18-19. In contrasting the work of Christ and the work

of Adam, the phrase "much more" shows that the two are not equal in power. Christ is supreme. In Jesus Christ believers have gained much more than they ever lost in Adam. Regarding the phrase "[just] as . . . so also," the emphasis is really on the "so also" clause—that is, what Christ has done. The "just as" is the obvious part. The "so also" is the good news: Christ has overcome! What Adam has lost, Christ has restored.

Let's look at four contrasts Paul makes in these verses. He contrasts (1) trespass and gift (5:15); (2) condemnation and justification (5:16); (3) death and life (5:17); and (4) disobedience and obedience (5:18-19).

Trespass and Gift (5:15)

You see an emphasis on "grace" or "the gift" in verses 15-17 appearing eight times. In Christ, God deals with us on the basis of grace. By grace we have a new identity, a new future, a new peace, and the promise of a new heaven and earth.

Adam's impact on humanity was negative, as "many died" physically and spiritually (v. 15). "Many" can mean a number of things, and we have to allow context to clarify how inclusive Paul is being. Here it means the totality of mankind (Morris, *Epistle*, 235). He has already said that death has spread to "all people" (v. 12).

Christ's impact was positive, as grace overflowed to many. Context will not allow "many" here to mean that "all" are actually saved. Salvation is offered to all, but people must "receive" it. Verse 17 is important for seeing that this passage is not teaching *universalism* (the belief that all people will be saved). Salvation is *offered* to all, all *need* it, but each must *receive* it.

So then, note the gracious work of Christ. Adam brought alienation from God. Jesus's grace and gift flourished for many. Paul wants the reader to marvel at Christ's grace. Paul piles up phrase after phrase to talk about God's amazing grace in Christ: "much more," "grace of God," "the gift," and "grace of the one man" "overflowed." The gift in view is probably righteousness (see v. 16).

Adam's transgression was fatal, but Christ's gift was life-giving and life changing. Sin and death will not triumph over us believers because the grace of Christ given to us will not allow it.

Paul is painting a dark picture of sin so that the good news of Christ will shine. It is like what a jeweler may do when putting a diamond on a black cloth, so as to make the diamond sparkle.

Condemnation and Justification (5:16)

Verse 16 focuses on the results that follow from Adam and Christ. Adam's work resulted in condemnation. Christ's work resulted in justification (being counted righteous). Everyone has one of these two statuses.

One of the repeated applications of Romans concerns one's *identity* or *status*. In the gospel we get a new identity. Believers are not in Adam; they are in Christ. This is like changing *locations*. We have gone from the swamp to a palace; from quicksand to the Rock; from the Dead Sea to paradise; or from a rat-infested apartment to the Bill Gates mansion (Bird, *Romans*, 191)!

What does this new identity mean? Our identity in Christ should impact everything about us. We should no longer seek to build our lives on our performance, our popularity, our power, or what our peers think of us. We must build our lives on our identity in Christ. We are justified before God, reconciled to God, and adopted by God. In the words of Romans 1:7, we are "loved by God." If you are renewing your mind by reflecting on these gospel realities, and if you are seeking to walk in this new identity, then you will become a more humble, grateful, generous, compassionate, and holy person. You become more conformed to the image of the Son (Rom 8:29; 12:2).

Death and Life (5:17)

What is the evidence for condemnation in Adam and justification in Christ? Paul tells us in verse 17. The evidence for universal condemnation is *the reign of death* over all people in Adam. The evidence for the gift of righteousness is *the reign of life* we believers share in Christ. Instead of Adam ruling over the world as God's agent, death ruled over him. By contrast, the justified in Christ will reign in life. To "reign in life" has an already/not yet focus. We have life now, and we will live and reign with Christ forever.

Robert Letham reminds us that each of us is on one of two teams:

> Paul's point is that we are not addressed merely as discrete individuals; instead, we are placed by God in solidaristic groups or teams. Adam was head or captain of a team of which we all were members. His sin plunged the whole team into sin, ruin, death, and condemnation. What Christ did for us was also done as the head of a team of which [Christians] are

part. He did it on our behalf, for us—and God reckons it to our account as a result of our being united, through faith, with him as the head of the team. Our justification is therefore grounded on union with Christ. (*Union with Christ*, Kindle)

It is good to be on Christ's team! Only in Christ can we triumph over sin and death!

Notice the phrase, "those who receive the overflow of grace" (v. 17). God's grace does not come to us automatically. The experience of new life—this new status, this reign of life—only comes to those who receive it, who believe on the Messiah. This is how you get on his team.

Stop and ponder the abundance of God's grace toward you, Christian. We have gone from death to life through Christ. Our church recently sent out one of our pastors, Matt, as a missionary/church planter to the western part of the nation in an unreached place. His story is remarkable, as Matt had been addicted to drugs and living out a depressing life. But he was awakened to faith through the preaching of the gospel by a pastor friend of mine in Alabama. My friend told me that Matt "looked like death" the first time he met him. But the Lord radically converted Matt and brought him to life. Now he is making the gospel known in a dark place. He received an "overflow of grace" and was brought to life. So have all of us who are in Christ Jesus. You may not have been on your deathbed, addicted to drugs, but before we were in Christ, we were in Adam. We needed spiritual life. Thanks be to God for bringing us to life—by this overflow of grace!

Disobedience and Obedience (5:18-19)

Paul picks up his argument that he began in verse 12. Adam's "one trespass" and "disobedience" are contrasted with Christ's "one righteous act" and "obedience." The obedience and righteous act are probably referring to the ultimate act of obedience, death on a cross (Phil 2:8), which of course has eternal significance because of his *whole life of obedience*.

Notice the outcomes. Adam's fall led to "condemnation for everyone" (v. 18). Jesus's work led to "justification leading to life for everyone" (v. 18). Justification is a forensic act. It involves being declared righteous. Paul joins this salvific concept with "life." This forensic act of justification also gives us spiritual life. And this life is available "for everyone."

Verse 19 essentially restates verse 18, but with an emphasis on the future and the transformative effect of Christ's work. In Adam we are "made sinners," and in Christ (by faith) we "will be made righteous." The two men represent us and appoint a certain status to us. The phrase "many *will be made* righteous" (emphasis added) could be about being declared righteous upon belief, or the future tense could be taken as a future reality; that is, we will be transformed on the final day. Both are true, for Christ's righteous obedience in the middle of history leads to our present justification, a future justification, and a future transformation.

Tim Keller reflects on verse 19, helping us ponder the importance of this "one man's obedience" and the wonder of it:

> Jesus' achievement was not simply to remove the penalty for our disobedience, wonderful though that is; it was to obey for us, as our representative head, throughout his life and supremely in his death. While Adam was told he would enjoy blessing if he obeyed God, and yet chose to disobey (Genesis 2:15-17; 3:6-7), the second Adam knew he would face agony and death if he obeyed—and yet he resolutely walked in obedience to his Father (Mark 14:32-36). When we read of Jesus' continual loving obedience in the Gospels, it is a matter of life and death to us; because that obedience is our obedience, if we are in Christ instead of Adam. (*Romans 1–7*, 132)

So we have the whole biblical story line in this passage. Applications abound, including this: Christianity gives the best explanation for the suffering and misery in the world. It is a result of living in what is now a sinful, fallen world. But it also gives the only solution to the problem in the second Adam, Christ. Jesus is the hope of the whole world. Paul describes the superiority of Christ to Adam in 1 Corinthians 15, reminding us of the hope we have in being united to Jesus:

> *So it is written, The first man Adam became a living being; the last Adam became a life-giving spirit. However, the spiritual is not first, but the natural, then the spiritual.*
>
> *The first man was from the earth, a man of dust; the second man is from heaven. Like the man of dust, so are those who are of the dust; like the man of heaven, so are those who are of heaven. And just as we have borne the image of the man of dust, we will also bear the image of the man of heaven.* (1 Cor 15:45-49)

If you are in Christ, you have this hope: you are united to the man of heaven. Believers, who bear the image of Adam, will one day be transformed into the image of Christ. We will behold him, and we will be like him. We will each have a resurrected, glorified body. So, this life is as bad as it will ever be! Soon suffering will be no more. We will be with him, and we will reign with him.

The Conclusion: Christ Has Overcome!
ROMANS 5:20-21

In verse 20 Paul concludes with the place of the Mosaic law in this grand view of history. A Jew may ask, How can you jump from Adam to Jesus? What about all the good stuff God did for Israel in between that time? Paul does believe in the rest of the Old Testament, and he has already affirmed that Israel had wonderful privileges. However, he is thoroughly convinced that the law does not solve the problem of sin. The law can count sin, but it cannot counter it (Bird, *Romans*, 185). It only serves to "multiply the trespass." The law did not bring relief from the sin problem. In a sense it made it worse. I do not think Paul is thinking about how the law actually stimulates more rebellion in people. Rather, he is thinking along the lines of Romans 4:15; that is, the law makes people accountable to a specific detailed series of commandments, thus bringing greater judgment (Moo, *Romans*, 185). It is not "trespasses" but "the trespass"—that is, the gravity of sin is weightier with specific laws.

The solution to sin is not Mosaic law but messianic grace, the gift of righteousness and life through Jesus. Paul declares, God's "grace multiplied even more." The only hope for humanity is grace, not the law. And grace has come in a person: Christ.

In verse 21 Paul first says that in Adam, sin has sway over us. In Adam sin rules us. We are under the dominion of death. But Paul concludes with the good news. In Christ grace reigns over us. We who have been declared righteous have life. We will share in the life of the world to come. We will share in the new creation. We will share in a cosmic renewal, the consummation of God's purposes.

Therefore, as we look back over the entire chapter, it is worth noting how the chapter begins and ends with the phrase "through Jesus Christ our Lord" (Rom 5:1,21). Through Christ, and Christ alone, we have victory over sin and death. What grace we have in Christ Jesus!

> Marvelous grace of our loving Lord,
> Grace that exceeds our sin and our guilt,
> Yonder on Calvary's mount outpoured,
> There where the blood of the Lamb was spilt.
>   Grace, grace, God's grace,
>   Grace that will pardon and cleanse within!
>   Grace, grace, God's grace,
>   Grace that is greater than all our sin!
> —Julia H. Johnston

Before moving to Romans 6, let's look back and consider what Paul has said in the first five chapters. Keller is again helpful here:

> The end of chapter 5 marks the end of a section in Paul's letter, a glorious section which has laid out the gospel of justification by faith. The second-century church father Tertullian said that, just as our Lord was crucified between two thieves, so this great doctrine of justification is continually being crucified between two opposite heresies. The gospel keeps two truths together.
>   1. God is holy, so our sins require that we be punished. The gospel tells us: *You are more sinful than you ever dared believe.* To forget this leads to license and permissiveness—to what we might call liberalism.
>   2. God is gracious, so in Christ our sins are dealt with. The gospel tells us: *You are more accepted in Christ than you ever dared hope.* To forget this leads to legalism and moralism.
>   If you eliminate one or the other of these truths, you fall into legalism or liberalism, and you eliminate the joy and the "release" of the gospel. Without a knowledge of our extreme sin, the payment of the gospel seems trivial and does not electrify or transform. But without a knowledge of Christ's completely debt-satisfying life and death, the knowledge of sin would crush us or compel us to deny and repress it. (*Romans 1–7*, 135; emphasis in original)

Indeed, according to Romans 1:18–3:20, we are worse than we think! But according to Romans 3:21–5:21, those who are in Christ are more loved and accepted than we could ever imagine!

Paul will now address more questions about sin and grace in the following chapters as he helps us think about our union with Christ, and as he exhorts those in Christ to live a gospel-driven life by the power of the Spirit.

Reflect and Discuss

1. How does Romans 5:12-21 compare with 5:1-11? What are the similarities and differences of these passages?
2. How does Romans 5:12-21 provide a glimpse of the true story of the whole world?
3. How is Adam a "type" of Christ (v. 14)?
4. What does this passage teach us about salvation by grace? How is grace emphasized?
5. What does this passage teach us about Adam and Christ as being representatives of humanity?
6. How does Paul connect the concept of justification by faith to "life" (v. 18)?
7. How does this passage magnify the person and work of Christ?
8. What does Paul say about the law in verses 20-21?
9. What are the practical ministry implications from this passage? What does it say about the need to evangelize, about counseling others, or about how we articulate the Christian worldview?
10. Believer, spend some time thanking God for the salvation you have in Christ Jesus. Unbeliever, will you consider what this passage says and turn to Christ now for salvation?

Raised to Walk in Newness of Life

ROMANS 6

Main Idea: Through our union with Christ, believers receive the glorious benefits of salvation and are enabled to walk in newness of resurrection life.

I. **Truths We Must Know (6:1-10)**
   A. We died to sin (6:2).
   B. We have died with Christ in baptism (6:3).
   C. We share in Christ's resurrection life (6:4-5).
   D. Our old selves were crucified with Christ (6:6-7).
   E. We will also live with Christ (6:8-10).
II. **Actions We Must Take (6:11-23)**
   A. Reckon ourselves dead to sin and alive to God in Christ (6:11).
   B. Offer ourselves to God (6:12-19).
   C. Remember the superior benefits of serving God (6:20-23).

We planted our church about eight years ago, and some of our most memorable days have been Baptism Sundays—that is, particular Sundays when converts read their testimonies to the congregation, declaring Jesus as Lord, and then get immersed in water as a visible display of their union with Jesus. We have done these baptisms in various places (in a portable baptistery at a storefront, at a lake, and now a built-in baptistery at our current church building). But regardless of the location, joy and gratitude have characterized those moments.

In our Baptist tradition it is common for the one administering the baptism to say to the person being baptized something like, "Based on your profession of faith, I baptize you my brother [or sister] in the name of the Father, the Son, and the Holy Spirit." Then the minister adds, while lowering the person into the water, "Buried with Christ in baptism . . ." and then joyfully declares, while raising the person out of the water, ". . . raised to walk in newness of life." The baptized person is proclaiming to the world, "I'm with Jesus. He is my Lord. I am new in him." It is also a statement saying, "I'm with Jesus's people. I am united to my fellow believers as my brothers and sisters." Further, it is a proclamation to the demonic realm that the risen Jesus Christ is Lord and that one day he will reign, putting all his enemies under his feet.

Baptism is indeed a powerful picture of our union with Christ, which Paul unfolds in Romans 6. Through our union with Christ, we receive the glorious salvation benefits we have in Christ, and we are brought into communion with the living Christ. We have died with him, and we have been raised to walk in newness of life. Kevin Vanhoozer says this about baptism:

> [Baptism] is also an object lesson, a visual demonstration of a doctrinal truth concerning union with Christ. Water baptism inserts the disciple, in a very visible and tangible manner, into the story of Jesus. Baptism marks a disciple's setting out on Jesus' way by ritually enacting the death of the old self and the birth of the new. . . . It is a communicative act that corresponds to the disciple's new reality in Christ. . . . In submitting to baptism, a person publicly and symbolically performs union with Christ and membership in the company of the gospel, for the baptized disciple has theatrically identified with the death and resurrection of Jesus. . . . It is a rich theological lesson that also grips the church's imagination, particularly when congregants are exhorted to "remember your baptism" as they watch the baptism of someone else. (*Hearers & Doers*, 151)

How do we live the Christian life? It involves remembering our baptisms. It involves walking in newness of life that we now have through our union with Christ. In certain parts of the world, new believers are literally given new names. In other places, unbelieving family members who do not support the baptized person's decision are shamed by such a confession and consider the new believer "dead." In these instances, the believer's brand-new identity is experienced on multiple levels.

While Paul is not writing about the ordinance of baptism here, this chapter is important for understanding the truths that point to the truth of baptism. Paul is expounding the glorious doctrine of our union with Christ.

We cannot overstate the importance of this doctrine. Throughout church history some have called it the central truth of the whole doctrine of salvation. Everything else flows from our union with Christ. The chief benefit that comes from Christ's salvation is Christ himself. Much of what is true of him is true of us. His death was our death; his resurrection was assurance of our resurrection; his appearance in glory will mean our arrival in glory. Union with Christ means we have a new identity, new security, new power, and a new destiny (cf. Col 3:1-4)

In Romans 6 Paul speaks of the glory of our union with Christ, teaching us much about these benefits, and he touches on some important aspects of our *sanctification*—that is, the believer's growth in Christlikeness. *Justification* (the primary doctrine addressed in the previous chapters) involves being saved from the *penalty* of sin. *Glorification* (which Paul will address more fully in chapter 8) involves being saved from the *presence* of sin. *Sanctification* is about being saved from the *power* of sin. All three aspects of our salvation are related, and union with Christ is related to each aspect, but Romans 6 focuses on sanctification. Because of our union with Christ, we each now have power to pursue a holy life that glorifies God. Sin does not have dominion over us any longer because of this blessed union with Jesus.

As Paul unfolds this passage, he reminds us of two big ideas regarding our growth in Christlikeness: truths we must know and actions we must take. Regarding the former, he reminds the believer of his or her union with Christ. Notice the word "know" in verses 3 (ESV), 6, and 9. Knowing who we are is critical for our discipleship. Regarding the latter, he reminds us that sanctification is not a passive matter. We must consider ourselves dead to sin and alive to God (v. 11); we must say no to sin and say yes to God as people now empowered for righteousness (vv. 12-19); and we must remember the superior benefits of serving God instead of sin (vv. 20-23).

Paul has been extolling the triumphs of God's grace in salvation (5:1-21). His has been a glorious picture of grace reigning and increasing (5:20-21). But this leads to a question about how a Christian is to now live between justification and final glorification. Some seemed to believe that Paul espoused a version of the faith that minimized sin (3:8) and encouraged a "live as you want to" kind of Christian experience. But Paul does not have a passive attitude toward sin. His theology does not encourage lawlessness. Through the believer's union with Christ, one can triumph over sin in one's daily life, and indeed one must make a serious commitment to do so.

Truths We Must Know
ROMANS 6:1-10

In light of all this talk about grace, the question is posed, "Should we continue in sin so that grace may multiply?" (v. 1). Paul clearly rejects *antinomianism*, the idea that God's grace in salvation gives one a license to live lawlessly (v. 2, see also v. 15). Quite the contrary, Paul argues strongly, giving several reasons grace is not a license to sin (Stott, *Message*, 168–69). These reasons are important for understanding Christian identity and how we now live the Christian life as people united to Christ.

We Died to Sin (6:2)

Paul poses the rhetorical question, "How can we who died to sin still live in it?" The phrase "died to sin" refers to vanquishing the tyrannical and dominating power of sin. Because we are no longer in Adam but in Christ, the power of sin is broken.

Paul is speaking here of the dying to sin that takes place when one becomes a Christian. We who know God's saving grace in Christ have said goodbye to the world of sin. We are new. This does not mean we are not capable of sinning anymore but that our relationship to sin has changed. We died to it. We no longer live under its dominion; we cannot and do not want to go back to that way of life. Bird puts it well:

> For believers, sin is no longer their status, their state, or their master. . . . You cannot live in Sin-land when the government posts your obituary in its local newspaper. Why would you want to remain there anyway when you recently received a letter notifying you that you had just inherited Grace-land. (*Romans*, 195–96)

We Have Died with Christ in Baptism (6:3)

Paul now elaborates on how we have died to sin (cf. 1 Cor 10:2; Gal 3:27). Paul here reminds us of the incompatibility between baptism and remaining in sin (Bird, *Romans*, 196). His statement about baptism recalls the believer's conversion to Christ. When we were baptized into Christ spiritually, we were baptized into his death. The person who thinks grace is a license to sin does not realize what it means to die with Christ.

Becoming a Christian is not just about adding a little something new to your life. It involves a brand-new personal identification with Christ, and part of this new identity involves dying with Christ. Keller says, "When we believe, we are united to Christ, so that whatever is true of him is now legally true of us. Since Christ died, and dead people are freed from sin, so we are freed from sin" (*Romans 1–7*, 140). This is just another reminder that sin no longer has dominion over the Christian.

We Share in Christ's Resurrection Life (6:4-5)

We not only share in Christ's death but also in his resurrection (v. 4). Paul says we have been "buried with him." We have shared in Christ's death. Burial speaks of the end of a life. We cannot go back to our old way of life because that way of life is dead and buried. Further, there is a purpose for the burial: resurrection. We have been buried in order to walk in "newness of life." What God did for Christ in raising him from the dead, he also does for believers at conversion; he liberates them from the power of sin and gives them new resurrection life—a life that begins in conversion but will be completed on the day of resurrection (Stott, *Message*, 174).

In verse 5 Paul seems to speak of this end-of-time resurrection. Notice the future tense: "We will." While we share in Christ's resurrection benefits now (Col 3:1), we await the consummation of this grace later (cf. Phil 3:20-21). How? Because we are united to him. What gives you any confidence that you will rise from the dead? We cannot suggest that we are strong enough to overcome death on our own! Our assurance is based on the fact that we are united with him in a resurrection like his.

Our Old Selves Were Crucified with Christ (6:6-7)

Paul continues by speaking of the results of dying with Christ. In verse 6 Paul says our old, unconverted selves were crucified (cf. Gal 2:20). The person a believer used to be in Adam was crucified (Stott, *Message*, 176).

Then Paul uses two "so that" clauses to explain the results of this action. Our old selves were crucified "so that the body ruled by sin might be rendered powerless." His point is straightforward: believers are no longer ruled by sin. Paul then adds, "so that we may no longer be enslaved to sin." Because sin's power has been broken, we should realize the new freedom we now have. Sin should not characterize the Christian, but a life of freedom from sin and a freedom for righteousness should characterize the Christian. Paul's statement in verse 7 supports his claim in verse 6. Those who have died with Christ have been set free from sin's tyranny. Schreiner comments, "Justification cannot be separated from sanctification. Only those who have died with Christ are righteous and thereby enabled to conquer the mastery of sin" (*Romans*, 319).

We Will Also Live with Christ (6:8-10)

Paul continues elaborating on his central statements from verses 3-5. These verses rehash what Paul has previously said: dying with Christ entails rising with him too (v. 8). Why should the believer not serve sin? We have resurrection life! We are spiritually alive now in Christ, and we will be physically raised later.

In verse 9 Paul explains that Christ's resurrection means he will not die again. He has triumphed over death. Because Christ has conquered death, we who are in him will also conquer death (Moo, *Romans*, 198). What is true of Christ is true of his people! In verse 10 Paul explains that Christ's death and resurrection formed a "climactic and non-repeatable action whereby he was removed from sin and given a never-ending and incorruptible life with God in his resurrection" (Bird, *Romans*, 200).

Consider what benefits our union with Christ brings! Recently I played in a golf scramble, where four of us played on a team. Each player hits the ball at the same spot, but he uses the farthest-hit ball for the next shot. For the entire round, our team shot seventeen under par. (For you nongolfers: that is remarkable!) But the secret was this: we had a golf pro on our team. So his score was credited to me! In the tournament you could say of your teammate, "If he shot it, I got it." In a greater way, we receive the benefits of being with Christ: he won the ultimate battle, and his victory is the believer's victory.

Actions We Must Take
ROMANS 6:11-23

Here in verse 11 Paul gives the first of several imperatives. Our new life in Christ must result in new actions. We can break it down into three broad exhortations.

Reckon Ourselves Dead to Sin and Alive to God in Christ (6:11)

We must "reckon" or "consider" something, namely, that we have died to sin and are alive to God in Christ. Until we grasp that our old lives have ended, that our penalty has been paid, and that Christ's resurrection life is ours, we will not have an appropriate view of our own sanctification. We must recognize that everything has changed, as verses 2-10 explain. We have died to sin. We have a new desire for righteousness. And we have power to obey God.

The emphasis on "consider" (*logizomai*) is important. It means one should judge that one is dead to sin and alive to God because this is true! Our incorporation into Christ has made this a reality. This does not mean that we are unable to sin but that the reign of sin has ended for all who are in Christ. Not only has the reign of sin ended, but also being "alive to God" has begun. God is our master, not sin (Schreiner, *Romans*, 322).

This kind of identity formation is critical for growth in Christlikeness. Our identity in Christ is our most fundamental and important identity. It should shape everything. It should stimulate our affections for Christ, give us a deep sense of gratitude, and fill us with hope as we live for God's glory in this fallen world.

Offer Ourselves to God (6:12-19)

Paul gives a series of exhortations regarding things Christians should and should not do. The basic idea is that we should say no to sin and say yes to God. He elaborates on this point in verses 15-23. Here in verses 12-14 he says that believers must "not let sin reign" (v. 12). While we have been freed from the power of sin, we must act. Putting away sin is not an automatic process (Moo, *Romans*, 200). We must exercise our will so that the desires of sin do not reign over us. This is a call not to make peace with sin but to declare war on it. Do not let it reign!

In verse 13 Paul makes a similar point but with more concrete expression. He urges us not to present ourselves to sin but instead to God. We must choose to present ourselves to God. While we may still be tempted by sinful desires (v. 12), we must not let these desires have control over us; we must instead surrender ourselves to God. The phrase "as those who are alive from the dead" is important. It reminds us that we share in Christ's resurrected life (vv. 4,11). We have power not to let sin reign! We can live a different kind of life now because of our union with Christ.

Paul closes this section with a promise (v. 14). The promise is that sin will not rule over us. The tyranny of sin has been broken. We must obey God and not let sin reign, but the ability to obey is a gift of God's grace and power.

Paul then says why sin will not master the believer: "You are not under the law but under grace" (v. 14). Here, Paul connects the believer's liberation from sin with liberation from the Mosaic era (Schreiner, *Romans*, 326; see Gal 4:3-5). Believers in the new covenant are enabled to obey God by the Spirit and to bear fruit for God (Rom 7:6). We have new life in Christ and new power in this new covenant to offer ourselves to God.

In verses 15-19 Paul magnifies the liberating power of Jesus, showing us that we have power to offer ourselves to God. He builds on verses 12-14 as he reminds believers that they have been set free to serve righteousness.

In verse 15 he (re)states that grace is not a license to sin. The idea that grace is a license to sin is morally and spiritually absurd! Paul affirms that we are *not* "under the law." We have been removed from the old Mosaic era. We were guilty lawbreakers. We could not keep the law. And the law actually intensified sin (3:20; 4:15; 5:20). He affirms that we are "under grace." We have entered the new era in which we have been declared righteous by grace. Christ kept the law fully and died in our place. He is our righteousness. Consequently, we do not fear the penalty of sin, and we have power to overcome remaining sin.

So then, grace is not just a gift but a *power*! We have power to live in righteousness. Grace not only justifies, but it also *transforms*. Grace gives us new "want-tos." It changes our desires. Now a willing obedience comes from a new heart and a renewed mind. This is why sinning in the name of grace is a total misunderstanding of grace.

The exodus account may be in Paul's mind throughout this chapter. The Israelites were freed from Egyptian bondage, but they were not just freed *from* something; they were freed *for* something—namely, to serve God! We know the better Moses, the Lord Jesus. Through his death and resurrection, he ushered in a new exodus. Jesus has made us a new people, and we delight to serve our God now.

In verse 16 Paul reminds us that we cannot serve two masters. The metaphor of slavery dominates these verses. Words related to it are used about eight times. Paul is not condoning slavery here but assuming a familiarity with it, and he is using an analogy to make a point (v. 19). The point is, a slave serves his or her master. The master we obey is evidence of whose we are. You can serve sin/Satan or righteousness/God (vv. 18-19,22). Being slaves to sin results in *death*. But an obedient servant of God leads to *righteousness*. Sin does not bring freedom. It only brings slavery/bondage/prison. Being a slave to righteousness/God does not mean *slavish fear* but childlike love—obeying with a glad heart.

Paul, like Jesus, is emphasizing the impossibility of compromise (cf. Matt 6:24). You can serve sin or God. It cannot be both. Again, Paul is not saying that one who has submitted to the lordship of Jesus will never commit a sin. He is saying that we are no longer under condemnation, and we are no longer in bondage to sin. Christian, you are not a slave to sin, so do not live like you are!

In verses 17-18 Paul erupts into praise as he considers the freedom from sin Christ has given us. Paul praised God because we who were once slaves have become obedient from the heart. How did we get free? God did it! God in his grace has broken the shackles of sin, so now we glorify him. By his death on the cross, Jesus has destroyed the enslavement camp and rescued us.

Verses 17-18 include the Romans' testimony. Paul speaks of their conversion when he states that they have "obeyed from the heart" (v. 17). The Greek aorist tense points to the decisive act of obedience (which springs from faith, 1:5) when they turned to God. Conversion is not just a mental ascent to the facts but a heart transformation. The next phrase, "that pattern of teaching to which you were handed over," is striking. This "teaching" refers to the gospel, accepted Christian teaching. "Pattern" carries the idea of being "molded." The Scripture forms us. And Paul says that they were handed over to it. God delivered the believer from slavery to sin to a new pattern of teaching. Being a Christian involves being under the authority of Christian teaching. This is fundamental to our growth in Christlikeness. Paul calls this becoming "enslaved to righteousness" (v. 18). We are free from the condemning power of sin *and* from its enslaving power. Now we give ourselves to God completely.

In verse 19 Paul reemphasizes what he said in verse 13. Living out our new identity involves daily sacrifice—a daily offering of ourselves to God in righteousness. Paul tells believers of their past, in which they used to live passionately for sin, but says, "so now" you must live passionately for God as "slaves to righteousness." This is a call to act. It is a call against passivity. Sanctification involves action. This offering our parts involves a holy sacrifice (v. 12; 12:1-2). Holy living involves offering yourself to God as an act of worship.

So Christian, let's offer ourselves to God in holiness. Let's remember that sanctification involves saying no to sin and saying yes to God.

Let's not serve sin but serve our God, who is worthy of our lives. Let's remember that we are not powerless! We have entered a new relationship with God through Christ. We have new power not to let sin reign but instead to serve righteousness.

Remember the Superior Benefits of Serving God (6:20-23)

Paul concludes this section by giving us additional motivation. In case you are tempted to think it is better to serve sin instead of God, Paul makes clear that this is not the case!

In verse 20 Paul reflects on their pre-Christian days. They had been "free with regard to righteousness." Leon Morris says,

> This did not mean that they had never done anything that was right (evil people do good things). But it meant that they were not subject to the rule of righteousness; they saw no compulsion to do what was right. Their freedom was a grim one. (*Epistle*, 265)

In verse 21 Paul speaks of the corresponding fruit of serving one of these two masters. Slaves of sin produced shame and "death." When they were the slaves of sin, they were not ashamed of those things (cf. Jer 8:12). A mark of a sin-dominated life is shamelessness. When they became Christians, they saw things differently.

The superior benefits of serving God are stated in verse 22: "sanctification" and "eternal life." The little phrase "but now" introduces a contrast. Being a Christian means you are new (cf. 2 Cor 5:17) and that you bear fruit. Paul does not say what the fruit is, only that it leads to sanctification, the process of becoming holy. The end of it all is "eternal life." This statement leads to verse 23, which is a fitting conclusion to the whole chapter.

What God in his grace offers is not payment for works rendered but a gift in the form of eternal life (v. 23). Eternal life is undeserved; it is not earned. The whole contrast made in verse 23 reflects much of Romans:

The Master One May Serve	Sin or God
The Outcome of That Service	Death or Eternal Life
How That Outcome Is Obtained	Wages Earned or a Gift Received

So, whom do you serve? Do you see the outcome of that service? Will you receive the gift of eternal life?

How do all these benefits come to us? "In Christ Jesus our Lord." Our Master is full of grace. Our Master laid down his life for us. In him there is liberty, fulfillment, and eternal life.

So let's put it all together. How do you live the Christian life? First, there are some truths you must know about your new union with Christ. You must remember who you are! And second, there are some actions you must take. Regarding those actions, you must reckon these things to be true about yourself: you are dead to sin and alive to God in Christ; you must act by the new power that is yours, saying no to sin and saying yes to God; and you must remember the superior benefits of serving God over sin. Our thoughts, actions, and motives are all important as we seek to live a sanctified life to the glory of God through our Lord Jesus Christ.

Reflect and Discuss

1. Explain *justification, sanctification,* and *glorification.*
2. Why is it important to remember one's identity in Christ when it comes to sanctification?
3. What does Paul say about the believer's union with Christ in Romans 6:1-10?
4. What does Paul teach the believer about having power over sin?
5. Explain how Paul teaches the believer to say no to sin and to say yes to God in 6:12-13. Why are both decisions important?
6. What does it mean to be "under grace"?
7. How does Paul answer the objection about grace giving people a license to sin (6:1,15)?
8. What does it mean to be "slaves to righteousness" or "enslaved to God"?
9. How does Paul contrast being a slave of sin and a slave of God?
10. How might you use this passage to help new believers?

Wretched Man, Wonderful Messiah

ROMANS 7

Main Idea: Paul describes how Christians have been released from the law and wedded to Jesus, enabling them to now serve in the new way of the Spirit (7:1-6). Before unpacking this more fully in chapter 8, he addresses God's purpose for giving the law, reminding the readers of the law's goodness, but then he dramatically describes how one cannot keep the law perfectly, thus magnifying our need for the Messiah (7:7-25).

I. **Wedded to Christ, Serving in the New Way of the Spirit (7:1-6)**
   A. The legal principle (7:1)
   B. The marriage illustration (7:2-3)
   C. The application (7:4)
   D. A further contrast (7:5-6)
II. **Thankful for Christ, Longing for Deliverance (7:7-25)**
   A. The value of the law (7:7-12)
   B. Human inability to keep the law (7:13-23)
   C. Thanks be to God through Jesus Christ our Lord (7:24-25)!

Throughout Romans Paul articulates the nature of the good news of salvation in Christ by grace alone through faith alone, at the same time affirming the value of the Old Testament. He boldly proclaims the good news, but he also defends the unity of the Scriptures. Many Jews raised objections to Paul's preaching (as the synagogue sermons in Acts demonstrate), so Paul constantly had to defend his position against these objections. In Romans Paul goes out of his way to show the priority of Israel in God's plan, the privileges they enjoy, and the promises they received—but he also shows how none of these truths are inconsistent with what he preaches. The coming of Christ is the fulfillment of all of these hopes and longings, and thus Paul weeps over Jewish unbelief.

Here in Romans 7 is another example of "confirming" the gospel and "defending" the gospel (Peterson, *Commentary*, 10–11). Paul confirms the truthfulness of a "released from the law and wedded to Christ" gospel (vv. 1-6) but then defends his argument, insisting that this in no way devalues the law (vv. 7-25). When properly understood, the law should lead us to Jesus who alone can deliver us from the penalty of sin, from the controlling power of sin, and eventually from the presence of sin. The law reveals the holiness of God. It shows us our sin. It condemns us. It cannot acquit us or change us (Bird, *Romans*, 255). Only the gospel can do that. We need something more than the law. We need the law-fulfilling and sin-bearing substitute, Jesus Christ. Through our union with Christ, we have the power of the Spirit to bear fruit for God.

Romans 7:7-25 is a highly controversial passage centering around two related questions. First, to whom does the "I" refer? At first glance, one may say, "Obviously, Paul is speaking autobiographically. He is speaking about himself." But is he? Paul speaks representatively elsewhere (cf. 1 Cor 13:1-3), so is he doing that here? Is Paul speaking of *himself*, of *Adam*, of a *God-fearing Gentile* who wants to keep God's law but cannot, or of *Israel*? Or is Paul speaking in a way that encompasses all the above (a composite character: Paul, Adam, Israel, and God fearers)? Second, is Paul speaking about a believer or unbeliever? How one answers the first question will impact how one answers this second question. If one thinks Paul is simply speaking of his own present experience, it is easier to conclude that he is writing about his experience as a Christian. But if one sees this as a style of writing in which Paul is representing those trying to please God under the law, it is easier to say that Paul is not speaking of a believer's struggle with sin but of an unregenerate person who is hopeless apart from Christ.

These are not easy questions. Scholar Tom Schreiner says, "Some think this text isn't difficult, but I have wrestled with the passage over and over, and I suppose I am not finished yet" (in Justin Taylor's "5 Questions, 5 Scholars"). If Schreiner is not finished with Romans 7, I do not merely "suppose" I am not finished with it; I *know* I am not finished with it!

Regardless of what position you take on these questions, the primary point remains the same. The law cannot deliver any person from sin and the flesh; it cannot produce obedience to God. That is true for both believer and unbeliever. The law can neither justify nor sanctify (Moo, *Letter*, 409). We need the gospel to transform us and the Spirit of God to empower us for obedience. Peterson says,

> Simply agreeing with God's law and desiring to keep it is
> not the way forward for the Christian. . . . Thankful for what
> Jesus has accomplished for us and confident about ultimate

deliverance from "this body of death," we need to seek the direction and empowerment of the Spirit to live in a way that pleases him (cf. Rom 8:1-17). (*Commentary*, 302)

Thankfully, God has given the believer such grace in Christ (5:20; 6:14,15-23).

So, we should bear in mind that the main issue here is *the law*. Morris rightly states, "We should be clear that Paul is writing about the law, not trying to answer the questions that modern people ask" (*Epistle*, 276). Bird also states, "Romans 7:7-25 should principally be understood as Paul's apologia for the Torah. . . . Paul mentions the law sixteen times in 7:7-25" (*Romans*, 232). Moo even contends, "One can preach this paragraph in its basic intention, without even making definite identification of the *egō* ["I"]" (*Letter*, 443).

That said, these questions are still important and should be considered (as Moo also points out). Nevertheless, keeping our eyes on Paul's main concern—the value of the law and its salvific inability—must remain a priority.

Wedded to Christ, Serving in the New Way of the Spirit
ROMANS 7:1-6

Paul reminds the Roman Christians of their new status and new power with the use of a legal principle, with a marriage illustration, with an application, and finally with further elaboration/contrast.

The Legal Principle (7:1)

Paul is speaking about the Mosaic law here, not Roman law (Schreiner, *Romans*, 346). The rabbis said, "If a person is dead, he is free from the Torah, and the fulfilling of the commandments" (in Moo, *Letter*, 218). Even many of the non-Jews in the Roman church were former God fearers, and thus familiar with the Mosaic law. Paul states that the law has authority over a man only as long as he lives. But this authority is limited to this life. Death annuls it. Death delivers you from your common obligations.

The Marriage Illustration (7:2-3)

This illustration is straightforward: if a husband dies, his wife is released from the marriage vows. The law binds her, but his death frees her. And this release is complete. Death makes her free to remarry.

The Application (7:4)

There is a shift in the metaphor. Now Paul has the wife dying and remarrying (not the husband)! Some want to make fun of Paul, claiming he is like the person who cannot tell the punch line of a joke! They say Paul was not very good at sermon illustrations.

Well, I disagree. Remember this is an illustration. Paul is not developing an allegory in which every detail of the picture corresponds exactly to something in the reality. The point is simple: death ends the obligations to the law. The point of his illustration is this: Christ's death has secured our release from marriage to the law and our remarriage to him.

At the cross we believers shared in *the death of Christ*. We died with him, as we saw in Romans 6. How did we die to the law? We died to the power of the old regime (6:14-15). In redemptive history the era of the law has come to an end with the saving work of Christ (Moo, *Letter*, 219). Believers have been newly related to Christ, and now the Spirit enables us to obey. Further, we no longer have the condemnation of the law (8:1). We have a new status, a new power, and a new security.

Marriage is a fitting illustration of the Christian life. Becoming a Christian is like getting married. It is about loving Christ our groom, our head, our good shepherd. It is the best of all relationships. Think about this: you are united to the resurrected Christ! Because we are united to him, we have glorious status, supernatural power, and future security.

What is the goal of this new union? It is that we might "bear fruit for God." In Colossians 1:9-14 Paul prayed that the Colossians would bear fruit in every good work. What does this mean? Fruitfulness involves manifesting the character of Jesus, the one with whom we are united: "love, joy, peace, patience, kindness, goodness, faithfulness, gentleness, and self-control" (Gal 5:22-23). Fruitfulness involves certain actions as well, like giving praise to God (Heb 13:15). Jesus told the disciples that in bearing fruit they prove to be his disciples (John 15:8). Paul prayed that Philippian believers would be "filled with the fruit of righteousness that comes through Jesus Christ to the glory and praise of God" (Phil 1:11). If we are united to Jesus Christ, then by the Spirit we will bear fruit.

A Further Contrast (7:5-6)

Paul concludes this section with two important verses that help us grasp not only this passage but passages to come later. Our sinful passions were aroused by the law prior to conversion. We were provoked to rebellion, as Paul will elaborate in verses 8-12, and we bore fruit for death. But in Christ we are free to "serve in the newness of the Spirit." This new age is essentially the age of the Spirit. The Holy Spirit writes God's law in our hearts. Our old lives involved a brutal bundle: *law, sin,* and *death* (v. 5). But the believer's new life makes us servants of God through the power of the Spirit (v. 6). Now, as believers, we *want* to obey God. We are not attempting to earn salvation. We want to obey because we have been changed. We still want to serve in a way that reflects the righteousness of the law, but we have new power to do this: the Holy Spirit.

Thankful for Christ, Longing for Deliverance
ROMANS 7:7-25

Having reached this point, Paul could have gone straight to Romans 8. But he does not pick up the thought of 7:6 until 8:1. Before Paul gets to Romans 8, he defends his comments regarding the law. He talks about the value of the law, our inability to keep it perfectly, and our ultimate deliverance in Christ. He does not mention the Holy Spirit again until chapter 8.

The Value of the Law (7:7-12)

Given what Paul has said, objectors may ask Paul if he thinks the law is actually an evil thing. But Paul denies this emphatically (v. 7). While we Christians are not under the written code, we still need to see the value of the law. The law has great value in several ways.

First, the law shows sin in its true colors (7:7-8). Paul illustrates this fact with *coveting.* Like a mirror, the law exposes our failures (Jas 1:22-25). In Galatians Paul says it is like a "tutor" leading us to faith (Gal 3:23-24 NASB). Here Paul says that he was made aware of coveting through the law. The law continues to have this kind of value today. No one comes to Christ in faith without a clear recognition of his or her sin. This is a gracious thing—for one to recognize his or her sinfulness.

Second, the law reveals the human proclivity to sin (7:8). Being enticed by forbidden fruit is as old as the garden. The problem is not the law but one's reaction to it. You can tell a kid in a grocery store, "You can't have that one," and her reaction sounds something like, "You never give me anything!" In our sinful condition, we do not react rightly to God's law. Instead, the human reaction often sounds something like, "No one is going to tell me what to do, not even God!" What Paul is saying is that sin twists the good function of the law. We cannot blame the law for proclaiming God's will. The problem is not with the law but with our sinful nature.

Third, the law exposes our need for spiritual life (7:9-11). Paul has already spoken in the first person, but in verses 9-11 he now talks about the "I" being trapped between law and sin (Bird, *Romans*, 239). It seems clear here that Paul is not strictly speaking about himself but about a particular person or class of persons who can identify with what he is saying (ibid.). All three of these verses speak of the commandment in relation to death.

Verse 9 is difficult. Paul is saying that he (or others he is representing) was alive before the law. This may connote a God-fearing Gentile (who was previously unaware of the sinfulness of sin before knowing the law), or Paul may have the garden in mind and/or Sinai. If Sinai, then we know that Israel was not sinless before the Mosaic law was given, but they were made more aware of the specificities of sin, the gravity of sin, and the resulting judgment when they received the law. In any case, once the law came, then awareness of sin and death came. The Mosaic law did not bring life but death (v. 10). Sin was magnified and judgment came as a result.

In verse 11 Paul speaks representatively about this experience of sin and death, stating that sin twists the law, like the serpent in the garden twisted it, and it brings death. As an Israelite, he can affirm that the giving of the law at Sinai also resulted in death.

Fourth, the law shows the nature of the Lawgiver (7:12). God's law reveals his attributes, such as holiness, righteousness, and goodness. You can imagine many Jews contesting what Paul has said up to this point regarding the law. So Paul states the holy, righteous, and good nature of the law. There are no unholy commandments because God is holy (Lev 19:2). There are no unrighteous commandments because God is righteous (Dan 9:14). There are no evil commandments because God is good (Mark 10:18). The problem is not with the law but with our sinful human condition.

Human Inability to Keep the Law (7:13-23)

Before dealing with these verses, let's deal with the controversy. To whom is Paul referring in this first-person discourse? I used to hold the position that this was Paul's autobiography and that he was speaking of his own present experience as a believer. This made sense since Paul says "I." Further, experientially, I know that as a Christian I still fight sin, so this reading has brought comfort. I also know that the idea of fighting sin is taught elsewhere in the New Testament, including in Romans (e.g., Rom 8:9-11; 13:14; cf. 1 Cor 3:1; Gal 5:13,16-18). Further, many of my favorite preachers take this position, and it is hard to go against your heroes! Moreover, Paul also switches to the present tense in verse 14, and that always helped tip the scales for me in favor of reading this as Paul's experience as a Christian. He seems to be speaking about his present experience. Added to these points is the phrase, "I delight in God's law" (v. 22), which has always seemed like a Christian rather than a non-Christian to me.

While I concur that believers are in a war with sin and will never fully overcome it in this life, and while there are good arguments for this passage being about Paul's own experience as a Christian, I take the other view: that it does *not* describe one's Christian experience. I see Paul speaking of his former life as a Jew under the law and writing with a dramatic style representing others under the law who are trying to please God but cannot. It is not just *a fight* with sin that Paul is describing here in 7:14-25; it is misery and *defeat*. The wretched man needs a wonderful Messiah. Schreiner offers four important reasons for holding the pre-Christian experience view:

1. The structure of the passage.

When we look at Romans 7 as a whole, we find a clear structure. This is outlined in 7:5-6. Verse 5 depicts pre-Christian experience, describing a time "when we were in the flesh," and explains that the flesh produced "death." Verse 6 refers to Christians in four terms: "But now," "released," "died" (to our old life), and "Spirit." Virtually all commentators agree that verse 5 refers to unbelievers and verse 6 to believers. But here is the key point: *Romans 7:7-25 unpacks verse 5, and Romans 8:1-17 unpacks verse 6* [emphasis added]. . . . Romans 7:5-6 forecasts what Paul is about to say in remarkably clear terms.

2. The Holy Spirit.

The Holy Spirit is never mentioned in Romans 7:7-25. But Paul refers to the Spirit 15 times in Romans 8:1-17, suggesting that the person described in Romans 7:7-25 is one who doesn't have the Spirit in his life. . . .

3. The question asked in Romans 7:13.

Paul proceeds to ask another question in Romans 7:13: "Therefore, did what is good cause my death?" The "good" here is clearly the law. But notice the question asked: did the good law cause my death? The answer is then given in Romans 7:13b-25. But this is a powerful argument supporting pre-Christian experience since Paul explains how sin used the law to bring about our death. The flow of the argument fits perfectly with what Paul says about unbelievers in Romans 7:5: the law worked in our members while we were outside of Christ to separate us from God, to kill us.

4. The total defeat described in Romans 7:13-25.

Many Christians throughout history have identified with the despair and inability of the "I" in Romans 7:13-25. We read these verses and think: That's my story; that's my experience. *Their instinct is right, but their interpretation is wrong* [emphasis added]. . . . Yes, we continue to struggle with sin. Yes, we fall short every day. But Romans 7:13-25 is talking about total defeat. As Paul says in verse 14, "I am of the flesh, sold under sin." In other words, he is describing complete and total captivity to sin. We see the same thing again in verse 23. . . . Paul isn't just talking about struggling with sin with frequent failures; he describes complete and abject defeat, being utterly enslaved to sin. The "I" is a prisoner of sin. Again and again in this passage, Paul says he wanted to obey but couldn't; the obedience didn't come and couldn't come—since he was unregenerate. The total defeat described in Romans 7 contradicts how Paul describes Christian experience in Romans 6 and 8. Paul proclaims in Romans 6 that we're no longer slaves to sin (6:6), that we're free from the sin that enslaved us when we were unbelievers (Rom. 6:16-19).

Yes, we still sin, but we aren't slaves to it anymore. As Romans 8:2 declares, "The law of the Spirit of life has set you free in Christ Jesus from the law of sin and death." Such freedom from sin doesn't accord with the person described in Romans 7:13-25, since that person is still enslaved to sin. As Christians we enjoy substantial, significant, and observable (though not perfect) victory over sin in this life. Though we fail every day, we are dramatically changed by the grace of God. (Schreiner, "Romans 7 Does Not Describe Your Christian Experience")

After addressing the argument of the "present tense" shift and the issue of "delighting in the law of God," Schreiner concludes:

> The reason we differ is that I see Romans 7:13-25 as describing total defeat, and that isn't our story as Christians since the Holy Spirit also empowers us to live in a new way. (Ibid.)

Likewise, Doug Moo believes Paul is referring to an unbeliever. He provides six reasons for this reading, which are similar to Schreiner's reasons:

1. The strong connection of *egō* ["I"] with "the flesh" (7:14, 18, and 25) suggests that Paul is elaborating on the unregenerate condition mentioned in verse 5: being "in the flesh."

2. *Egō* throughout this passage struggles "on his/her own" (cf. "I myself" in 7:25), without the aid of the Holy Spirit.

3. *Egō* is "under the power of sin" (7:14b), a state from which every believer is released (6:2,6,11,18-22).

4. As the unsuccessful struggle of 7:15-20 shows, *egō* is a "prisoner of the law of sin" (7:23). Yet Rom. 8:2 proclaims that believers have been set free from this same "law of sin (and death)."

5. While Paul makes clear that believers will continue to struggle with sin (cf. e.g., 6:12-13; 13:12-14; Gal 5:17), what is depicted in 7:14-25 is not just a struggle with sin but a defeat by sin. This [in 7:14-25] is a more negative view of the Christian life than can be accommodated within Paul's theology.

6. The *egō* in these verses struggles with the need to obey the Mosaic law; yet Paul has already proclaimed the release of the believer from the dictates of the law (6:14; 7:4-6). (Moo, *Letter*, 445)

For the reasons listed by Schreiner and Moo (along with Mike Bird's argument), I see Paul as speaking representatively when he says "I." I think he is referring to himself as a Jew under the law, while also echoing Adam and Israel and providing application to God fearers trying to live under the law. It is not necessarily Paul's specific experience in every detail, but it is the general experience of those Paul represents. He is speaking as an unbeliever trying to obey God's law and finding it impossible. Only through Christ can we be set free from the law of sin and death (7:24; 8:1-2).

Now to the verses! Verses 13-25 have a similar flow to 7:1-12. Paul raises a question and then emphatically denies it. Is the law the cause of death? Paul says, "Absolutely not!" (v. 7). That is, the law is not inherently fatal (Bird, *Romans*, 241). Paul once again exonerates the law and places the blame on sin. The law, though good and holy, brought death so that *sin* may be seen as the killer (ibid.).

Paul then launches into the first-person speech in character. Notice the "we" in verse 14, as Paul speaks representatively of those in the same situation. How could sin work death in Paul when the law is good? Paul says it is because while the law is spiritual, he is of the flesh. The following verses support his fleshly nature (as a preconverted Jew). Paul explains in verses 15-21 his miserable inability to do that which he knows to be right (Moo, *Letter*, 453). He is controlled not by that which is spiritual but that which is fleshly, and because he is a slave to sin, the law has become this instrument of death (ibid.). Only Christ can give him life.

Once again the phrase "sold as a slave to sin" (v. 14) tips the scale for me on the issue of whether this is a Christian. Some argue that this phrase can be used of a Christian dealing with indwelling sin. While Christians do sin and fight sin, I do not think this reading is best. Paul seems to be saying more than, "A Christian will struggle with sin." It is hard to read Romans 6 and say Romans 7:14 is speaking of a Christian.

In verses 15-23 Paul begins this lament that is so famous. He dramatically states how he cannot do that which he knows is right. Try reading it fast! It is almost as hard as interpreting this passage! I will make only a few comments on these verses in light of what I have already stated about it. Verses 15-20 are about inner conflict, of his frustration with his inability to keep the law. He is a conflicted man with conflicted desires (v. 15). He knows the law is good, but his disobedience proves that he is under the control of his sinful nature (vv. 16-17). Because nothing good dwells in him, he does not have the power to carry out the good (v. 18). He persists in doing evil though he does not want to do it (v. 19), thus proving the enslaving power of sin (v. 20). Verse 21 is Paul's principle that he draws based on the conflict: when he wants to do right, evil is at hand. Verse 22 is the statement of a pious Jew who has a real delight in the law of God (which many Jews would profess; cf. Pss 19; 119; Rom 10:2), but he/she must also admit that his/her failure leads to defeat (v. 23) and eventually to despair (v. 24).

Paul's preconverted description in Philippians 3:5-6 is often used as an argument against reading this passage as Paul speaking of himself as an unbeliever. In the Philippians text Paul says that prior to conversion he was "blameless" under the law (3:6). That does not sound like this individual in Romans 7, does it? Again I am indebted to Moo and others who argue that, as a believer, Paul now views the law with a different perspective: "He now sees it as a unity, an expression of God's will for his people that, when broken in any part, is broken in the whole" (Moo, *Letter*, 456). In response to this question about Philippians 3:6, Bird adds,

> [B]efore his conversion on the Damascus Road, Paul thought he was doing alright, and he was certainly not fixated on his moral inadequacies. He was probably more like the hypothetical Jewish teacher in Romans 2:1-11, 17-24, who is confident in his election, convinced of the goodness of his own moral effort, and believes he has earned a right to be comparatively boastful over others. In which case, the moral struggle of the "I" narrated in 7:7-25 is probably retrospective and reflects the inner anxiety about keeping the law that is only perceptible from the vantage point of faith. It spells what Douglas Campbell calls "the horrifying view backward." The person speaking is saying, "Ah, yes, in coming to Christ now I can see the struggle I formerly had, a struggle to obey the law, a struggle I could not win, because the law could not help me overcome the flesh." Paul, from a Christian perspective, can now view his mix of pricked conscience and presumption of righteousness as part of the deception and death that he experienced under the law. (*Romans*, 235; see also n. 16).

Thanks Be to God through Jesus Christ Our Lord! (7:24-25)

Paul now gives a title to his prior condition: "wretched." He then rejoices in the fact that the wretched man has a wonderful Messiah who gives him the victory. Certainly those who espouse that Paul has been speaking of his experience as a Christian may rightly say that we recognize our failure and long for final glorification, where sin will be no more (8:23). But it seems that Paul's word is stronger than simple failure and frustration (Moo, *Letter*, 465). It is more along the lines of the individuals described in Romans 3:9-20. Who can deliver the non-Christian? Nobody except Jesus the Messiah.

Paul's cry for deliverance could be read as a cry for resurrection and ultimate deliverance (8:23), or it could be read as a non-Christian crying out for rescue from condemnation. I think the latter is the most likely view, given the aforementioned arguments and what is coming in Romans 8:1. Apart from Christ, Paul and those like him are under condemnation and desperate for rescue. Thankfully, Jesus rescues wretches! Paul cannot jump to 8:1 before mentioning the inner conflict one more time (v. 25b). Regardless of one's view of the "I," both views anticipate the victory to come (cf. 8:1,10,23).

While I have tried to put forward a particular reading of this passage, Moo is correct that this does not mean the passage only has relevance for nonbelievers (*Letter*, 465). For Christians, we can read this text and be reminded that our only hope for obedience is through our union with Christ and the empowerment of the Spirit, as we saw in verses 1-6. The law not only cannot bring justification (the view of Paul the Jew under the law), but it cannot bring sanctification either (the view that Paul is describing his Christian experience). The passage should, on either reading, make us thankful that wretched people have a wonderful Messiah. And we can all share Paul's statement: "Thanks be to God through Jesus Christ our Lord!" In Christ we are saved, and through Christ, by the Spirit, we can bear fruit to the glory of God. This tone of triumph continues now into chapter 8, in what is one of the greatest chapters of hope, encouragement, and security in the Bible.

Reflect and Discuss

1. What is Paul trying to articulate in Romans 7:1-6 with the analogy of marriage?
2. Why is marriage a good illustration of the Christian life?
3. Compare the two types of fruit in verses 4 and 5.
4. Give some examples of what these two types of fruit might look like.
5. How is Romans 7:6 tied to 8:1-11?

6. How does Paul defend the value of the law in Romans 7:7-12?
7. How can the law be good and holy but also produce death?
8. What are two big questions to answer for understanding Romans 7:13-25?
9. What does Paul say about his inner conflict in 7:13-25?
10. Describe Paul's personal summary and praise in verses 24-25a.

The New Way of the Spirit

ROMANS 8:1-17

Main Idea: To begin one of the most celebrated chapters in all of Scripture, Paul describes believers' new life in the Spirit in verses 1-17.

I. **The Spirit of Life (8:1-13)**
   A. A new freedom (8:1-4)
   B. A new mindset (8:5-8)
   C. A new indwelling presence (8:9-11)
   D. A new obligation (8:12-13)
II. **The Spirit of Adoption (8:14-17)**
   A. A new identity (8:14)
   B. A new intimacy (8:15-16)
   C. A new inheritance (8:17)

Sinclair Ferguson tells the story of two pastors from the Czech Republic who attended a conference in the southern part of the United States many years ago. On Saturday afternoon, the visiting pastors were taken to a massive supermarket—unlike anything they had ever seen. After looking around at the vast number of products, their first instinct was to burst into tears. Then they turned to their host and asked, "Does this store belong to the American government?" To them, it was inconceivable that this store could be *for all the people.* They were stunned to learn that everyone had access to the items. In a similar way, when we read of the gospel privileges in Romans 8, we want to turn to Paul and ask, "Do these privileges belong to every Christian?" Paul would answer, "Yes. They are for all who are in Christ" (Ferguson, "His Transforming Spirit"). These riches in Romans 8 are not reserved for only a select few Christians, but they are for all who are united to Christ and indwelled by the Spirit.

It is no wonder Christians love Romans 8. It is a storehouse of gospel blessings. Many have heralded it as the greatest chapter in the whole Bible. It begins with "no condemnation" and ends with "no separation" (Moo, *Letter*, 468). These bookends highlight the theme of *assurance* in Romans 8.

Further, not a single imperative is issued in the entire chapter (Morris, *Epistle*, 299). What we read are glorious privileges believers enjoy through our union with Christ.

This chapter also magnifies the work of *the Holy Spirit*. The word *pneuma* ("spirit") occurs twenty-one times in this chapter, and all but two refer to the Holy Spirit (Moo, *Letter*, 468). Paul's emphasis on the Spirit (especially in 8:1-17) picks up his thought from Romans 7:6: "But now we have been released from the law, since we have died to what held us, so that we may serve in the newness of the Spirit and not in the old letter of the law." Bird comments, "The central claim of 7:6 about dying to sin and law and the liberation of the Spirit finds its sequel in 8:1-17" (*Romans*, 256).

There are two main sections in verses 1-17. Paul first speaks of "the Spirit of life" (vv. 1-13) and then "the Spirit of adoption" (vv. 14-17). In both sections Paul explains the new life believers enjoy in Christ and the Spirit's work of liberation, empowerment, transformation, and assurance.

The Spirit of Life
ROMANS 8:1-13

The prophets foretold the new age of the Spirit in which God would put a new spirit in his people (cf. Ezek 11:19; 36:26). With the arrival of Jesus, the Messiah, believers enjoy the reality of this new age in their new lives in the Spirit. Verses 1-13 list four new privileges.

A New Freedom (8:1-4)

The Spirit does what the law could not do: give life. The believer has been set free from the law of sin and death described vividly in Romans 7:7-25. This has happened through the work of Christ and the liberating work of the Spirit.

Ponder verse 1 for a moment. "No condemnation" is the flip side of "justification." Because we have been justified through faith in Christ, we do not fear judgment. Paul's use of "therefore" reaches back from 3:21 onward. The opening statements on justification of Romans 5:1 and 8:1 complement each other; 5:1 is stated positively and 8:1 is stated negatively. In 8:3 Paul says that this happened by God's condemning our sin in Christ (cf. 8:33-34).

The word "now" in verse 1 is also important. Something new has happened! God has intervened in redemptive history. The verdict that was over us because of the aftermath of Adam's sin has been changed from guilty to *free* (Bird, *Romans*, 258; cf. Col 2:14).

To bolster your sanctification (your continued growth as a Christian), remind yourself of this verdict. When Satan afflicts you and brings up your past, dwell on Romans 8:1. Dwell on who you are in Christ. Dwell on the fact that there is *no* condemnation—not a bit of it. None. There is no "modified condemnation." The message is not "Jesus paid it all . . . mostly" or "Jesus paid a lot of it," but rather, "Jesus paid it all!" Do not revert to this line of thinking: "I'm forgiven for 95 percent of my failures, but that big thing that I did is still hanging over me." No! Jesus paid it all! Satan likes to bring up our pasts, but you need to remind him of Jesus's past. We are not under condemnation because Christ was condemned in place of us! "In my place condemned he stood," as the hymn says (Philip P. Bliss, "'Man of Sorrows,' What a Name").

Remember who is writing this: Paul! He oversaw the death of Stephen. He persecuted Christ's church. But do you see him thinking he needs to pay God back for his past? No! He is the one who says, "There is now no condemnation for those in Christ Jesus." Professor Mounce puts it well: "To insist on feeling guilty is but another way of insisting on helping God with our salvation. How deeply imbedded in human nature is the influence of works-righteousness!" (Robert Mounce, *Romans*, 174).

Allow Romans 8:1 to give you peace about the future, and allow Romans 8:1 to lead you to sing. Liberated people are singing people! People in oppressive religions do not sing because works-based righteousness does not fuel praise. But grace fuels praise! Recall Acts 12 and Acts 16. In Acts 12 Peter is in prison, sleeping soundly. In Acts 16 Paul and Silas are singing passionately. Though they were physically chained, their hearts were free. The gospel is the reason we can sleep and the reason we can sing in the midst of the difficulties of life. We know our greatest problem has already been solved in Christ!

In verses 2-3 we find *the reason for this glorious freedom: what Christ has done for us.* The phrase "in Christ Jesus" is so important. The believer does not fear condemnation because Christ has freed us from the law that condemned us. Paul is repeating the great themes of justification and our union with Christ. We who are in Christ, justified through his blood, have been liberated by the Spirit.

The phrase "the law of the Spirit of life" (v. 2) refers to the powerful work of the Spirit to bring liberty. The Spirit, as the outflow of Christ's work on behalf of sinners, follows through on God's purpose of redemption and applies Christ's work to our hearts, thereby freeing us. And as the text goes on to show, Christ's work for me is confirmed by the Spirit's presence in me. Because of Christ Jesus, by the power of the Spirit, we are set free from the penalty of sin and the ruling power of sin. Verse 3 magnifies God's provision in Christ. The law could not justify us because of the weakness of our human condition (cf. 7:14-24). It was not the law's fault; look what it had to work with! The Torah could not fix us. Only Jesus could do that. And God in his grace made provision for us, sending "his own Son in the likeness of sinful flesh" (8:3). This refers to the incarnation. It is a statement that affirms Jesus's humanity. The word "likeness" is Paul's attempt to avoid saying that God sent Jesus in "sinful flesh." Bird states, "What Paul wants to say is that Jesus's humanity was the same as ours and yet not totally like ours to the point that he was tainted with sin" (*Romans*, 260).

Further, God sent his Son to be "a sin offering." You can see the sacrificial allusion here. The phrase "sin offering" refers to sacrifices used to atone for guilt (see Lev 5:6-8,11; 6:25; Num 6:16; Ezek 42:13). The sacrifice of Jesus has removed the stain, burden, and penalty of sin.

Moreover, God's provision involved God's condemning "sin in the flesh." God judged our sins in the sinless humanity of his Son, who bore them in our place. There is no condemnation, since the condemnation we deserve has already been fully borne by Christ.

In verse 4 Paul shows us *the results of this freedom: sanctification.* One goal of the work of Christ was to bring us justification; but in this verse, Paul focuses on another goal, namely, our sanctification. Freedom in Christ is not a freedom to sin but a freedom from sin. Paul has already stated that his apostolic purpose involved bringing the Gentiles to the "obedience that springs from faith" (1:5 my paraphrase). Here we see the ethical implications of the gospel. The Spirit writes God's law on our hearts. We want to obey God now. Moo states,

> God not only provides in Christ the full completion of the
> law's demands for the believer, but he also sends the Spirit
> into the hearts of believers to empower a new obedience to his
> demands. (*Letter*, 485)

A New Mindset (8:5-8)

Paul now makes a contrast between flesh and Spirit. Paul states that the flesh brings death but the Spirit brings life. Paul is using the Greek word for "flesh" (*sarx*) not to describe this muscular tissue that covers our skeletons but to refer to our corrupt and unredeemed nature. That is, our fallen, egocentric, sin-dominated self.

Paul says there are *two types of people* (8:5). What Paul says in verses 8:8-9 makes clear that the contrast between flesh and Spirit is a contrast between Christian and non-Christian. He is not yet describing the temptation Christians have to live in the flesh; he will do that in verse 13. Here he is describing the two basic natures of Christians and non-Christians. To become a Christian involves being transferred from a realm dominated by the flesh into a new realm dominated by the Spirit (Moo, *Letter*, 486). A Christian has a new mind—that is, a new attitude, orientation, bent, pattern of thinking, and affections. This text should make us thankful to God for what he has done for us! He has taken us out of darkness, flesh, rebellion, and death into light, the Spirit, obedience, and life! Though he or she will fail at times, a Christian's basic orientation and his/her affections are for the things of the Spirit.

In verse 6 Paul comments on the *two spiritual states of people: life and death*. In other words, a mindset has eternal consequences. The mind of sinful man is "death" (now and forever). Sadly, this person does not celebrate Romans 8:1. But the mind controlled by the Spirit is "life and peace." Or as Paul put it previously, believers are "alive to God" (6:11). We are alert to spiritual realities and thirsty for God. We have peace with God (5:1).

In verses 7-8 he says there are *two fundamental attitudes of people: hostility or peace* (with peace being implied from the previous verse). He says the mind of the flesh has animosity toward God. This person is disinterested in God. He or she has no interest in his name, his kingdom, his Word, or his people. Observe that Paul does not give a list of gross sins. He speaks more about the attitude of *the heart* toward God and his Word. This attitude is one that focuses on self, ignoring God. Because of this, God is not pleased (v. 8). Paul highlights the corruption of this mindset, saying that those living in the flesh do not submit to God's law, for they cannot (v. 7). The attitude of those in the Spirit is implied: empowered for obedience to the glory and pleasure of God.

This bring us to the third privilege of our new life in Christ.

A New Indwelling Presence (8:9-11)

Paul now focuses more specifically on those individuals who are in the Spirit, the regenerate ones. Paul points out several important truths regarding the indwelling presence of the Spirit here.

He reminds us that *if anyone does not have the Spirit of Christ, then he or she does not belong to Christ.* The Spirit assures believers that they belong to Christ (see also vv. 14-17). The word "if" (vv. 9,10,11) should not be read as a cause for doubt. Paul is actually stressing what is true. It could be paraphrased, "if (as is the case)" (Morris, *Epistle*, 308). Jesus promised this: "He remains with you and will be in you" (John 14:17; cf. 1 Cor 6:19).

When people repent and trust in Christ, the Spirit comes to indwell them. There are richer experiences of the Spirit's work throughout the believer's life, but the presence of the indwelling Christ is ours from the beginning. This does not mean believers will not at times quench the Spirit—they will (1 Thess 5:19). Nor does it mean believers will not at times grieve the Spirit—they will (Eph 4:30). Nor does it mean believers will never sin—for they surely will. It means believers possess the Holy Spirit, and they will be manifesting the fruit of the Spirit.

Notice also *the relationship between the "Spirit of God" and "Spirit of Christ."* Only three times in the New Testament do we read, "Spirit of Christ" (also Phil 1:19; 1 Pet 1:11; Bird, *Romans*, 263). Moo puts it well: "The indwelling Spirit and the indwelling Christ are distinguishable but inseparable" (*Letter*, 491). This relationship makes sense for a number of other theological reasons: (1) the Trinitarian nature of God; (2) the Spirit raised Christ from the dead (Rom 1:4; 8:11); (3) Christ is the giver of the Spirit (John 14:26; 15:26; Acts 2:38); and (4) Christ and the Spirit work together in salvation (1 Cor 6:11; Bird, *Romans*, 263).

In verse 10 Paul declares that *"the Spirit gives life" to believers.* An implication of having the Spirit dwell in you is that you have *life.* The Spirit guarantees us this life. Although we are bound to earthly bodies, we have the Spirit in us. This means we enjoy a freedom from condemnation now, and we await resurrection and transformation of our bodies in the future (Moo, *Letter*, 492).

The phrase "because of righteousness" (v. 10) either refers to God's righteous character displayed in salvation or to our status as being "declared righteous" (imputed righteousness) in Christ. I prefer the latter interpretation (see 5:18, "justification leading to life").

In verse 11 Paul elaborates on how *the Spirit assures believers of future resurrection.* This verse focuses on our future security. The Spirit is in us now, and this assures us of our future life in the resurrection. The prerequisite for resurrection is the Spirit's indwelling presence.

Ponder this for a moment: The same Holy Spirit who raised Jesus from the dead dwells in you, believer! This fact is astonishing and assuring! If the Spirit raised Christ, he will raise us. We will have transformed bodies.

Paul says that we now have a fourth privilege.

A New Obligation (8:12-13)

Paul moves from the privileges to the present responsibility. The logical conclusion of what has been said in 8:1-11 is that believers have no obligation to live in the flesh. So even though positionally we are in the Spirit, practically we have not been fully removed from this sinful world and temptations of the flesh. But we owe the flesh nothing! Our obligation is to the Spirit, to live according to his holy desires. As a believer, remember who you are, and remember the power that is yours. Do not go "back to Egypt," listening to the voice of your old master.

The first part of verse 13 contains a warning: if you live according to the flesh, you are going to die. Paul does not believe Christians can lose their salvation (a dominant theme in Romans 8 is the believer's security in Christ). But Paul is aware that some in the "Christian crowd" may not actually have the Spirit. Some may not actually be Christians, and consequently they are living in the flesh and will die.

In the second part of verse 13, Paul calls on Christians to "mortify the flesh" (as the old divines used to call it). It speaks of "killing" sin. Paul does not have *masochism* in mind (taking pleasure in self-inflicted pain) or *asceticism* (resenting and rejecting good gifts from God as an act of piety; Stott, *Message*, 228). It is a call to renounce sin and put it to death (cf. Col 3:5-11). This verse is what John Owen commented on when he famously said, "Be killing sin or it will be killing you" (*Mortification of Sin*, 50). We are to put to death "the deeds of the body," that is, to terminate every use of our bodies that serves our sinful, selfish appetites rather than God.

How does mortification take place? It is something we have to do. We put something to death. We must be ruthless in putting sin to death. In the words of Romans 6:12, "Do not let sin reign in your mortal body." Do you have that instinct with sin—with pride, self-pity, anger, selfishness, lust, or other sins? Do you see these temptations as something to kill, like when you see a venomous snake in your yard? John Stott is instructive here:

> If temptation comes to us through what we see, handle or
> visit, then we must be ruthless in not looking, not touching,
> not going, and so in controlling the very approaches of sin.

Positively, we are to set our minds on the things the Spirit desires (5), set our hearts on things above, and occupy our thoughts with what is noble, right, pure and lovely. In this way "mortification" (putting evil to death) and "aspiration" (hungering and thirsting for what is good) are counterparts. (*Message*, 229)

I love that—mortification and aspiration. Say no to sin and say yes to God! Why should we practice mortification? Notice Paul's words: "You will live"! Real life is experienced when we live according to the Spirit. The emphasis seems to be on the present life now—this is the satisfying life. We enjoy this life when we put to death the misdeeds of the body, contrary to the way the world thinks. Many people think you have to give up pleasure to pursue holiness, but you actually find pleasure in the pursuit. You find life. You find joy. Sin never satisfies and gives life. But living for the glory of God by the Spirit of God is the path to true and lasting joy.

The Spirit of Adoption
ROMANS 8:14-17

As we continue strolling through this supermarket of gospel blessings in Romans 8, we come to the glorious doctrine of adoption, which is also an already-not yet salvific reality (see v. 23). These four verses serve as a transition in Romans 8, building on the Spirit's work in the believer (vv. 1-13) and preparing us for a discussion of our future hope (vv. 18-30).

In verses 14-17 Paul tells us that our adoption, or our "sonship," involves a new identity, a new intimacy, and a new inheritance. The word "for" links it to the previous verse, where Paul says the believer is not obligated to the flesh. Instead, we are the grateful adopted children of God who are led by the Spirit of God.

A New Identity (8:14)

Being an adopted child of God provides the believer with a new identity. The concept is prominent in these four verses: "God's sons" (v. 14), "adoption" (v. 15), "God's children" (v. 16), "if children, also heirs" (v. 17), and "adoption" (v. 23). This is who you are, Christian!

The Greek word for "adoption" (*huiothesia*) means "to have the place of a son" (Bird, *Romans*, 267). It appears five times in the New Testament (8:15,23; 9:4; Gal 4:5; Eph 1:5). The Roman world was familiar with the concept of adoption, and Paul uses this concept to describe the glorious privilege of being adopted by the only Sovereign (see Burke, *Adopted*, 60–66). The Christian has been adopted into God's royal family with all the rights and privileges of a natural child (cf. Gal 4:6-7).

The language of Romans 8:14-17 also has echoes of the exodus story. We have been taken out of slavery and made "sons of God" (cf. Exod 4:22). We are now led by the Spirit as the Israelites were led by the pillar of cloud in the wilderness. Gentile Christians have been grafted into this sonship, being among the number of the family of God (Bird, *Romans*, 266).

The question of identity has always been a subject of intense discussion, and it continues to be so today. For the Christian this question is answered. Who am I? I am an adopted child of God! If you do not get your *identity* right, you will not get your *community* right, and you will not get your *purpose* right.

The challenge for every Christian is to live in view of this new identity. Believer, your identity is not in your performance, your popularity, or your pedigree. You are an adopted child of God. We have not earned this identity; we have received it as a gift. Our adoption is ordained by the Father, purchased by the Son, and applied by the Spirit (cf. Eph 1:1-14).

The passage also speaks of the horizontal dimension of adoption: "we are God's children" (v. 16). Another basic identity question is not only "Who am I?" but "Who are *we*?" If you get the first right, you can get the second right. For Jews and Gentiles to call one another "brother and sister" was radical. (We use that language often in the church when we forget someone's name!) But this is what the church is: adopted brothers and sisters who call on *Abba* Father. The church is a family.

My wife and I have five adopted children. We have four kids from Ukraine and one child from Ethiopia. I will never forget my Ethiopian son's first Christmas. He walked into his grandparents' home in Virginia and asked me (in broken English), "Papa, are all these people our family?" I said, "Yes." He was beginning to understand that when you get adopted, you not only get a new dad, but you get a new family. So it is with our spiritual adoption. We have a big family of diverse brothers and sisters!

Many view the church as a building you visit occasionally or as an event you attend for a few hours. While events and buildings are important, the church is fundamentally a family. Paul will expound many important principles for our life together in Romans 12–16.

So if you get your identity right, you get community right, and you can also then get your purpose right. Our new identity has produced in us a desire to glorify our Father and to reflect our elder brother, Jesus (v. 29), by the power of the Spirit. In the biblical period, and even today in various parts of the world, your vocation was based on your father's vocation. In a similar way, our vocation involves being about our "Father's business." We are to let our light shine before others, so that they may see our good deeds and glorify our Father who is in heaven (Matt 5:16).

A New Intimacy (8:15-16)

Second, being an adopted child of God provides the believer with a new intimacy. Paul outlines several ways the Spirit brings intimacy with the *Abba* (this is a term of closeness and affection).

He says the Spirit *confirms the status change that has taken place*. We know we belong to God by the Spirit of God. The phrase "Spirit of adoption" means essentially the "Spirit who confirms adoption" (Moo, *Letter*, 502). Notice verse 16: "The Spirit himself testifies together with our spirit that we are God's children." To the Galatians, Paul says, "And because you are sons, God sent the Spirit of his Son into our hearts, crying, '*Abba*, Father!'" (Gal 4:6). The Spirit of God confirms that we are God's children.

Additionally, Paul tells us that *the Spirit replaces fear with acceptance and security* (v. 15a). We do not live in fear but in this new position of acceptance. The slavery of our old life saw God as our Judge to be dreaded. But now we see God as our Father to be adored. Freedom and security now rule our lives instead of bondage to fear. We are at peace with God now. We have security. We are not insecure, fearful orphans; we are loved and protected children.

Moreover, this intimacy with the Father is powerfully underscored as Paul says that *the Spirit enables us to cry out* "Abba, *Father*" (vv. 15-16). This *Abba* cry relates to the phrases before and after it. Because we are adopted children, fear is replaced with acceptance, and we cry out to our Father knowing he hears us and loves us. In times of desperation and profound weakness, we can cry out to our Father, as Jesus cried out in the garden of Gethsemane (Mark 14.36). Sometimes you can only manage to say "Father" in your prayer because you are so brokenhearted over the stuff of life. But even then your Father hears you. We can cry out to him in prayer not just on our best days but on our worst days as well. Even when you cannot formulate a prayer, the Spirit of God gives you the instinct to cry to the Father, "Father, oh, Father." He hears our groaning, and in that cry you are given assurance that you are an adopted child of God.

Regarding this new intimacy, the last and related thing is that the Spirit *stirs up affections for the Father* (vv. 15-16). As adopted children of the Father, we love him. Interestingly, in Galatians 4:6 *the Spirit* is sent to our hearts, crying "*Abba*, Father." But here in Romans 8:15 Paul says, "*We* cry out, *Abba*, Father" (emphasis added). So, who is crying "*Abba*, Father?" Us or the Spirit? It appears to be similiar to what Paul says in 1 Corinthians 12:3: no one says, "'Jesus is Lord,' except by the Holy Spirit." That is, when we say, "Jesus is Lord," it is the fruit of the Spirit's work in us. And here in Romans 8, when we cry, "*Abba*, Father," it is the fruit of the Spirit's work in us (Ferguson, "His Transforming Spirit"). Just as the Spirit gives us affections for the Savior, so he too gives us affections for the Father. Adopted children of God are not interested in *using* God; they are interested in *adoring* him. The Spirit has created this intimate fellowship with *Abba*.

A New Inheritance (8:17)

Finally, the adopted child of God has a new inheritance. Paul tells us that adopted children are heirs of the Father. The best is yet to come for all of God's children. We went from slavery to being heirs with the Crown Prince of the universe! Paul develops the concept of glory in the following passage (vv. 18-30).

Why does Paul say "sons" at the beginning of this passage and not "daughters"? In Paul's day only the sons received the inheritance. In the gospel all Christians are "sons" (Gal 3:28). Male or female, in Christ, all receive this inheritance.

So then, adoption has an "already" dimension and a "not yet" dimension. We are heirs waiting to receive our inheritance. Burke says,

> The alpha point, the already, is the present reality of the "Spirit of *huiothesia*" (Rom 8:15), which believers now have, but the omega point, its completion, still lies ahead: "as we wait eagerly for our adoption as sons" (Rom 8:23). (*Adopted*, 44)

The Spirit is the firstfruits of our inheritance, guaranteeing the harvest to follow. The Spirit of God assures us that we are God's children and also assures us that we are heirs. Our adoption is true and real but not yet complete. We are not home yet. We are awaiting glory. In the meantime, we have the Spirit of God to empower us and to enable us to cry out to *Abba*. There will be a lot of suffering in the meantime, but press on, child of God, glory is coming (v. 18).

The doctrine of adoption is a wonderful unifying concept of the Christian life. It touches on so many key concepts, like the nature of God, salvation, authority, identity, ecclesiology, purpose, morality, destiny, worship, prayer, suffering, and glory. Being adopted by God changes everything! So do not just believe the doctrine of adoption in your head. Allow it to change your heart and shape your worldview.

Reflect and Discuss

1. What is the relationship between Romans 7:6 and 8:1-17?
2. How does the phrase "no condemnation" relate to the doctrine of justification?
3. How has the Christian been set free?
4. Compare the mindset of the *flesh* and the *Spirit* (8:5-8). What is most striking about this contrast?
5. What marks a true Christian according to Romans 8:9?
6. What do you find assuring and astonishing in Romans 8:9-11?
7. What does Romans 8:12-13 teach us about killing sin?
8. How does the doctrine of adoption speak to Christian identity, community, and purpose?
9. How does the Spirit give us intimacy with the Father?
10. Describe the already-not yet dimension of adoption. Why is this encouraging?

Future Glory, Present Help

ROMANS 8:18-30

Main Idea: God's children are people of hope; they will groan in this fallen world, but they have a glorious future ahead of them and divine help for their present trials.

I. **Hope for Waiting Saints (8:18-25)**
    A. Glory is coming (8:18).
    B. The creation will be set free (8:19-22).
    C. God's adopted children will be redeemed fully (8:23-25).
II. **Help for Weak Saints (8:26-30)**
    A. Rest in the Spirit's intercession (8:26-27).
    B. Rest in God's sovereign plan (8:28).
    C. Rest in the golden chain of salvation (8:29-30).

The doctrine of glorification gives Christians hope in the midst of their present sufferings. That is one of the reasons we should meditate on it regularly. We will suffer in this fallen world, and we need unshakable hope to endure.

Many saints through the ages have taught us the value of meditating on the glory to come. For instance, Richard Baxter passed on this legacy to us. He was a faithful pastor who discipled a whole village where he served. We still use his book, *The Reformed Pastor*, originally printed in 1656. He published some 140 books. Yet he lived with unrelenting sufferings, so ill on one occasion that doctors thought he would die. One of the secrets of Baxter's endurance was that he determined to spend at least thirty minutes per day thinking about future glory, usually on a walk before dinner (in Donald Whitney, "Think Much about Heaven"). He lived to age seventy-six. It was precisely because he was so heavenly minded that he was of such earthly good.

Or consider John Newton's example. In describing the suffering saint's glorious inheritance to come, the author of "Amazing Grace" vividly wrote,

> Suppose a man was going to New York to take possession of
> a large estate, and his [carriage] should break down a mile

before he got to the city, which obliged him to walk the rest of the way; what a fool we should think him, if we saw him wringing his hands, and blubbering out all the remaining mile, "My [carriage] is broken! My [carriage] is broken!" (Quoted in Piper, "John Newton")

Newton reminds us that the saint only has "a mile" to go! So let's not murmur and complain in light of the glory to come. That was Newton's message. John Piper adds (with a reflection on Rom 8:18-30),

> John Newton's habitual tenderness is rooted in the sober realism of the limits of redemption in this fallen world where "we groan awaiting the redemption of our bodies" (Romans 8:23); the all-pervasive humility and gratitude for having been a blasphemer of the gospel and now being a heaven-bound preacher of it; and the unshakable confidence that the all-governing providence of God will make every experience turn for his good so that he doesn't spend his life murmuring, "My carriage is broken, my carriage is broken," but sings, "Tis grace that brought me safe thus far, and grace will lead me home." ("John Newton")

I cannot help but believe that if Christians would practice a similar pattern of pondering the promises of the world to come, we too would be more faithful, productive, and joyful. Baxter, Newton, and others have given us an example of following Paul's words to the Colossians:

> *So if you have been raised with Christ, seek the things above, where Christ is, seated at the right hand of God. Set your minds on things above, not on earthly things. For you died, and your life is hidden with Christ in God. When Christ, who is your life, appears, then you also will appear with him in glory.* (Col 3:1-4)

Let's set our minds on things above for a few minutes daily that we may endure faithfully until we appear with Christ in glory.

Paul introduces this idea of future glory in Romans 8:17 and then develops the thought in verses 18-30. It is a section filled with eschatological hope. This first section speaks of "waiting" (see 8:19,23,25) for future glory. Verses 26-30 speak more of the help and the promises we have while we wait.

We know that all who follow the suffering Christ will also endure suffering. And we know that the glorified Christ will take his redeemed to glory. In his high priestly prayer Jesus prayed that his people would be with him, see his glory, and share in his love (John 17:24). But Paul's teaching on suffering here is put into a broader creational context. In verses 18-22 he speaks of the groaning of creation itself. In verses 23-25 he speaks of the groaning of God's adopted children, of the hope that the waiting redeemed possess. He then goes on to speak of the Spirit's groaning in prayer on our behalf in verses 26-27, which we will consider under the theme "help for weak saints," where Paul also reminds the redeemed of the assuring purposes of God (8:28) and the comfort of the "golden chain of salvation" (8:29-30).

Hope for Waiting Saints
ROMANS 8:18-25

Paul's vision of the future is *not* what we call an "overrealized eschatology" (a misguided expectation of complete sanctification and satisfaction in this present life). Paul knows better (just read some of his own personal experiences, e.g., 2 Cor 6:4-10). Paul knows we are not yet in glory. So he writes with realism about the present but also with gospel optimism about the future. Christians are people of hope because of what they have now and what is promised to come.

Glory Is Coming (8:18)

The word "for" connects this verse with the previous verse on glorification (v. 17). As Paul builds on this theme, he reminds us that the path of glory is through suffering. Previously he taught that our suffering produces character and hope (5:3-5), but here he focuses on the greatness of glory that comes after our suffering.

Notice the contrasts of glory and suffering. Paul says the suffering is "not worth comparing" with the glory to come. In other words, calculate it rightly. Consider your suffering from a heavenly perspective. You will find that in the scope of eternity, it is like comparing a thimble of water with the ocean. Paul said elsewhere,

> *For our momentary light affliction is producing for us an absolutely incomparable eternal weight of glory. So we do not focus on what is seen, but on what is unseen. For what is seen is temporary, but what is unseen is eternal.* (2 Cor 4:17-18)

When you contrast the glory that is coming with the present suffering, you find fresh strength. You see how small, momentary, and light these afflictions actually are. In the words of Theresa of Ávila, "In light of heaven, the worst suffering on earth will be seen to be no more than one night in an inconvenient hotel" (in Bird, *Romans*, 277). The phrase "glory . . . revealed *to us*" is interesting. It is also translated "in us" (NIV) and "for us" (NJB). However one translates it specifically, each rendering is true theologically. For those in Christ, glory will be shown "to us" and shown "for us," and it will in a sense reside "in us" when we are transformed fully.

The Creation Will Be Set Free (8:19-22)

Poetically and prophetically, Paul describes the creation anticipating future glory (8:19-21). The creation, personified here, is straining forward, anticipating the future. Paul is describing how the fallen world is in pain and waiting for its liberation, renewal, and transformation.

Paul says that the creation is eagerly anticipating the revelation of "God's sons" (v. 19). I like the Phillips paraphrase: "The whole creation is on tiptoe to see the wonderful sight of the sons of God coming into their own." Right now there is something very ordinary about God's people. On the surface we are normal people, weak people, and even "clay pots" (2 Cor 4:7 GNT). At the same time, there is something spectacular about a Christian, which will be revealed in the future. In the end God will lift the veil and reveal his children. And all those who are in Christ Jesus will be glorified. The creation is on tiptoe to see this!

In verse 20 we see the reason for creation's longing. Creation knows that after the revelation of the sons of God, it is next in line to receive this glorification. Creation will be released from futility, slavery, and corruption. It will be released from all that the curse has caused. As a result of the fall, floods, hurricanes, droughts, tornadoes, earthquakes, bloodshed, death, sickness, and more are common. But this corruption, slavery, and futility will one day give way to a renewed earth, as the curse will be reversed.

The author of Ecclesiastes wrestles with the futility of life in this fallen world. Paul actually uses the same word that the Septuagint (Greek version of the Old Testament) uses in Ecclesiastes 1:2 here in Romans 8:20 (*mataiotēs*/"vanity") as he talks about the curse. Because of disobedience, we now find life frustrating and broken. But there is hope! Creation is screaming for rescue, and Paul proclaims that rescue here in verses 20-21.

The phrase "because of him who subjected it" (v. 20) refers to God, who allowed creation to be drawn into the decaying effects of Adam and Eve's sin (Bird, *Romans*, 278; see Gen 3:17-19). But God's divine design was a design for good, as it was subjected "*in the hope* that the creation itself will also be set free" (vv. 20-21, emphasis added; see Isa 24–27; 65–66). So creation, like the redeemed, possesses an eschatological hope. For creation, this hope consists of being "set free from the bondage to decay into the glorious freedom of God's children" (v. 21). Slavery and decay will be replaced by freedom and renewal as creation shares in the glorification of God's children (cf. Gen 3:15; Rom 16:20; 1 Cor 15:20-28; Phil 3:20-21). Sin brought death and destruction, but the redeemed wait for the day in which they will dwell in a new heaven and new earth, made possible through our Lord Jesus Christ (2 Pet 3:10-13; Rev 21:1).

The creation was marred through the sin of humanity, and the creation will be restored when the children of God are glorified. Paul summarizes verses 20-21: "For we know that the whole creation has been groaning together with labor pains until now" (v. 22). This is some vivid language—groaning with labor pains! We share this groaning with creation (v. 23). The analogy of labor pains also calls to mind the joyous outcome of a successful birth: the arrival of new life (Moo in Bird, *Romans*, 279). Creation and the saints are called to push through the pain in order to experience the joy of the glorious life to come.

God's Adopted Children Will Be Redeemed Fully (8:23-25)

Paul tells the church of the groaning they share in common with creation (8:23). In the film *Princess Bride*, there is that memorable line, "Life is pain, highness. Anyone who tells you differently is selling something" (in Bird, *Romans*, 285). Christianity is not trying to "sell something" to the world. That is, Christians are not hiding the fact that there is pain in the world. Quite the opposite. The Bible is a book filled with statements about suffering and examples of suffering. And we worship a Savior who was the Suffering Servant (Isa 53). We will groan because of the manifold sufferings common to humanity: cancer, AIDS, infertility, persecution, violence, war, etc. And because we have the Holy Spirit, we live frustrated, for our salvation—though already real—is not yet consummated. We groan because we are not yet home.

Verse 23 highlights the doctrine of adoption again (recall vv. 14-17). Our adoption has an "already" but "not yet" dimension. One of the "not yet" aspects of our salvation is "the redemption of our bodies." We each will have a new body, free from corruption, decay, sin, and death (cf. v. 11). Paul's doctrine of adoption is written in the context of *suffering*. Meditating on the already-not yet message of adoption provides tremendous hope to troubled saints. We should elevate the importance of this doctrine in the Christian life. J. I. Packer wrote in his classic book, *Knowing God*,

> If you want to judge how well a person understands Christianity, find out how much he makes of the thought of being God's child, and having God as his Father. If this is not the thought that prompts and controls his worship and prayers and his whole outlook on life, it means that he does not understand Christianity very well at all. For everything that Christ taught, everything that makes the New Testament new, and better than the Old, everything that is distinctively Christian as opposed to merely Jewish, is summed up in the knowledge of the Fatherhood of God. "Father" is the Christian name for God. . . . Our understanding of Christianity cannot be better than our grasp of adoption. (*Knowing God*, 201–2)

Indeed, when we understand the doctrine of adoption, we get a wonderful grasp on the Christian life. We sense the privilege of being God's children; we begin to see the church rightly, as a family of adopted siblings; we get caught up in adoration as we consider the glory of our Father; and we enjoy an unshakable hope, knowing that the glorious "not yet" dimension is still to come!

It is this *hope* that Paul underlines next (vv. 24-25). By "hope" Paul is not speaking of wishful thinking. He is speaking of the confident future that the saints possess. Christian salvation involves past events, present belief, and the promise of a glorious future. This last element (the promise) is what is meant by being saved "in hope." But since we have not experienced the culmination of our salvation, we must wait with patience. Soon we will inherit the renewed world (4:13). We cannot yet see it, touch it, taste it, or smell it—but we will. Our faith will end in sight. We should have this certain confidence because the promise rests on the character of our God, who is the God who always keeps his promises.

Soon the creation and the redeemed will experience the end of groaning and experience the glory. Until then we wait. But as Paul goes on to say, this does not mean we are just twiddling our thumbs until then, nor does it mean we are helpless in our present suffering. We have the intercession of the Spirit and the wonderful promises of God.

Help for Weak Saints
ROMANS 8:26-30

These next five verses are some of the most comforting words in all of Scripture. Weary saints find rest in the Spirit's intercession, in God's sovereign purpose, and in his sovereign plan of redemption.

Rest in the Spirit's Intercession (8:26-27)

The phrase "in the same way" (v. 26) links the next two verses with the previous section (vv. 18-25). In this groaning world we groan. And in our groaning the Spirit groans for us. Verses 26-27 remind weak saints where our help comes from. In our frailty and timidity, the Spirit intervenes on our behalf in this mysterious act of intercession.

What kind of "weakness" (v. 26) does Paul have in mind? It is that "we do not know what to pray for" in the midst of this suffering world. It is not only that we do not have the right *words*; it is that we do not always know God's *will* in particular situations (v. 27). In this time the Spirit "also helps us" with "inexpressible groanings" (v. 26) or "groanings too deep for words" (v. 26 ESV).

John Piper applied this ministry of the Spirit to his congregation this way:

> So what is it that we don't know what to pray for in this weakness? I think the answer is: we don't know the secret will of God about our sicknesses and our hardships. We don't know whether we should pray for healing or for strength to endure. Of course, both are right and it's not wrong to pray for either. But we long to pray with great faith, and we groan that we are not sure what God's way will be with this sickness or this loss or this imprisonment. We just don't know.
>
> We can see some examples of this in Paul's life. Consider his thorn in the flesh in 2 Corinthians 12. He asked three times that it be removed. And finally Jesus revealed to him

that his will was not to take it away. Surely that experience would leave Paul wondering with every sickness and pain and hardship and imprisonment what God's will was: Healing or not? Deliverance or not?

And when he was in prison in Rome he seemed—at least for a time—to be unsure what to pray for—life and ministry, or death with courage [Phil 1:22-24].

Now this is painfully relevant to many in this church now. And it will become increasingly relevant as the price of being a Christian and a missionary increases in the years to come. Not only are there many who are sick, but there are some now and there will be many over the next years who are in danger somewhere in the world, and wonder, "How should we pray?" Should we pray for a safe escape? Or should we resolve to stay and pray for protection? Or should we stay and pray for courage to suffer and even die? ("The Spirit Helps Us in Our Weakness, Part 1")

It is indeed relevant, for what church does not have people who are physically ill, and many of our churches have missionaries on the front lines, some in dangerous places. It is of great comfort to know that when we do not know what to pray for, the "Counselor" (John 16:7) comes to our aid in this glorious intercession.

Of course, this does not mean we should not search out the will of God, but it does give us wonderful comfort. Moo says,

Our failure to know God's will and consequent inability to petition God specifically and assuredly is met by God's Spirit, who himself expresses to God those intercessory petitions that perfectly match the will of God. (*Letter*, 526)

So do not despair, weary saint: the Spirit is doing his glorious work on your behalf!

Throughout the years some have argued that this groaning intercession involves speaking in tongues (1 Cor 14:15-17), but that view should be rejected (by both those who affirm speaking in tongues still happens and those who deny it). Tongues speaking is associated with thanksgiving and blessing in the Corinthians passage, and it also includes someone interpreting. Further, only some of the Corinthians spoke in tongues, but here in Romans 8:26 all Christians experience the Spirit's groaning intercession on their behalf. All believers can cry out, "*Abba*, Father" (v. 15) in their weakness, and all believers have the Spirit's work of intercession taking place in their weakness. For this we should pause and give God praise.

This ministry of the Spirit takes place in our "hearts" (v. 27). That is, it is imperceptible to us (Peterson, *Commentary*, 330). Paul is not talking about believers praying quietly but rather the Spirit's work of taking our needs before the Father. Later in the chapter Paul says that the glorified Christ is taking our needs before the Father (v. 34). Thus we see the unity of the triune God. However this mysterious intercession works, it is good news for suffering saints! Moo says,

> There is one in heaven, the Son of God, who "intercedes on our behalf," defending us from all charges that might be brought against us, guaranteeing our salvation in the day of judgment (8:34). But there is also . . . an intercessor "in the heart," the Spirit of God, who effectively prays to the Father on our behalf through the difficulties and uncertainties of our lives here on earth. (*Letter*, 527)

What good news for weak saints!

Verse 27 includes the biblical concept that God "searches our hearts" (cf. 1 Sam 16:7; 1 Kgs 8:39; Pss 44:21; 139:1-2,23; Prov 15:11; Jer 17:10). He who knows the hearts of all knows the intention of the Spirit's inarticulate groanings for the saints. The "saints" are the sanctified community of the new covenant (Moo, *Letter*, 330). Therefore, the triune God is sustaining his saints through the Spirit's effective intercession.

So be encouraged, Christian. You are not expected to know the secret will of God in every situation, but there is One who knows (Piper, "The Spirit Helps Us")! Be comforted by the fact that God knows your heart, that God is working for you (cf. v. 31), and that the Spirit's prayers are always effective (ibid.).

Rest in God's Sovereign Plan (8:28)

Paul continues with one of the most treasured promises in the Bible (v. 28). Paul begins with the expression "we know" to introduce something with which he believes the saints will agree. And then, in the order of the Greek, he says "that for those who love God, all things work together for good." Many things could be said about the saints, and

Romans 8 highlights a number of them. But here is a basic quality of God's people: they *love* him. Numerous biblical texts highlight love as a primary aspect of a relationship with God (e.g., Exod 20:6; Deut 5:10; 6:5; 7:9; Josh 22:5; Matt 22:37; Mark 12:30; Peterson, *Commentary*, 331). Why do the saints love God? Because God loved them first! Paul has already made this point in Romans (5:5), and he will go on to herald it in 8:31-39. Recall how Paul opened the book: "To all who are in Rome, loved by God, called as saints" (1:7). Saints are those who are loved by God and those who love God.

Those who love God have confidence that "all things work together for the good." Paul magnifies God's superintending sovereignty in this amazing and sweeping promise. This does not mean everything feels or seems good to the saint. Joseph did not enjoy being abused by his brothers, sold into slavery, and so on. But he could later confess, in a Romans 8:28 kind of way, "You planned evil against me; God planned it for good to bring about the present result—the survival of many people" (Gen 50:20). We may struggle to detect God's goodness in the midst of our various pains and trials too, but when viewed in light of the end of history and our future glory, we will stand convinced of God's good and sovereign plans (Bird, *Romans*, 282).

Further, the saints' love for God is evidence of God's calling of them, "who are called according to his purpose." Those who love God are those who have been summoned to become the recipients of God's salvation (cf. 1:6). God's "purpose" involves all that God has planned to do in the future (cf. Rom 9:11; Eph 1:11), and for the saint, God's salvific plan is that believers be conformed to the image of the Son and share in his glory (Rom 8:29-30; Moo, *Letter*, 530–31). God's calling, then, elicits love for him and gives the saint confidence in God's sovereign purposes (Bird, *Romans*, 282).

John Stott says, "Romans 8:28 is surely one of the best-known texts in the Bible. On it believers of every age and place have stayed their minds. It has been likened to a pillow on which to rest our weary heads" (*Message*, 246). Rest in this promise, Christian. God is at work. God is working out all things for the good of his people. Nothing is outside the scope of God's providential rule. "Life is not a random mess which it may sometimes appear," as Stott notes (ibid., 248). God is working for our good, working to conform us to the image of his Son, and he promises to take us to glory. On this, we rest.

Rest in the Golden Chain of Salvation (8:29-30)

Paul goes deeper into God's sovereign calling in these two verses. The word "for" in verse 29 reflects on the previous concept. Verses 29-30 have commonly been called "the golden chain of salvation." That is, the order or the way in which God saves sinners. Peterson says,

> God is the subject in each case [foreknows . . . predestines
> . . . calls . . . justifies . . . glorifies], grounding the Christian's
> certainty in the continuity of [God's] actions. (*Commentary,*
> 333; emphasis in original)

One cannot miss the emphasis here: God alone saves. Salvation from start to finish is the Lord's doing (cf. Jonah 2:9).

Paul says first that God "foreknew" his people. This does not mean that God looked down through the corridor of time and saw who would choose him and then on that basis elected them to salvation. Paul is speaking of God's personal, intimate knowledge of individual persons (cf. Gen 18:19; Exod 33:12; Jer 1:5; Amos 3:2). It speaks of God's decision to set his love on his saints (cf. Rom 9:11-13; 11:2; Acts 2:23; Eph 1:5; 2 Tim 1:9; 1 Pet 1:2). God "fore-loved" individual believers.

Those whom he foreknew, God also "predestined." This sovereign action relates to God's purpose of election also. God decided ahead of time that his children be "conformed to the image of his Son" (v. 29). The phrase "image of his Son" reflects the language of Genesis 1:27; 1 Corinthians 15:49; 2 Corinthians 3:18; Philippians 3:21; Colossians 1:15; and 1 John 3:1-2. We could group these verses in three categories: *creation, anticipation,* and *participation.* We were *created* in the image of God (Gen 1:27). But because sin entered the world, that image has been marred. Through Christ, who is the visible "image of the invisible God" (Col 1:15), we are redeemed and reconciled to God, and now we *anticipate* the promises of bearing "the image of the man of heaven" (1 Cor 15:49; cf. Phil 3:21; 1 John 3:1-2). In the meantime, by the Spirit we *participate* in something that is presently happening: we are being transformed into his image (2 Cor 3:18). Paul then proclaims that one day, we the redeemed will be just like our elder brother, Jesus, and right now, through the Spirit's sanctifying work, we are being made more and more like Christ.

But we should not miss the communal emphasis of verse 29: "brothers and sisters." While election is personal, it is not individualistic. Bird notes, "God's before-the-ages plan was to create a Christ-shaped family, a renewed humanity modeled on the Son" (*Romans*, 283). God has always purposed to have a people for himself, individuals chosen in divine love, who will together be conformed to the image of the Son to the praise of God's glorious grace.

This has great implications for your local church. You should not view your brothers and sisters from a human perspective but from this divine perspective. God has set his everlasting love on them, so let's never cease to worship and serve our God together with gladness in our hearts and with deep love for one another. And when one of your brothers or sisters relocates or is sent out of the church on mission, remember that you will have all of eternity to fellowship with him or her! When we send our church planters and missionaries, we call these send-offs "gospel goodbyes." It hurts to say goodbye to faithful saints, but we can make the short-term sacrifice for the sake of Christ and the mission, and we can do so with the joyful knowledge that we will spend eternity with them in the brightness of Christ's glory. This certainty comes from rock-solid promises like Romans 8:29.

God's foreknowledge and predestination ensure what we read next: his calling, justification, and glorification (v. 30). "Calling" picks up what Paul said in verse 28. This calling refers to God's "effectual call" that results in an individual's salvation—not the "general call" that goes out to all through the preaching of the gospel (Acts 16:14; 1 Thess 1:4-5; 2 Thess 2:13-14). This fact is made plain by the next statement. Justification, a major doctrine in the entire book of Romans (3:25,28; 4:5; 5:1; 8:32), is here connected to God's sovereignty in salvation. Those God calls believe in Christ and are justified before God.

Finally, those who are fore-loved, predestined, called, and justified are also "glorified." God has decreed that those who are justified will experience glorification. True believers can be assured of this reality, as this entire passage (vv. 18-30) shows.

Therefore, God's saving actions form an unbreakable golden chain of salvation. Christian, you are in God's hands. He chose to love you and to declare you righteous in Christ. You belong to him, along with many other brothers and sisters, now and forever. Reflecting on the whole passage, Bird says,

> Believers form a forgiven family of Jews and Gentiles, groaning for glory, sustained by Spirit-inspired prayer, with creation anxiously waiting for the unveiling of the glorious freedom of these children in the age to come. (*Romans*, 284)

Amen! As Newton said, we only have a mile to go! And as Baxter did, let us (weary and weak saints) meditate on this glory regularly, in our own personal lives and in our life together as brothers and sisters in the church, in order that we may faithfully endure until we see the risen and glorified Christ!

Reflect and Discuss

1. Sometimes you hear, "That person is so heavenly minded that he/ she is no earthly good." Do you agree with that statement? Why or why not?
2. How does the doctrine of glorification help us endure hardship?
3. What does this passage teach us about the effects of the fall on the creation?
4. How does this passage emphasize Christian hope?
5. How is the doctrine of adoption an already-not yet reality?
6. Describe the work of the Holy Spirit in verses 26-27. Why is this encouraging?
7. Explain how the phrases "called according to his purpose" and "those who love God" relate to each other.
8. What does verse 28 teach the saint about God's providential control?
9. What aspect of the "golden chain of salvation" do you find most difficult to grasp? Which aspect do you find most glorious to celebrate?
10. How does this passage emphasize not just one's personal salvation but also the family of God?

God Is for Us

ROMANS 8:31-39

Main Idea: In this celebratory passage, Paul assures the saints that God is for them and that nothing can separate them from the love of God in Christ Jesus.

I.   Who Can Be against Us (8:31-32)?
II. Who Can Bring a Charge against Us (8:33)?
III. Who Will Condemn Us (8:34)?
IV. Who Can Separate Us (8:35-39)?
V.   Applications

I am not sure who first popularized the sports cheer, "Who dat?" but several teams use it, like the New Orleans Saints. Saints football fans passionately chant, "Who dat? Who dat? Who dat say dey gonna beat dem Saints?" I like to think of Romans 8:31-39 as Paul's "Who dat?" section of Romans! Paul asks four "who questions" in these verses in order to proclaim the fact that no one will ultimately beat "dem saints"! Yet it is not due to the greatness of the saints but due to the grace of God in Christ Jesus.

Paul's triumphant answers to these four questions provide believers with gospel-centered assurance:

Questions/Answers on God's Love and Our Security in Christ[1]	
Who can be against us? (8:31-32)	Nobody! God, having not spared his own Son, will give us all things.
Who can bring a charge against us? (8:33)	Nobody! God has justified us!
Who will condemn us? (8:34)	Nobody! Christ Jesus died, rose, and intercedes for us!
Who can separate us? (8:35-39)	Nobody! God's love in Christ has made us superconquerors.

[1] Adapted from Bird, *Romans*, 291.

Paul triumphantly declares that *nobody* can ultimately prevail against those who belong to Christ. God is for us; God has justified us; Christ has died, he rose, and now he intercedes for us; we are more than conquerors through him who loved us; and nothing can separate us from the love of God in Christ Jesus.

In this celebratory passage Paul proclaims the believer's security in Christ and the certainty of God's love for his saints. Weaving together several previous themes in Romans, Paul exults in the work of God for us through Christ and the love of God for us in Christ. This passage is one of the "awe passages" of the Bible. It should stimulate our love and adoration for our triune God. It is a fitting conclusion to a remarkable chapter, a chapter that begins with "no condemnation" and ends with "no separation" (Morris, *Epistle*, 299). Schreiner says, "The magnificent and exalted style in these verses is immediately apparent, and the beauty of the text may be unrivaled in all of Pauline literature" (*Romans*, 456). Let's meditate on this beautiful passage and then draw some applications for our lives.

Who Can Be against Us?
ROMANS 8:31-32

Paul actually begins with a previous question in the first part of verse 31 before raising the "who" question in the second half of the verse: "*What, then, are we to say about these things? If God is for us, who is against us?*" (8:31; emphasis added).

What exactly does Paul mean by "these things"? Paul has more in mind than just Romans 8. Most commentators believe Paul is at least thinking of Romans 5–8 (Bird, *Romans*, 292), but others assert that Paul may have all of Romans in mind (Schreiner, "God Is for Us!"). Paul is about to finish a large section of Romans (chs. 5–8) and launch into a new section (chs. 9–11). So Romans 8:31-39 serves as a summary and transition passage. It seems like Romans 5 onward is at least in view. But of course, you cannot really understand chapters 5–8 without the previous four chapters. So then, it is like Paul is asking, "What do we say about all that has been said thus far in Romans?" It is like a test question, How do you summarize the first 8 chapters of Romans?

We have covered a lot of ground. When you begin the letter, you see Paul showing how the gospel has its roots in the Old Testament (1:1-5). Then he calls believers those "who are also called by Jesus Christ

. . . loved by God, called as saints" (1:6-7). But when you read the first three chapters of Romans, you wonder how on earth you could be loved by God and be a saint, given how sinful humanity is! It is only because God has intervened in Christ Jesus, as Paul declares in Romans 3:21-26. Beginning in 3:21 ("But now"), Paul has been relentlessly unfolding the good news of the gospel. He has shown that, through Christ, we believers are *justified before God*, we are *reconciled to God*, we enjoy *peace with God*, we are *indwelt by the Spirit of God*, we are *not condemned before God*, we are *adopted by God*, we have glorification *hope in God*, we have *help in the Spirit of God*, we are *called by God*, and we have the certainty that all things are *working for the good of those who love God* (3:21–8:30).

So, what do we say about *these things*? I think Paul's answer is found in his question, "If God is for us, who is against us?" (8:31). Here is a short summary of the good news of Romans for every child of God: *God is for us*. In many ways the rest of the verses in this chapter expound this dominant point. Many will oppose us, but, ultimately, God is for us.

In this fallen world there will be pain and hardship, but we must not let the pain and hardship deceive us. If we are in Christ, we can be assured that God is for us. In our Christian experience we will encounter spiritual warfare. But though all the powers of the evil one may come against us, they will never prevail since God is on our side.

It is hard to imagine anything greater than this truth. Almighty God is not opposed to us; he is for us (cf. Ps 56:9). Schreiner says, "He [God] will vanquish any enemies that present themselves before believers" (*Romans*, 458).

Now, this is a somewhat dangerous statement in the sense that many religious fanatics who do great harm and even violence to people claim that their God is for them. Terrorists may say this while they wage holy war against others. But of course, they are completely wrong. Even though people will wrongly make this statement, Christians should not let misuses deter them from claiming this wonderful promise. This is the good news of Romans! The triune God who calls, justifies, and glorifies sinners is for those who belong to Christ Jesus!

Verse 32 reinforces the point. So, how do we know God is for us? I mean, it sounds good to say, "God is for us," but how can we be sure? Notice the verse. Something has happened in space, time, and history to prove once and for all that God is for us. If you want to know if God is for us, simply look to the cross! The cross provides the believer's ongoing assurance. God's work in Christ for us at Golgotha ensures us of God's continued grace toward us now and forever.

Romans 8:32 employs the greater to the lesser style of argument (or "harder to easier"). The great gift (the hard thing): God "did not even spare his own Son." You can hear an echo of Genesis 22. Abraham offered up Isaac, but God spared Isaac. The Father's own beloved Son, Jesus, was not spared. He "gave him up for us," in place of us, instead of us (cf. Isa 53; Rom 4:25; 1 Cor 15:3; Gal 1:4). This is the supreme act of love. Paul says if God has done the hard thing—give up his own Son—then we can rest assured that he will also do the lesser or easier thing—"grant us everything." That is, he will give us everything necessary to conform us to the image of his Son and everything necessary to get us to glory (8:17-31).

We should not read Paul saying God will give us everything we have ever wanted. This is not a prosperity gospel verse. Paul is saying that God does not redeem us to leave us. He redeems us to conform us. He will continue working out his sovereign purposes in our lives, conforming us to the image of his Son (8:28-30; cf. Phil 1:6).

Perhaps an illustration of the greater to the lesser would be helpful. If I take my kids to Disney World, it will cost a fortune. But love spares no expense, as they say. So let's imagine that I pay for this expensive family trip. And on the way to the theme park, I see a sign that says, "Parking: $50." What if I then look to my bride, Kimberly, and say, "I'm not doing it. I'm drawing the line. We're not paying $50. We're going home." What would she say? Among other things she would say, "Oh yes we are doing this! We have spent hundreds to go to Disney World! We're going to pay $50 to park!" Paul is saying, in Romans 8:32, that God has already made the big purchase at the cross; he's going to take care of our parking. If God is going to put forward his own beloved Son in our place, he is going to see to the ongoing work of our salvation. He will see us through to glory. The cross assures us of the ongoing, unfailing, everlasting love of God for his saints.

Who Can Bring a Charge against Us?
ROMANS 8:33

The apostle continues, "Who can bring an accusation against God's elect?" (8:33). Once again the answer is, Nobody!

You can hear the judicial language of Romans again here. Regarding those the Lord has chosen for himself, who can successfully charge them with a crime? Paul gives a God-centered answer, saying that no prosecution can succeed because God has justified us. That is, you cannot go higher than Almighty God. When the omnipotent, righteous Judge of all the earth says, "Not guilty," then you are not guilty (cf. Isa 50:8-9).

Paul is glorying in the good news of justification by faith that he has been articulating in the previous chapters (cf. 3:21–5:21; 8:1,30). The gavel has come down. Case closed. If you are in Christ, you are justified—regardless of who accuses you. The accuser, Satan, will certainly try to accuse you, bringing up your sins and your past. When this happens, you need to go back to the gospel and realize that the verdict has already been pronounced. God has justified us through faith in Christ (Rom 5:1). Therefore, we do not have to fear future condemnation:

> Believers can face the day of judgment with confidence, for
> those whom God has chosen as his own will certainly not
> be accused on the day of judgment. God has declared them
> to be right in his sight, and thus those who would accuse
> believers will not successfully establish their case. (Schreiner,
> *Romans*, 462)

Who Will Condemn Us?
ROMANS 8:34

This is the same basic question as verse 33 with a Christ-centered response. Who can condemn us? Again: Nobody!

Sometimes our own hearts will try to condemn us (1 John 3:20). And Satan will try to accuse us as well (Rev 12). Our critics, enemies, or the dark forces of evil may try to condemn us, but again, they will not prevail. Not only has God chosen us and justified us, but the Savior has died for us, been raised for us, and is now interceding for us. Who will condemn us? Not Christ! He died in place of us (cf. Rom 5:8)! He rose for us (cf. 4:25)! He is also interceding for us at the Father's right hand (cf. Ps 110:1). Moo says, "With such a defense attorney, it is no wonder the prosecution loses its case!" (*Romans*, 283).

Marvel at this verse. Christ died for us. He died for the sins that would have condemned us (cf. v. 3; Gal 3:13). Christ has been raised.

The crowd declared him guilty, but God raised and vindicated his Son. The resurrection said, "They are wrong! He is the Messiah!" The resurrection demonstrated that the Father accepted the Son's sacrifice. And if we are in Christ, then Christ's victory is our victory.

Christ Jesus is at the right hand of the Father, occupying the highest place of authority and honor. The author of Hebrews tells us, "After making purification for sins, he sat down at the right hand of the Majesty on high" (Heb 1:3). Now he is our heavenly advocate and high priest (Heb 4:14-16; 7:25). Stott says, "His very presence at the Father's right hand is evidence of his completed work of atonement, and his intercession means that he 'continues to secure for his people the benefits of his death'" (*Message*, 257, quoting Hodge, n. 192).

This is indeed a most comforting passage for the saints. It is hard to imagine anything more peace giving than to know you are the subject of Christ's intercessory prayers. Consider a few of the following quotes as you ponder this fact:

John Chrysostom: "If then the Spirit even 'maketh intercession for us with groanings that cannot be uttered,' and Christ died and intercedeth for us, and the Father 'spared not His own Son,' for thee, and elected thee, and justified thee, why be afraid any more? Or why tremble when enjoying such great love, and having such great interest taken in thee." (Quoted in Schreiner, *Romans*, 456, n. 15)

Louis Berkhof: "It is a consoling thought that Christ is praying for us, even when we are negligent in our prayer life; that He is presenting to the Father those spiritual needs which were not present to our minds and which we often neglect to include in our prayers; and that He prays for our protection against the dangers of which we are not even conscious, and against the enemies which threaten us, though we do not notice it. He is praying that our faith may not cease, and that we may come out victoriously in the end." (Quoted in Justin Taylor, "Christ Is Praying for Those Who Are His")

Robert Murray M'Cheyne: "If I could hear Christ praying for me in the next room, I would not fear a million enemies. Yet distance makes no difference. He is praying for me." (Ibid.)

Christian, see how committed Christ is to you. Jesus is more committed to you than you are to him. He has you. When you stumble and fumble, remember that Christ is praying for you—unceasingly, fervently, and successfully.

Who Can Separate Us?

ROMANS 8:35-39

Because God is for us, we will never be separated from the love of God in Christ Jesus our Lord. Paul's answer to this question is the same (Nobody!), but he spends double the amount of time on it! Why does Paul answer in this way? Why not just raise the question in verse 35 and simply answer, "Nobody. Chapter 9." I think it is because Paul is after more than just the right answer. He is going after our hearts.

It is possible to know the Bible but be cold spiritually. This does not have to be the case. Gospel truths should warm our hearts. But Paul knows that Christians can sometimes fail to be deeply moved by the love of God, so he "puts the rhetorical pedal to the homiletical metal" to convince Christians of the love of Christ for them (Bird, *Romans*, 290). He wants us to know that Jesus not only defends us; he also loves us. Jesus enters a relationship with us, and nothing can separate us from him.

In verse 35 Paul lists some possible "separators." The first two are similar: *affliction* and *distress.* Can outward affliction or inward distress separate us from Christ's love? One may think that Christ's love is absent during these kinds of moments. But while the distressed Christian may not feel particularly loved, Paul reassures us: we are not outside the grip of Christ's grace.

Persecution takes affliction/distress to another level. Suffering for the gospel was a reality for the early church, as it is today for many Christians around the world. But persecution cannot separate the faithful witness from the love of Christ either. Actually, this would be a wonderful passage to meditate on should one face persecution.

Famine and *nakedness* speak of the absence of our basic necessities. In a time of physical desperation, one may be tempted to ask, "Have I been untied from God's love?" But again the answer is no. The saint in this condition should not take such experiences to mean that he or she has been unfastened from the love of Christ.

Danger reminds us of the reality of living out our faith in risky contexts. Paul certainly knew of danger (2 Cor 11:23-28). The apostle was not a cold philosopher or an armchair theologian. He endured danger, persecution, hunger, and more.

What about the *sword?* Does execution mean the Christian has been separated from Christ's love? No! Not even death can separate the child of God from the Savior (8:38; cf. Phil 1:21)!

Paul then supplies a quick scriptural reflection from Psalm 44:22. This particular psalm is about the suffering of God's people. Paul's point seems to be this: suffering is a normal part of the Christian life. It is par for the course. So suffering should not surprise the saint, and he or she should never think for a moment that Christ's love has been removed from his or her life.

In verse 37 Paul gets around to answering the question directly: "No." Then he makes the celebratory exclamation. It is "*in* all these things" (emphasis added) that we are more than conquerors. God does not always take us *out of* these things! You may actually go through danger, persecution, affliction, and so on. What you can know is that you are secure in the love of Christ in the midst of these trials and that God is sovereign over it all.

This is a striking phrase: "more than conquerors" (v. 37). What does that mean? How can you be more than a conqueror? Schreiner puts it well: "To be more than a conqueror over affliction, distress, persecution, and so on indicates that *these enemies are actually turned to the good of believers* through the power of God" (*Romans*, 460; emphasis added). So not only can we endure these sufferings and be assured of Christ's love in the midst of them, but we can also know that God is using them for our good and his glory. The phrase "in all these things" is connected back to verses 28 and 32. God is at work in all these things for our good and his glory. So, suffering Christian, do not ever let these trials deceive you. You have not been separated from Christ's love, and God is for you!

Again, how can we know God is at work in the midst of these trials and that he is for us? Notice the last two words of verse 37, through him who "loved us," which again highlights Christ's love displayed at the cross (cf. Gal 2:20; Eph 5:2). This is how we know God is for us and will even use our trials for our good. The cross is the ongoing assurance of Christ's love that our fickle hearts must return to again and again.

Therefore, we do not muddle our way through the Christian life. We are victors who have found the ever-present love of Christ holding us, our sovereign Father working for us, and the indwelling Holy Spirit empowering us.

Paul underscores our need for divine help with the phrase "through him" (v. 37). The apostle is not proclaiming groundless triumphalism. That is the kind of thing you hear in pop music: "All *I* do is win." No, it is "through him." Jesus is the champion! Apart from him we are not conquerors. Apart from Christ, we will be conquered by sin and death. But in him we are not destroyed; we are victorious. Through our union with him, we have the indwelling presence of the Spirit, access to our Father, and rock-solid assurance of victory.

This kind of gospel-centered assurance will enable us to endure adversity and opposition in this life. Kent Hughes reports how such promises upheld the famous preacher John Chrysostom (AD 347–407):

> When Chrysostom was brought before the Roman Emperor, the Emperor threatened him with banishment if he remained a Christian.
>
> Chrysostom replied, "Thou canst not banish me for this world is my father's house."
>
> "But I will slay thee," said the Emperor.
>
> "Nay, thou canst not," said the noble champion of the faith, "for my life is hid with Christ in God."
>
> "I will take away thy treasures."
>
> "Nay, but thou canst not for my treasure is in heaven and my heart is there."
>
> "But I will drive thee away from man and thou shalt have no friend left."
>
> "Nay, thou canst not, for I have a friend in heaven from whom thou canst not separate me. I defy thee; for there is nothing that thou canst do to hurt me." (Hughes, *Romans*, 171)

That is a man living in Romans 8! When you grasp that you have been liberated from condemnation, that you will never be separated from Christ's love, that God is for you, that the Spirit of God is indwelling you, that God is using suffering to make you more like Jesus, and that the Spirit and the Son are interceding for you, then you say no to the cravings of this world and boldly follow Jesus in the face of opposition, just as Chrysostom did.

In verses 38-39 Paul closes with a final celebration of God's love. He begins with his own assurance of God's love in Christ: "I am persuaded." Paul now wants the Roman Christians to be persuaded too. He wants them to be convinced that nothing can separate them from Christ's love. Here we see one of the essential actions of preaching, disciple making, and counseling: working to *convince* fellow believers of the unfailing love of Christ. But to do this well, we need to be convinced ourselves!

Paul then goes on to list four pairs of threats (more potential separators), with the word *powers* thrown in between the third and fourth pair. The first list in verse 35 deals more with hardships in this life, while the list in verses 38-39 contains a more universal and cosmic list of threats. Paul passionately asserts that for those in Christ, nothing in the realm of human existence, or even in the experience of death, can separate them from Christ's love ("death nor life"); nor can anything in the spiritual realm ("angels nor rulers" [or "demons," NIV]); nor any event in history, either past or future ("things present nor things to come"); nor any dark "powers"; nor anything above us or below ("height nor depth"); nor anything in the created order ("any other created thing"). None of these things can separate the saint from Christ's love. How can we have this assurance? Why are the glorious promises of Romans 8 true for every saint? It is because we are "*in Christ Jesus* our Lord" (emphasis added)! If we are united with Christ, nothing can separate us from the love of God.

What promises we have as God's adopted children! He does not promise us that life will be easy, but he promises to be with us. He promises that nothing will unfasten us from his love. He promises to take us to glory. Ray Ortlund draws a parallel to the beloved Psalm 23 with Romans 8:31-39:

> "Surely goodness and mercy shall follow me all the days of my life, and I shall dwell in the house of the Lord forever" (Psalm 23:6). The Romans 8:31-39 of the Old Testament. Glorious assurance. (Quoted on Twitter, June 24, 2019)

Glorious assurance indeed!

Applications

Romans 8:31 is true. God is for us. Verses 32-39 assure us of this fact. Let's pause to reflect prayerfully on these hope-giving words. Allow me to offer four ways we may apply this text to our hearts and to the hearts of fellow believers.

First, allow these truths to lead you to worship. This text should cause us to sing and celebrate with joy. It should inspire awe and devotion. Paul goes to great lengths to impress the love of Christ on the hearts of the saints here. He not only wants us to affirm that Christ loves us, but he also wants us to feel it, rejoice in it, and celebrate it. If your affections are cool, then slowly and prayerfully ponder the truths of this passage so that you may adore the God of your salvation.

Second, allow these truths to lift you from despair. If you look back over this text, you find three things that can lead a saint into discouragement: sin, suffering, and death. But we must apply the truths of Romans 8:31-39 to our hearts during these times. This is a most encouraging text!

This passage has lifted saints for years. For example, Kent Hughes describes how much Philip Melanchthon loved Romans 8:31. Melanchthon served with Martin Luther during the Reformation and was a gifted scholar and preacher. When Melanchthon died, his body was lowered next to Luther's. (One can visit the graves at the Castle Church of Wittenberg today.) What truth made Melanchthon able to endure the adversity of the Reformation? According to Hughes, Romans 8:31 is quoted more by Melanchthon than any other Scripture in his lectures and correspondences. Moreover, Hughes comments,

> When Melanchthon sensed he was dying he asked to be placed on the traveling bed in his study because that is where he was happiest. When the pastor read Romans 8:31, Melanchthon exclaimed, "Read those words again!" The pastor read, "If God is for us, who can be against us?" Melanchthon murmured in a kind of ecstasy, "That's it! That's it!" This text had always been the greatest comfort to him. In the darkest hours of his life when destruction threatened, he comforted himself again by reciting, "If God is for us, who can be against us?" (*Romans*, 166)

Melanchthon allowed this passage to lift him; let it lift you too—in times of disappointment and discouragement, and even in the face of death.

Third, allow these truths to show you what unites diverse believers in community. Look back through the passage and notice the plural language. Look at verse 31: "What, then, are *we* to say . . . ? If God is for *us*, who is against *us*?" (emphasis added). Paul does not say, "What am *I* to say?"

or "If God is for *me* . . ." A believer should certainly apply this text to his own personal life, but the passage is not individualistic. It is corporate. It is familial. Read right through the passage and notice the "we" and "us" emphasis in verses 32-39. Paul is writing to diverse believers in Rome, Jews and Gentiles, and it is *the gospel* that unites them—and it is *the gospel* that unites believers today! (This subject of God's saving purposes for the Jew and Gentile will be worked out in Romans 9–11.)

Fourth, allow these truths to embolden you for mission. Assurance should never lead us to apathy. Gospel assurance should lead to gospel advancement. Having the promises of Romans 8 should make us bold and courageous. We can plant churches in hard places because Romans 8 is true. We can testify boldly to the claims of Christ in a skeptical world knowing that God is for us, Christ has died for us, and the Spirit of Christ indwells us. We can go to unreached people groups and herald the gospel, though we may face opposition, knowing that nothing will separate us from the love of God in Christ Jesus our Lord. We can live missional lives, knowing that we can cry out to *Abba* Father at any moment and that all things are working together for our good and God's glory. We can suffer now because we know glory is coming. So be filled with hope, Christian! Be set ablaze by the gospel and allow the joy in your heart to spill over into worldwide witness. Romans 8 made Paul the greatest missionary ever, and it can make us more faithful in mission as well if we will embrace these truths wholeheartedly and live in light of them passionately.

Reflect and Discuss

1. Why is the phrase "God is for us" a good summary of Romans 1–8?
2. How do we know God is for us?
3. How does Paul argue from the greater to the lesser in Romans 8:32? Why should this verse encourage Christians?
4. In Romans 8:31-39 Paul reminds us of some of the doctrines he has previously taught. What are some of them?
5. What does this passage teach us about the redemptive work of Jesus?
6. Believers may be tempted to believe that they have been separated from Christ's love. What are some of those potential separators, according to this text? What does Paul say about them?
7. Why do you think Paul spends so much time waxing eloquently about the love of Christ in verses 35-39?

8. What does it mean to be more than a conqueror? How can we be more than conquerors?

9. Why should this passage lead us to worship and lift us from discouragement?

10. Why should this passage embolden us for mission?

God's Word Has Not Failed

ROMANS 9:1-29

Main Idea: After expressing his burden for unbelieving Israel, Paul defends the idea that God's word has not failed by explaining God's sovereign purposes in redemptive history.

I. Setting the Stage for the Argument: The Tragedy of Israel (9:1-5)
II. Truth 1: God Is Working Out His Sovereign Purposes in History (9:6-13)
III. Truth 2: God's Ways Are Just and His Salvation Is Merciful (9:14-18)
IV. Truth 3: God Has the Right of a Potter over His Clay (9:19-23)
V. Truth 4: God's Promises Include Many Gentiles and a Jewish Remnant (9:24-29)
VI. Applications

After shouting, "Yeah!" at the end of Romans 8, some readers react to Romans 9 with, "Say what?" We might expect Paul to go from that exalted language of God's love straight to the application of the good news, but he does not provide such practical, day-to-day application until he arrives at chapter 12. What we find in Romans 9–11 is a complex portion of the letter.

In Romans 16:22 we learn that Tertius was Paul's scribe. James Dunn says that he could imagine Paul telling Tertius after chapter 8 to go home for the rest of the day and get some sleep before starting on chapters 9–11 (in Bird, *Romans*, 304).

Though these are challenging chapters, they should not be neglected. They have much to teach us about God's sovereign freedom, his mercy and justice, and his saving and surprising grace and love. They are also integral to the letter as a whole, as Paul's burden to explain the relationship between Jew and Gentile is observable throughout Romans.

I am saying chapters 9–11 because you need to read these three chapters as a unit. If you study only chapter 9, you may be tempted to think everything is up to God and we have nothing to do, as the focus is on God's sovereignty, election, choosing, and outworking of his purposes in history. But if you study only chapter 10, you will be tempted to believe everything is up to you, as the focus is on human responsibility, the necessity of believing, and the urgency of evangelism. Then in chapter 11, Paul puts both God's sovereignty and human responsibility together, concluding with this beautiful doxology:

> *Oh, the depth of the riches*
> *and the wisdom and the knowledge of God!*
> *How unsearchable his judgments*
> *and untraceable his ways!*
> *For who has known the mind of the Lord?*
> *Or who has been his counselor?*
> *And who has ever given to God,*
> *that he should be repaid?*
> *For from him and through him*
> *and to him are all things.*
> *To him be the glory forever. Amen.*

Notice his language. Paul says God's ways are "unsearchable" (11:33). We should humbly keep this in mind as we study this unit of Romans. Here is an inspired apostle saying that God's ways are "unsearchable." How do you hold to both God's comprehensive sovereignty and humanity's responsibility? It is mysterious. And this is not a cop-out answer. If you think you have everything here figured out, then you know more than Paul. We should remember, "The hidden things belong to the LORD our God" (Deut 29:29).

We should also notice what acknowledgment of God's sovereign and mysterious ways does to Paul. It leads him to *worship*. These chapters should lead us to worship before our sovereign God as well. Paul is not writing as a cold philosopher but as an awe-inspired worshiper. Romans 9–11 is a God-centered portion of Scripture: "For from him and through him and to him are all things. To him be the glory forever" (11:36).

So, let's keep these three chapters in view as we study one at a time. Doing so will give us a needed balance on sovereignty and human responsibility, it will keep us mindful that we are dealing with the infinite wisdom of God, and it will encourage us to have an attitude of praise.

The big question in Romans 9–11 is simple: Has God's word failed? Romans 9:6 is the thesis of Romans 9–11. That much should not be disputed. The argument then climaxes with Paul's statement about the eschatological salvation of Israel in 11:26-29.

Can God be trusted to do what he said? Is God's word reliable? The reason the question is asked is because of *Israel*. What is Israel's place within the promises and purposes of God? That is the problem with which Paul is wrestling. Did God not promise to send the Messiah to Israel in order to bless his people? Why then is the church made up largely of Gentile believers? Just look at the book of Acts. Who was more likely to believe, Jew or Gentile? Gentile. Who were Paul's harshest opponents? Jews. So, what is up with this?

In addition to this primary issue regarding Jew and Gentile, a practical question arises for the believer. If God's word failed in regard to Israel, then how can we know that we can trust him? In the final analysis we will see that God's word has not failed concerning Israel (cf. Rom 3:3-4), and in this we should rejoice; because of this, we should rest secure: we can trust our God!

So now, let's consider Romans 9:1-29, which highlights the sovereignty of God. After we set the stage in verses 1-5, we will see four truths to affirm in verses 6-29. I will then offer some final applications for our reflection and edification.

Setting the Stage for the Argument: The Tragedy of Israel
ROMANS 9:1-5

Paul contrasts Israel's privileges with her current state. They were given so many privileges but did not act on them (cf. 3:1-2).

The apostle is deeply concerned for his Jewish kinsmen according to the flesh. His primary identity was "Christian," and he was the "apostle to the Gentiles" (11:13), but that did not mean he did not love his Jewish kinsmen. In verses 1-2 he confirms his anguish. Some Jews were suspicious of Paul's loyalty to them, so he says, "I speak the truth" and "I am not lying." You can hear Paul's brokenheartedness at Israel's state with the words "great sorrow and unceasing anguish." Paul goes from pleasure and wonder in chapter 8 to grief and burden in chapter 9. He longs for his unbelieving kinsmen in Romans 9 to know the joy and hope of Romans 8.

Consider also the remarkable extent of Paul's anguish (9:3). I have heard about having a "burden for the lost," but this is another level. Paul would be willing to trade places with unbelieving Jews, who stood under condemnation.

Why such agony? It was because these Jews were not saved (cf. 10:1). To be a missionary-evangelist like Paul means not only to share his *theology*; it means also to share his *burden*. While we may not be able to grasp all the nuances of God's sovereignty in chapter 9, every Christian should have a burden for those separated from Christ.

In verses 4-5 Paul lists some of Israel's privileges:

- *They are a special nation.* "Israelites" had a special position in salvation history.
- *They were adopted.* Paul implies a national adoption (Exod 4:22), but not the type of adoption that refers to *salvation*, as in 8:16,23.
- *God revealed his glory to them.* God's presence was with Israel.
- *They have been given the covenants.* God made an everlasting covenant with them.
- *God gave them his law.*
- *They had the privilege of worshiping God.*
- *They were given promises.* The greatest promise: the Messiah.
- *They had a godly ancestry.* That is, the patriarchs.
- *They are the people from whom Christ came.* This Christ, Paul adds, "is God" (something most Jews did not believe).

Israel had all of this and yet did not believe in Jesus. John writes, "He came to his own, and his own people did not receive him" (John 1:11). Paul says later, "They stumbled over the stumbling stone" (Rom 9:32). This Jewish rejection broke Paul's heart, and it sets the stage for the following section.

In Romans 9:6-29 Paul helps us think through the question, Has God's word failed? In so doing, he shows us four truths to affirm concerning God's sovereign freedom.

Truth 1: God Is Working Out His Sovereign Purposes in History
ROMANS 9:6-13

Paul states his main idea: "Now it is not as though the word of God has failed" (v. 6a). By the "word of God" he means *God's promise to Israel.* Notice how clear Paul is. Has God's promise to Israel failed? Absolutely not!

Paul then gives the explanation for his clear declaration: "Because not all who are descended from Israel are Israel" (v. 6b). In other words, God never promised that every Israelite would be saved. Not every physical child of Abraham will be saved. That *is* not the promise, and it never *was* the promise. The fact that the Jews did not believe did not and does not contradict God's promises because he never promised that they would all be saved. Further, God has always chosen some within the nation of Israel to be his true people (a "remnant," v. 27).

There is an Israel by birth, and there are some who have been called to belong to *true* Israel. Paul has already made this sort of statement in 2:29. In 9:8 he adds that there are "children of the promise" and children of "physical descent." God has reserved the sovereign right to determine who his people will be (vv. 7-29). Moreover, God can and has chosen to include the Gentiles in this believing company (vv. 24-29).

So then, if only a minority of Jews embraced Jesus as Messiah, that would not be out of step with God's ways. God is working out his purposes in history. To underscore this idea, Paul gives some biblical illustrations in verses 7-13.

Isaac over Ishmael (9:7-9). To show that his teaching is not novel, Paul reaches back to Isaac and Ishmael. Abraham had these two sons. But God's covenant was established through Isaac, not Ishmael. God had given Abraham a grand promise of children (Gen 12; 15), but he and Sarah had seen no child. Abraham then had Ishmael by Hagar, an Egyptian maid of Sarah, when he was eighty-four years old. By this action Abraham thought he would have the offspring he needed to make the promise come true. But no. In Genesis 17:19 God promises that Abraham's barren wife will have a son and that God will establish his covenant with him.

In the second part of verse 7 Paul quotes Genesis 21:12 to ground his assertion. God determined that Abraham's offspring would be traced through Isaac. The chosen offspring was the result of a *miracle*, not *human achievement.* Salvation is of the Lord!

In verse 8 Paul says that only "the children of the promise" are Abraham's offspring. There is an Israel within Israel. In verse 9 Paul gives a loose quotation from Genesis 18:10,14. It reminds the reader of God's gracious miracle, which enabled aged Sarah to bear the child of promise.

We should not miss the application here. Salvation is not based on birth but on God's gracious intervention. Salvation is not by birth or works but by grace.

It is also important to keep in mind that God's promise to Abraham was for all the earth to be blessed. Eventually, through this line, through this promise, the ultimate offspring would come: Christ. Now all who call on him will be saved. God's sovereign election had *the nations* in view.

Jacob over Esau (9:10-13). Paul makes the same point with his second biblical illustration. One might think, *Well, it was because of Ishmael's status that God chose Isaac instead of Ishmael. He was the son of Hagar, an Egyptian maid.* Or perhaps God chose Isaac instead of Ishmael because Ishmael mocked Isaac (Gen 21:9). One line was chosen by merit. But Paul goes one generation down to say otherwise.

Paul again presses home the point that salvation has nothing to do with status, works, or ethnicity, but rather it comes down to God's grace. Jacob and Esau not only had the same mother, but they also had the same father: Isaac. Furthermore, they were *twins!* Rebekah's twin sons were the product of one single act of conception (v. 10).

In verses 11-12 Paul highlights God's sovereign freedom. Jacob's story illustrates that salvation is not based on doing "bad or good" but based on God's electing grace (v. 11); and it illustrates that salvation is not based on works but on "the one who calls" (v. 12). God's sovereign freedom is also highlighted in that God promised, "The older will serve the younger," that is, the birth order was not the basis of salvation either. Jacob's status was the result of sovereign grace. What is more, God did not look into the future and see Jacob doing good deeds and on that basis decide to choose him, for Jacob was a deceiver.

So then, we see that salvation is not based on your descent or your good deeds. God did not choose us for anything good in us. Charles Spurgeon put it well:

> I believe in the doctrine of election, because I am quite sure that if God had not chosen me I never would have chosen him; and I am sure he chose me before I was born, or else he never would have chosen me afterward. (Spurgeon, *Lectures to My Students,* 227)

In Romans 9:13 Paul quotes Malachi 1:2-3. God chose to set his saving love on Jacob, not Esau. Moo points out that "hated" may be best understood as "rejected" in the context, since the focus is not so much on God's emotions but on God's actions (*Letter,* 587). We should also keep in mind that neither of them deserved to be saved. The context of Malachi is that the kingdom of Edom (descended from Esau) will suffer devastation, and their efforts to rebuild will be thwarted, whereas Jacob's descendants (Israel) have failed to be grateful, but they will still experience God's gracious restoration (Bird, *Romans,* 329). God set his love on Jacob, even though he did not deserve it.

Some modern interpreters take these names to mean "nations" or the "political fortunes" of Jacob and Esau, since in Malachi they represent nations. So they argue for "corporate election" in this text, not "individual salvation." I, however, agree with Moo and Schreiner that corporate idea is unlikely for several reasons (Schreiner, *Romans*, 501–3; Moo, *Letter*, 585–86). First, Paul has not left the topic of personal salvation (cf. vv. 1-5). He was not willing to be cut off from Christ because things were going bad politically or nationally; these verses are about salvation. Second, Paul uses the phrase "God's children" (v. 8), and Paul always uses that phrase in the context of salvation. Third, Paul uses the word "election" in verse 11, which usually has personal salvation in view. Fourth, Paul contrasts works/calling in verse 11, which is also personal salvation language (cf. 8:29-30). Fifth, Paul's question in verse 14, which follows this present paragraph, "Is there injustice in God?" and his subsequent answer in verses 15-18 have individual salvation in view, not corporate or national election. Finally, I do not think Paul would have rehearsed the details of the lives of Isaac and Jacob if he did not have personal salvation in mind. It is hard to imagine that he would shift to a corporate idea without any warning in verse 13.

Of course, affirming God's sovereign election does not mean we believe humans are puppets in God's hands, having no personal responsibility. We affirm several truths that are hard to reconcile; for example, Christ's divinity and humanity as well as the divine and human nature of Scripture. We also affirm God's sovereignty and human responsibility. They are friends, not foes. Remember: chapter 10 (which magnifies the necessity of personal belief) follows chapter 9!

So then, the point is clear: God's word has not failed. It was and is being fulfilled in an Israel within Israel. In sovereign freedom, God has always chosen a people for himself. And he continues to work out his sovereign purposes in history.

Truth 2: God's Ways Are Just and His Salvation Is Merciful
ROMANS 9:14-18

If you struggle with the idea of election, then you should know you are not the first to have questions! Paul, like a good teacher, anticipates a question: "What should we say then? Is there injustice with God?" Paul's empathic answer is "Absolutely not!" (v. 14).

Paul cannot fathom the thought of God being unjust. The Judge of all the earth always does what is right. To make this point, Paul again draws on Old Testament examples for proof.

In verses 15-18 Paul uses references from Exodus concerning God's mercy expressed to Moses and God's judgment on Pharaoh to address the issue of God's justice. He first appeals to God's sovereign freedom and mercy from Exodus 33:19. Far from unjust, God is merciful, gracious, and compassionate! No one deserves God's saving mercy, so if you are in Christ, you should praise God in humility and awe. John Stott puts it well:

> The wonder is not that some are saved and others not, but that anybody is saved at all. For we deserve nothing at God's hand but judgment. If we receive what we deserve (which is judgment), or if we receive what we do not deserve (which is mercy), in neither case is God unjust. If therefore anybody is lost, the blame is theirs, but if anybody is saved, the credit is God's. This antinomy contains a mystery which our present knowledge cannot solve; but it is consistent with Scripture, history and experience. (*Message*, 269–70)

As the kids would say today, "Mic drop."

Based on this reference from Exodus 33, Paul makes the point clear (v. 16). The word "it" stands for *salvation*—salvation does not depend on our willingness but on God's merciful action. Yes, we choose, but even that is a gift from God (Eph 2:8-10).

Paul then reaches further back in Exodus for another example of God's sovereignty in Exodus 9:16. God displayed his glory and publicized his name and power in the exodus event as Pharaoh refused to release Israel from bondage.

Following the same pattern as verses 15-16, Paul now (v. 18) makes an emphatic point based on this Exodus reference. God is free to leave some in rebellion, as he did with Pharaoh, and God is free to save others. God's actions are just. God is glorified in salvation and judgment. Again, Stott is helpful:

> The fact is, as Paul demonstrated in the early chapters of his letter, that all human beings are sinful and guilty in God's sight (3:9, 19), so that nobody deserves to be saved. If therefore God hardens some, he is not being unjust, for that is what their sin deserves. If, on the other hand, he has compassion on some, he is not being unjust, for he is dealing with them in mercy. (*Message*, 269)

Again, remember where all this is headed: to a doxology (11:33-36). If you are in Christ, you should give God glory for his mercy. And notice Romans 12:1-2. What attribute does Paul begin with? He says, "Therefore, brothers and sisters, *in view of the mercies of God*, I urge you to present your bodies as a living sacrifice" (12:1; emphasis added). In other words, God's mercy toward us in Christ should cause us to praise him with our lips and with our lives.

Truth 3: God Has the Right of a Potter over His Clay
ROMANS 9:19-23

Again, as a good teacher, Paul anticipates a follow-up question. He reflects on Old Testament imagery and texts to answer this particular question, also.

He anticipates this line of questioning: "You will say to me, therefore, 'Why then does he still find fault? For who resists his will?'" (v. 19). To ask it another way, "If God controls everything sovereignly, why does he still blame us?" Paul's response is interesting. He actually does not try to resolve the issue of divine sovereignty and human responsibility. (We should learn from him!) Rather, he gives a rebuke and then corrects the questioner's view of God. Paul is not opposed to humble questions, but he rebukes the proud individual who arrogantly refuses to believe in God's sovereignty.

In verses 20-21 he reminds the questioner that God has the right of a potter to shape his clay, and the clay has no right to talk back to the potter. Now Paul is playing offense. He has been playing defense in answer to the question about the success of God's word and about the justice of God. But now Paul raises the question, "Who are you . . . to talk back to God?" Paul reminds the objector of his or her creaturely status. Notice the phrase "a human being" (v. 20). Who do you think you are—with your limited knowledge and your sinful condition—to think you can tell Almighty God how to run the world? The proper attitude we should have is reflected elsewhere in Scripture, as in Psalm 115:3: "Our God is in heaven and does whatever he pleases."

Paul then alludes to a rich Old Testament background of a potter with his clay to illustrate God's work among people (Isa 29:16; 45:9; Jer 18:6-10; cf. Isa 10:15). Of course, humans are not mere lumps of clay, but the analogy is fitting: a potter is free. The clay does not make demands to the potter. So it is with God: he is free, and he has the right to do with the clay as he pleases. Some pots are used for honorable purposes, and others are used for dishonorable purposes.

So instead of talking back to God, the appropriate thing for us to do is bow down before God, the sovereign Potter. Like Moses we should take off our sandals, for we are on holy ground when we approach him. Like Job, after receiving God's rebuke, we put our hands over our mouths, and we submit to the godness of God (Job 42:1-6).

In verses 22-23 Paul goes on to say that God is merciful in salvation and just in his wrath. God "endured with much patience." God is patient, but he will exercise wrath, as Pharaoh experienced, and as those who have not bowed the knee to Christ will experience. Paul's statement about God's mercy demonstrates that mercy is most appreciated when considered against the backdrop of God's wrath (cf. Eph 2:3-4). So God acts in perfect accordance with his wrath and mercy. Both attributes glorify who he is.

Truth 4: God's Promises Include Many Gentiles and a Jewish Remnant
ROMANS 9:24-29

The shift from verse 23 to 24 is seamless, but there is a shift in emphasis as Paul cites more Old Testament texts to describe how believing Jews and Gentiles make up the people of God. God's choice of Israel and the remnant that was preserved always had the larger picture in mind: believing Gentiles from the nations.

Paul contends that God is free in dispensing his mercy, that God has chosen to include the Gentiles into his plan, and that this is the very thing he foretold in Scripture. God foretold the inclusion of the Gentiles and the exclusion of Israel except for a remnant. Again, God's word has not failed! God has called both Jew and Gentile to himself out of his free grace and mercy (v. 24). If anyone is saved, it is on the basis of God's grace, not one's ethnicity. What matters is grace, not race (Bird, *Romans*, 330). To summarize Romans 9:6-24, John Sailhamer states, "Not all Israelites are Israelites (vv. 6-8); not all Jews are God's chosen (v. 24); and not all God's chosen are Jews (v. 24)" (*NIV Compact Bible Commentary*, 529).

Paul uses two texts from the prophet Hosea to illustrate God's saving purposes. In verse 25 Paul cites Hosea 2:23; in verse 26 he cites Hosea 1:10a. Paul uses these two texts to support God's inclusion of the Gentiles. The promise in Hosea's day was directed to the northern kingdom of Israel, but Paul applies it to the Gentile believers. By God's gracious call, outsiders are made insiders; strangers are made family members. Consider your status, Christian: "Beloved." "My people." "Sons of the living God." All of this by God's sovereign grace. Glory to God!

Paul then uses a major prophet, Isaiah, to explain the inclusion of a Jewish remnant into the people of God. The background of both texts is one of national apostasy (Isa 1:2-15; 10:1-4), only this time from the southern kingdom of Judah. The people turned their backs on Yahweh, and they have been judged through the Assyrian invasion, so that only "a few survivors" remain (Isa 1:9). But God promises that Assyria will be punished for their arrogance (Isa 10:1-19) and that the believing remnant will return to the Lord (Isa 10:21-22; Stott, *Message*, 274). Paul will revisit this remnant idea in Romans 11:1-5. Bird says,

> What to take away for now is that the remnant is an important
> element as it shows that judgment has not overtaken Israel and
> there is an embryonic hope for the future of the rest of Israel.
> (*Romans*, 336)

The future of Israel will be teased out more in Romans 11:1-32.

By using both Hosea and Isaiah, Paul shows that God has called both Jew and Gentile to himself (v. 24). God preserved a remnant of Jewish believers within Israel and then expanded it to include the Gentiles as well (Bird, *Romans*, 335). This too proves Paul's thesis that God's word has not failed and that God's salvation is a work of God's sovereign grace and mercy:

> God's word has not been frustrated through the disbelief
> of the majority of Jews. He planned that only a remnant of
> Jews would believe and that many Gentiles would confess
> Jesus as Messiah in order to maximize his mercy (cf. 11:32).
> (Schreiner, *Romans*, 526)

Applications

What should we take away from this weighty chapter? After personal reflection on it, I would like to offer six exhortations.

First, share Paul's burden. Are you brokenhearted for those who are apart from Christ? This burden for those outside of Christ appears again in Romans 10:1. If Romans 9–11 does not give you a heart for lost people, you are not following the example of Paul. Let's share this burden.

Second, never doubt God's word. God's word never fails! Paul has gone to great lengths, with biblical example after biblical example, to prove his thesis in Romans 9:6 (cf. 1 Kgs 8:56). We can trust God's word!

Third, embrace the mystery of God's sovereignty and human responsibility. God is in control, and you are accountable. God is sovereign, and you must believe. This is a great mystery to affirm. The famous Charles Spurgeon line comes to mind. When someone asked him how to reconcile these ideas, Spurgeon said, "I never reconcile friends" ("High Doctrine and Broad Doctrine"). Doug Moo reminds us, "Divine sovereignty and human responsibility in salvation stand in some tension, but they are not logically contradictory" (*Romans*, 308). Or, as Spurgeon maintained, they're friends.

Fourth, allow this vision of God's sovereignty to increase your faith. As a Christian, you can rest in God's sovereignty as you live by faith. Because God is sovereign, you do not have to freak out. You can share the gospel with your friends, live out your faith in the midst of opposition, go to the nations with confidence, and trust God with every detail of life.

Romans 9 led thirty-four-year-old professor John Piper into the pastorate while he was writing a book on that chapter. He said that the Lord told him, in effect, "I will not simply be analyzed, I will be adored. I will not simply be pondered, I will be proclaimed. My sovereignty is not simply to be scrutinized, it is to be heralded" (Piper, "The Absolute Sovereignty of God"). If you believe in the God of Romans 9, you too will be driven to attempt great things for the glory of God—perhaps even risky things for his glory. But you can do this with confidence, knowing that God is sovereign. A big God will lead to big faith. Romans 9 helps us elevate our vision of his greatness.

Fifth, bow down before God's majesty. Remember where all of this is headed: Romans 11:33-36. This God is worthy of our devotion and our worship. So let's put away earthly trinkets and marvel at the majesty and wisdom of God here.

Finally, never get over the wonder of God's saving mercy and grace. May God's mercy and sovereign grace break you of ingratitude and cause you to praise him wholeheartedly. Praise him with your lips, and praise him with your life:

Chosen not for good in me,
Wakened up from wrath to flee,
Hidden in the Savior's side,
By the Spirit sanctified—
Teach me, Lord, on earth to show,
By my love, how much I owe.
—Robert Murray M'Cheyne

Reflect and Discuss

1. Why should we see Romans 9–11 as a unit?
2. Explain the unique emphases in each chapter: 9, 10, and 11.
3. How does Paul feel about his unbelieving, Jewish kinsmen (9:1-5)? What does Paul teach us about a burden for lost people here?
4. What privileges does Paul say the Jews possess (vv. 1-5)?
5. What does Paul mean when he says, "Not all who are descended from Israel are Israel" (v. 6)?
6. List the Old Testament texts that Paul cites in Romans 9. Why is Paul citing so many texts?
7. How does Paul defend the doctrine of election in verses 7-13?
8. How does Paul defend God's justice in verses 14-18?
9. What does Paul say about God's rights as the potter over his clay (vv. 19-23)?
10. What does Paul say about the Jewish remnant and the believing Gentiles in verses 24-29?

The Faithful Evangelist

ROMANS 9:30–10:21

Main Idea: Paul's heart for unbelieving Israel, his teaching on the necessity of faith in Christ, and his emphasis on the urgency of proclaiming Christ give us instruction and inspiration for modern-day evangelism.

I.   The Intensity of Paul's Burden (9:30–10:4)
II. The Necessity of Faith in Christ (10:5-13)
III. The Urgency of Proclaiming Christ (10:14-21)

Who was the first person to show you the beauty of Jesus? I was recently asked this question, and it seems like a good opening question for this portion of Romans. Here, Paul commends those with "beautiful feet," who faithfully proclaim the good news of Jesus to others. It is a wonderful passage for encouraging us to be faithful gospel witnesses in today's world.

My mother took me to church services at a young age, and through her witness and those in the church body, gospel seeds were planted. I watched her read the Bible every day. I watched her care for those in need. I watched her pray. I listened to her counsel me with Scripture. I did not start following Jesus until college, and when that happened, my relationship with my mother deepened. When I went to seminary, I would call her at least once a week to tell her all that I was learning.

While my mother was the first person to show me the beauty of Jesus, she was not the only one the Lord used to bring me to faith. I went to college to play baseball. I loved baseball but was not very interested in school. I certainly was not interested in Jesus. My mother made me take my Bible to college, but I did not open it until I was a sophomore. When I arrived on campus, I had no desire to study Scripture or pursue spiritual things. But the Lord placed two guys on my team—a second baseman named Stephen and a pitcher named Kenny—who showed me the beauty of Jesus. There were other faithful Christians on the team, and on our campus too, but these two guys (who were roommates with each other) were the spiritual leaders on our team. I would reluctantly go to church services with them. I remember one particular Sunday when I was watching Stephen taking notes. I watched in amazement at how a guy my age was actually interested in the Bible and sermons. Kenny was like him in this regard. I also would listen to them talk to my teammates about the faith in a way that I had never encountered. They gave good arguments for the faith, and they were also filled with grace. I felt safe around them, as if I could ask them any question I had. During my sophomore year I found myself searching for meaning, freedom, and joy. I sensed the Lord dealing with me. After my conversations with Stephen and Kenny, and after I attended some campus ministry events, the Lord brought me to himself.

These gospel witnesses never did anything sensational. They simply lived out their faith in the ordinary rhythm of life and had gospel conversations with me. I was not looking for Jesus, but God used these witnesses to open my eyes and draw me to the Savior. These witnesses did what every genuine Christian should do: commend Christ to unbelievers. God in his grace uses the word of Christ to bring people to faith in Christ (Rom 10:17).

Romans 9–11 deals with the problem of Jewish unbelief (Stott, *Message*, 279). After discussing God's sovereign purposes in the first part of chapter 9, Paul now focuses on human factors: the necessity of belief and the urgency of evangelism. In chapter 11 Paul will address the question of Israel's future belief.

While the passage has a focus on Israel, Romans 10 also has a broader application. There is something here for both the believer and the unbeliever. For the unbeliever, this passage shows that everyone, regardless of ethnicity and background, must believe in Christ in order to be saved. The focus on Israel gives particular relevance to the *religious* person who has yet to believe in Jesus for salvation. It is possible to be religious and miss out on God's gracious salvation. Regarding the believer, this passage shows us the priority of evangelism. Paul reveals the heart, the theology, and the practice of a faithful evangelist. Let's keep these things in mind as we consider the text in three parts.

The Intensity of Paul's Burden
ROMANS 9:30–10:4

Paul opens this section discussing Israel's failure to attain salvation and the Gentiles' experience of it. The majority of Jews trusted in their own religious works for salvation. They sought their own righteousness rather than receiving righteousness through faith in Jesus. The Gentiles did not obtain right standing by strict Torah observance, as indicated by the phrase "did not pursue righteousness" (v. 30). But they did obtain right standing with God by faith in the Messiah. Over and over Paul has been arguing that justification is obtained by faith alone (1:16-17; 3:22; 4:1-25; 5:1-11). This salvation is universally offered to the world.

Look again at verses 31-32. Paul states that Israel has pursued the wrong means of salvation in the wrong manner. They pursued "the law of righteousness" (v. 31)—that is, "they pursued a law for the purpose of righteousness, but did not succeed in attaining such a law or the righteousness they were looking for" (Bird, *Romans*, 347). What they ultimately needed was a righteous status that is attained by "faith," not by "works" (v. 32).

Paul adds that the majority of Israelites have actually "stumbled" over the right means of salvation: Jesus (v. 32). The apostle then adds a quotation from Isaiah 28:16: "Look, I am putting a stone in Zion to stumble over and a rock to trip over, and the one who believes on him will not be put to shame" (v. 33). God provided the way of salvation in Christ, but Israel failed to receive him. Salvation is centered on Jesus Christ. If you miss him, you miss salvation.

Paul says those who believe in Christ "will not be put to shame." By implication, some will be humiliated when they one day realize that they rejected the offer of salvation in Jesus.

This paragraph reminds us of how many people tragically try to find *one's own way* of salvation rather than looking to *the one way* of salvation. Works-based righteousness seems to be the default approach of the human heart. We cannot earn God's grace with religious rituals and good deeds, yet look at the world's religions and consider how many people live under oppressive works-based systems. The good news of the gospel is that Jesus Christ lived the life we could never live, obeying God perfectly, then died the death we should have died, and rose conquering the enemies we could not conquer. Now, by faith in him, we can have right standing with God. Works-based salvation is a dead-end road. Faith in Christ is the road to life and glory.

In Romans 10:1-4 Paul expresses an intense burden for Israel (cf. 9:1-5). We should never look down our noses at those who are apart from Christ. The proper heart attitude is heartbrokenness, not an air of superiority. Grace should humble us, and it should cause us to long for others to know the saving grace of God too. When we sing songs of

God's grace, we should long for the unbelievers around the world to sing songs of praise also (cf. Ps 67). And grace should cause us to pray like Paul (10:1). While Paul is praying for unbelieving Israel in particular, I think there is a general principle here for us to apply. To be an evangelist like Paul, we need to learn to pray for the salvation of others. C. S. Lewis quipped,

> I have two lists of names in my prayers, those for whose conversion I pray and those for whose conversion I give thanks. The little trickle of transferences from List A to List B is a great comfort. (in Ryken, "C. S. Lewis the Evangelist," 8)

May the Lord use us to help people transfer from list A to list B!

In verse 2 Paul adds to his list of reasons for Jewish unbelief. Paul does not question their zeal. He questions their decision making. They have not been zealous for the right thing, or we should say, for the right person, Jesus Christ. They were zealous for the law, the interpretation and application of the law, and for the Jewish way of life. To the Philippians, Paul shared his story of once having the same zeal (Phil 3:2-11). But eventually Paul saw the light, trusted in the Messiah, and had his zeal properly directed to the glory of Christ. He remained intense, but his passion became Christ centered (cf. Phil 1:21).

One of the common ideas promoted in our pluralistic society is, "It doesn't matter what you believe, just be sincere." That sounds nice, but how does that correspond to Romans 10:2? These unbelieving Jews were sincere. They were zealous! And they were sincerely wrong, according to Paul. As *The Message* paraphrases, "They are doing everything exactly backward." They were like the football player, Jim "Wrong Way" Marshall, who in 1964 recovered a fumble and ran over sixty yards for a touchdown—to the wrong end zone! He ran hard. He was zealous. But his running was not according to knowledge. We should pray for our unbelieving friends who are headed in the wrong direction.

In verse 3 Paul shows why Israel's knowledge was deficient. Notice the charge of ignorance. That is quite a charge for those who studied the Torah passionately. But that same charge appears in the early church's preaching (Acts 3:17). Paul could relate to such hostility and ignorance. He said of his preconverted life, "I acted out of ignorance in unbelief" (1 Tim 1:13). But the Lord saved him by grace (1 Tim 1:14-16), and that kind of transformation is what Paul longs to see in his Jewish kinsmen.

Paul wraps up this section and prepares us for the next one, exalting the saving provision of Christ (v. 4). Moo comments,

As Christ consummates one era of salvation history, so he inaugurates a new one. In this new era, God's eschatological righteousness is available to those who believe; and it is available to everyone who believes. Because the Jews have not understood that Christ has brought the law to its culmination, they have not responded in faith to Christ; and they have therefore missed the righteousness of God, available only in Christ on the basis of faith. (*Letter*, 641)

Verse 4, then, is a hinge verse for Paul, as he underscores Jewish preoccupation with the law and their refusal to accept the Messiah while also preparing the way for his statements about the accessibility of salvation for all who believe (vv. 5-13; Moo, *Letter*, 641).

It is possible to be a lost religious person or a lost irreligious person. One can be lost in legalism, or one can be lost in hedonism. Whether you are a rule follower or a rule breaker, Christ alone saves. The focus of this text is on the religious person who seeks salvation the wrong way— through religious works. The next paragraph shows you what you must do: believe on the Lord Jesus alone and be saved!

As believers, we should reflect on the posture of our hearts toward unbelievers. Consider the intensity of Paul's burden. Think about the people in your networks—people in your neighborhood, in your workplace, at your school, where you shop, where you play, and in your family. Can you say, "My heart's desire and prayer to God concerning them is for their salvation"? To step up our commitment to evangelism, we need to start here: our hearts. Jesus was moved with "compassion" as he looked at the shepherdless crowds of people (Matt 9:35-38). Let's pray for our unbelieving friends; and let's pray for the Lord of the harvest to send out laborers across the world.

The Necessity of Faith in Christ
ROMANS 10:5-13

Because of the work of Christ, Paul describes how right standing with God is accessible and available. He continues to contrast righteousness based on doing the law (v. 5) with the righteousness of God that is based on faith (vv. 6-13). Strikingly, Paul once again appeals to the Old Testament to make his claims in order to show the Jews that his teaching is consistent with the Scriptures. He also reveals a robust Christ-centered view of the Scriptures in his selection and application of texts.

In verse 5 Paul continues the thought of verse 4 as he quotes
Leviticus 18:5, where it says, "The one who does these things will live
by them" (cf. Gal 3:12). That is, if a person could keep the whole law
perfectly, that person would gain eternal life. From both the immediate context and the wider context of Romans, we know that no matter how virtuous a person is, he or she will not attain life in this way
because we all violate the law (1:18–3:20). The law, then, does not save
us by helping us to fulfill it. Rather, it points us to the law fulfiller and
Savior, Jesus Christ.

Righteousness based on faith (and not the law) is different. We cannot attain salvation by the law, and the good news is that we do not have
to! Paul says, "Do not say in your heart, 'Who will go up to heaven?'
that is, to bring Christ down or, 'Who will go down into the abyss?' that
is, to bring Christ up from the dead" (vv. 6-7). Drawing on more Old
Testament references (see "say to yourself" in Deut 9:4; and "heaven"
and "sea" in Deut 30:12-13), Paul says that righteousness by faith
looks away from self and looks to God's provision in Christ. Paul reads
Deuteronomy 30 in light of the new covenant, and in view of the whole
story line of Scripture, to show that Christ has fulfilled the law for us.
He died on behalf of us, thereby taking the curse for us, giving life and
blessing to us (cf. Deut 28–30; Gal 3:10-14). Paul omits the words "so
that we may follow it" from Deuteronomy 30:12-13, and he also inserts
"Christ" to the quotation when speaking of descending into the deep
and in being raised. He does this to show us that we cannot do it, but
God has done it *in Christ*. Paul reads the Bible with a Christ-centered
perspective. We cannot descend and be raised on our own, but Christ
has done it for us! By faith in Jesus, salvific blessing belongs to those who
have faith in him.

Paul only quotes a small part of Deuteronomy 9:4 when he says,
"Do not say in your heart" (Rom 10:6), but the rest of that passage is
significant because it supports what Paul is teaching about salvation by
faith. In Deuteronomy 9 God says that Israel is *not* going to enter the
land because of *their righteousness* but because of *his promise*—that is,
because of *God's grace and faithfulness* (Deut 9:4-5). Saving faith recognizes that righteousness does not come from ourselves, for we cannot
keep God's law perfectly (Rom 10:5); it is by God's grace alone through
faith alone that we are saved.

In verse 8 Paul quotes Deuteronomy 30 again (Deut 30:14). Paul
takes this claim in Deuteronomy and reads it in light of the whole story

line of Scripture, essentially saying that this word is the gospel; it is "the message of faith." One must believe the content of the gospel, the Christ of the gospel, which is what Paul declares in verse 9.

Reflecting back on 10:2, notice the focus is not on *the zeal* or *the degree* of one's faith but on *the object* of one's faith. We are saved by faith in someone—the Messiah. We are saved by sincerely believing in the crucified and risen Christ. At the heart of our faith is the lordship of Jesus. Therefore, saving faith says, "I believe the risen Jesus is Lord." Mike Bird summarizes the importance of Romans 10:9:

> This verse is perhaps the best explanation of what it means to be a Christian. A Christian is someone who professes to live under submission of King Jesus and believes that God has acted in Jesus to usher in the age to come. . . . At the time of Paul's writing, one can find inscriptions, papyri, and ostraca all attesting that "Nero is Lord," even the grandiose claim that "Nero, the Lord of the entire world" [sic]. (*Romans*, 359)

But the believer knows there is one Lord, Jesus Christ, and salvation comes through faith in him alone. This means resting on him fully and solely and committing one's self to follow him as King.

In verse 10 Paul reinforces his point on faith. Real saving faith arises from the heart and is professed through one's mouth. Paul then supports this claim in verse 11 by quoting Isaiah 28:16. Again, trusting in Christ for salvation is contrasted with works righteousness. The "shame" in view here seems to be end-time humiliation. Those who do not trust in Christ now will eventually be ashamed in judgment. Paul knows that the believer in Christ, on the other hand, will eventually be delivered and honored—though he or she may experience shame in this life (cf. Rom 1:16).

Paul has already mentioned the universal offer of the gospel in verses 4 and 11, but now he underlines it again. He states that the offer of salvation by faith in Christ is available to every person and to every ethnic group (vv. 12-13). Previously, Paul taught that every person, both Jew and Gentile, is guilty before God (1:18–3:20). Here he states that anyone can be saved through faith in Christ.

Notice the phrase "richly blesses" (10:12; Eph 1:7; 2:7). God bestows riches on those who call on him. But one must confess Christ as Lord to enjoy these blessings. One must admit that he or she cannot attain righteousness by the law but only through faith in Christ.

Verse 12 reminds us of God's promise to Abraham. God will have a people from all nations, and they will live under the Messiah's rule and reign. Today we have a foretaste of that day as we worship with people from various backgrounds. We get to be in community with diverse believers who call Jesus "Lord."

Verse 13 is a citation from Joel 2:32. Paul takes Joel's reference of "Lord" (Yahweh) to apply to *Jesus*. This verse thus supports not only a proper soteriology (salvation through faith alone) but also a proper Christology (Jesus is the fully divine Son of God).

Therefore, Paul has gone to great pains to show us that salvation is by faith alone. His message is consistent with Scripture. It is focused on the Messiah. It is a message offered to the world. And this good news unites believers from diverse backgrounds.

To be a faithful witness in this world, we need not only a *burden* for unbelievers (10:1), but we also need this *theological conviction* that a person must believe on Christ to be saved. I have heard Christians through the years deny this notion when pressed on it. When questioned about the exclusivity of the gospel, some are functional universalists. They think that on the last day God will be like a nice grandpa and let everyone into heaven. But you cannot hold this position if you follow Paul's line of thinking in Romans 10. While some Christians lack the heart of an evangelist, some lack the theological conviction. We need both. And we need what Paul addresses next: *a sense of urgency*.

The Urgency of Evangelism
ROMANS 10:14-21

Paul stresses the urgency of proclaiming the good news by weaving together various Old Testament passages. He first asks a series of rhetorical questions to emphasize the priority of evangelism, and then he draws on Isaiah (52:7; 53:1; 65:1-2), Psalm 19, and Deuteronomy 30 to support his various arguments related to evangelism.

He asks these rhetorical questions (vv. 14-15a). John Stott wisely notes that if we put these verbs in the opposite order then we will see the essence of Paul's argument: "Christ sends heralds; heralds preach; people hear; hearers believe; believers call; and those who call are saved" (*Message*, 286). Unless people are sent, the good news will not be announced. If the news is not announced, no one will hear. If no one hears, no one will believe the gospel; no one will call on the Lord and be saved. Therefore, messengers are essential!

Because of the importance of gospel messengers, Paul quotes Isaiah 52:7 (cf. Nah 1:15) to honor those who are faithfully proclaiming the gospel regularly: "How beautiful are the feet of those who bring good news" (Rom 10:15). The way to have beautiful feet is not through a pedicure but through proclamation! Leon Morris writes,

> Messengers normally travelled on foot and the feet were the significant members. They might be dirty and smell after a long, hot journey, but to those who eagerly awaited good news they were beautiful. (*Epistle*, 390–91)

In former days, one may have rejoiced at the arrival of a messenger who brought good news regarding deliverance from an enemy nation; but now, gospel messengers are bringing even better news of Christ's victory over sin and death.

While we must proclaim the gospel faithfully, Paul adds that the hearers must respond to the gospel rightly (v. 16). So, while hearing the gospel is necessary for faith, it does not guarantee faith. Paul says that while messengers have been sent out, not everyone responds to that message with an obedience that springs from faith (cf. 1:5; 16:26). Paul quotes Isaiah 53:1 to reinforce the point that not everyone will trust in the Messiah. Read through Paul's synagogue sermons in Acts, and you will find much Jewish hostility rather than positive receptivity.

But we must keep proclaiming the gospel faithfully because "faith comes from what is heard, and what is heard comes through the message about Christ" (v. 17). While Paul could discuss opposition, he also knew what it was like to see people respond in saving faith when the message about the crucified and risen Christ was proclaimed (cf. Acts 13:48; 16:14; 17:34; 19:18).

In verses 18-21 Paul speaks first about the general rejection of the gospel in the world and then about Israel's particular rejection. In noting Israel's rejection, Paul also includes a word about Israel's jealousy over Gentile belief (setting the stage for chapter 11).

Paul cites Psalm 19:4 to support the idea that the "world" has heard (v. 18). Paul seems to be using "world" here to mean the spread of the gospel in the world in general (cf. Col 1:6,23). Later, Paul says he wants to go to Spain, where Christ has not been preached (Rom 15:24), so he knew of parts of the world that needed to hear the gospel. But speaking broadly, the gospel was going out to the whole world, including to the Gentiles, which meant that the Jews had heard the gospel too.

Psalm 19 is usually used to describe "general revelation" (how creation testifies to the Creator; cf. Rom 1:18-32); but here Paul cites it as referring to special revelation (the gospel) being proclaimed throughout the world. Schreiner seems on target in saying, "God's general revelation thus functions as a type and anticipation of the gospel message that extends to all peoples" (*Romans*, 572). Stott states a similar position, drawing attention to the church's call to be worldwide witnesses:

> Paul of course knew this perfectly well [the original context of Ps 19]. It is entirely gratuitous to conclude that he misremembered, misunderstood or misrepresented his text. It seems perfectly reasonable to suggest that he was transferring eloquent biblical language about global witness from creation to the church, taking the former as symbolic of the latter. If God wants the general revelation of his glory to be universal, how much more must he want the special revelation of his grace to be universal too! (*Message*, 288–89)

Indeed, and what a privilege it is to share with the world the special revelation of God's grace in Jesus Christ!

Paul then argues that Israel did not understand God's plan for including the nations in his salvific purposes. He first quotes Deuteronomy 32:21: "Moses said, I will make you jealous of those who are not a nation; I will make you angry by a nation that lacks understanding" (Rom 10:19). Paul reads Moses's song as a prophecy that the Gentiles will come to faith, leaving Israel jealous. This point will be picked up in Romans 11, as it factors in significantly to the future of Israel.

Paul then quotes from Isaiah 65:1: "I was found by those who were not looking for me; I revealed myself to those who were not asking for me." Again, it is the same idea of Gentile acceptance and Jewish rejection. The majority of Israel rejected God's blessings, so God found a people far off. But this too was part of the plan announced to Abraham (Gen 12:1-3); therefore, God's word has not failed (Rom 9:6).

By quoting Isaiah 65:2, "All day long I have held out my hands to a disobedient and defiant people" (Rom 10:21), Paul again draws attention to the sadness of Israel's rejection. Why did they reject the good news? He has been telling us: They pursued saving righteousness by the law, not through faith in the Messiah. This is dramatic imagery: like a father inviting a child home and offering a warm hug and welcome,

God stretched out his arms to Israel, pleading with them to come home (Stott, *Message*, 289).

Looking back over verses 14-21, it is important to see God's plan for the nations and the urgency of evangelism. God will have a people for himself "from every tribe and language and people and nation" (Rev 5:9), and he is accomplishing this plan through gospel proclamation. "The gospel is only good news if it gets there on time" (usually attributed to Carl F. H. Henry) is a saying worth reflecting on. How will people believe unless they hear? Whether it is across the street or across the seas, let's commend the beauty of Jesus to others with a sense of urgency.

Looking back over the whole passage, Paul shows us *the heart* of a faithful evangelist, *the theology* that drives a faithful evangelist, and *the practice* of a faithful evangelist. This passage emphasizes human responsibility, but it is tucked in between two chapters that emphasize God's sovereignty, showing us that these two truths (responsibility and sovereignty) are not at odds with each other. With brokenhearted compassion and Christ-exalting passion, let's prayerfully proclaim the gospel to unbelievers and leave the results to our sovereign God, who brings the dead to life through the word of Christ.

Reflect and Discuss

1. Who was the first person to show you the beauty of Jesus?
2. How does Paul contrast righteousness by the law and righteousness by faith?
3. How do people today try to earn salvation through works? How does this passage address this problem?
4. How does Paul express his burden for his unbelieving Jewish kinsmen? How might you follow his example?
5. Explain how Paul gives a Christ-centered reading of the Old Testament in 10:5-12.
6. What does Paul say about the offer of the gospel for the world? How does this inform our view of missions?
7. How does Paul stress the importance of evangelism in this passage?
8. Go back and read Isaiah 52:7 and think about how Paul uses it here in Romans 10. How might you have "beautiful feet" today?
9. How does Paul prepare us for Romans 11 by speaking of Israel's jealousy and Gentile belief in 10:19-21?

10. Paul shows us the heart (burden/prayer), the theology (necessity of faith in Christ), and the practice (actually proclaiming the gospel) of a faithful evangelist. Which of these three do you need help with? Do you struggle more with having a heart for lost people, believing the exclusive claims of the gospel, or actually commending with boldness the good news? Have a discussion with a Christian friend about these things and pray for the Lord to make you a more faithful witness.

From Theology to Doxology

ROMANS 11

Main Idea: Paul explains the outworking of God's saving purposes in redemptive history, with particular emphasis on the future of Israel, and concludes by praising God with a glorious hymn.

I. **God Has a People, Chosen by Grace (11:1-10).**
   A. A personal example (11:1)
   B. A theological truth (11:2a)
   C. A scriptural example (11:2b-4)
   D. An application of the example (11:5-6)
   E. A recap of Israel's failure (11:7-10)
II. **God Will Continue Working Out His Saving Purposes in the Future (11:11-32).**
   A. Israel's rejection, Gentile inclusion, and gospel jealousy (11:11-15)
   B. Redemptive history, the olive tree, and Gentile arrogance (11:16-24)
   C. The mystery of Israel's future salvation (11:25-32)
III. **God Deserves the Glory Forever (11:33-36).**

Recently at a conference I was telling a young man that our church was studying Romans. He told me that his church was studying Romans also. But when his pastor made it to Romans 11, the pastor said, "Romans 11 is just too hard. I don't know what to say about it, and our VBS is coming up, so let's just pray about that and pick up with Romans 12 next time." So they totally skipped Romans 11!

I can sympathize with this pastor. Peter said that some of the things Paul wrote are hard to understand (2 Pet 3:15-16). Romans 11 would classify as a difficult portion of Pauline material, to be sure. But we need to engage it because it is God's Word and because it is such an important section in the book of Romans as a whole.

What is Romans 11 about? This passage is speaking about the outworking of God's saving purposes in redemptive history, with particular emphasis on the future of Israel.

You may wonder, *How is this lofty concept practical?* Let me go ahead and state four reasons this passage is practically significant for believers. *First, it is relevant for our evangelism.* You cannot read chapter 11 as a whole—or Romans 9–11 for that matter—without feeling Paul's passion for people to be saved! This entire discussion is based on a burden, a concern, for people to be saved. If Romans 9–11 does not lead you to zeal for evangelism, then you are ignoring Paul's example and burden.

Second, it is relevant for our unity. Paul is writing to the church in Rome, which was made up of both Gentiles and Jews, with the majority being Gentiles. So if you ask, Why is chapter 11 important for me, a Gentile? then realize that Paul apparently thought the Gentiles needed to hear it! Why? Because he desired unity in the church. The following chapters of Romans will draw out Paul's desire for unity. This chapter helps lay the foundation for that unity.

Third, it is relevant for our hope. This text should give us hope for the future. God is in control of human history, including the affairs of our day, and that should encourage us!

Finally, it is relevant for our worship. In the end Paul bows before the infinite wisdom and matchless mercy of God and worships. So should we. Good theology should lead to heartfelt doxology.

As we begin with these things in mind, consider the context. Chapter 10 ends with God holding out his hands to stubborn Israel (10:21). Now the apostle addresses the future destiny of the Jews. In the first part of chapter 11, he addresses the present situation of Israel (11:1-10). There is a remnant of believing Jews. In the second part of the chapter, he addresses the future hope of Israel (vv. 11-32). He then ends with a glorious doxology (vv. 33-36). Consider three truths that we glean from the three parts of this chapter.

God Has a People, Chosen by Grace
ROMANS 11:1-10

Paul begins with a question: "Has God rejected his people?" After all, they have stumbled over the stumbling stone (9:32). Is it over? Is hope gone? Answer: "Absolutely not!" God will never reject Israel totally. Paul then goes on to give three proofs to undergird his answer.

A Personal Example (11:1b)

Paul grounds his answer in the fact that he is an Israelite! He (as well as some other Jewish kinsmen) embraced Jesus as the Messiah.

A Theological Truth (11:2a)

Paul adds, "God has not rejected his people whom he foreknew" (cf. 1 Sam 12:22; Ps 94:14). Foreknowing involves God's choosing. It involves a relationship of love. It involves God's commitment to his people. God cannot "unknow the people whom he knows are his" (Rom 8:29; Bird, *Romans*, 381). Paul reminds the Romans that God is working out his electing purposes in history (cf. 9:6) with an Israel within Israel.

A Scriptural Example (11:2b-4)

Paul appeals to the famous Elijah story involving Mount Carmel. In Elijah's day the majority of Israel had turned away from God. But not all of them. After Elijah's mighty victory on Mount Carmel, he fled from Jezebel to Mount Horeb, where he lamented that he was the "only one left" among disobedient Israel (1 Kings 19). But the Lord assured Elijah that seven thousand men had not bowed the knee to Baal—even though the majority of Israel had indeed rebelled against Yahweh.

An Application of the Example (11:5-6)

Paul says what was true in Elijah's day is true in Paul's day. Just as God preserved a remnant in Elijah's day, he had a Messiah-embracing remnant now, even though the vast majority had rejected him (cf. 9:27-29). Schreiner points out here the need to always link "grace" with the doctrine of election:

> Many worry that the choosing of some and not all would be unjust, but this idea overlooks the fact that election is gracious. No one deserves to be elected, and thus the election of any is a merciful gift of God that cannot be claimed as a democratic right. (*Romans*, 582)

God graciously chose a remnant in Elijah's day, and the God of grace had done so in Paul's day as well.

In verse 6 Paul underscores the nature of grace again. Paul says that this grace ceases to be grace if someone mixes it with works. If anyone is ever converted—whether Jew or Gentile—it is by the grace of God, not human performance (cf. 9:16). Let's rejoice in the saving grace of God! This leads to the larger question of unbelieving Israel. Is there any hope for them? Yes! Paul says there is a remnant now, and, as Paul will go on to describe, there will be a greater number of believers in the future (v. 12). This chapter starts with a remnant but expands to include many more Jews.

These verses about the remnant should also motivate us to *be faithful.* While we may each at times feel like we are the only Christian around— at work, in our school, in secular cities, or among unreached people groups—we should remember the example of Elijah and Paul's words here. God is at work around the world forming a people for himself, by his grace and for his glory; and it is good to be in that number. Be faithful even when it seems like you are alone. Be OK with being different, with being set apart. This is far more important than being cool, or popular, or successful. Live for God's glory above all things.

A Recap of Israel's Failure (11:7-10)

Paul begins by asking what the remnant idea has to say about Israel as a whole. He alludes to 9:30-32, where the majority of Israel wrongly pursued works-based righteousness. However, the elect within Israel obtained righteousness because they trusted in Christ (9:30; 10:6,8-11; 11:20). Paul says that those who have not believed are "hardened." That is a judicial act of God. He then cites Deuteronomy 29:4; Isaiah 29:10; and Psalm 69:22-23 to support the idea of spiritual blindness that exists among many (Rom 11:8-10). A lot of Jews were persisting in this kind of unbelief. And this is the case today, as the vast number of Jews do not believe in Jesus as Messiah.

Before moving to the next part of Romans 11, we should recognize Paul's emphasis on grace. We are saved by grace alone through faith alone in Christ alone (cf. Rom 3:21-26; Eph 2:8-9). Yet this is not the default understanding of the human heart. People will try everything to get rid of their guilt and to deal with an unsettled conscience: therapy, exercise, diets, medicine, and exotic trips. Or they will adopt a works-based religion. Or perhaps they will give up and just self-medicate. But you cannot drink your guilt away; you cannot burn your guilt off with plank walks and jumping jacks or yoga; you cannot work it off with job performance, with more education, or through more religious rituals. We are saved by undiluted grace, God's unmerited favor to those who repent and place their faith in the Messiah. Christian, stand in grateful awe that God extended grace in Christ to you.

God Will Continue Working Out His Saving Purposes in the Future
ROMANS 11:11-32

In verse 1 Paul asked if Israel's rejection was *total*. In verses 11-32 he asks whether it was *final* (Stott, *Message*, 291). Paul argues that Israel has not fallen to irreversible ruin. Are they down for the count? Is this a permanent fall? "Absolutely not!" The same answer in verse 1 is expressed here in verse 11: No! Israel's rejection *is not total, and it is not final.*

Israel's Rejection, Gentile Inclusion, and Gospel Jealousy (11:11-15)

Ethnic Israel's fall does not mean they have no hope in the future. Paul shows the interlocking destinies of Jews and Gentiles. Israel's rejection of Jesus has given occasion for the Gentiles to believe on him and be saved (cf. Acts 13:44-48). Paul borrows from Deuteronomy 32:21, saying that the Gentiles' salvation is not the end of the matter. It is intended to "make Israel jealous" (v. 11; cf. 10:19). This is a positive form of jealousy, not a sinful jealousy. In Deuteronomy 32:21 jealousy was intended as a curse, but here it becomes a means of drawing Israel back to God (Bird, *Romans*, 384). Gospel jealousy can provoke an "I want in on the riches of Christ!" mentality. What sticks out here is that God really does want to save Israel.

Paul continues by saying that Israel's full inclusion will bring greater blessings to the Gentiles. If Israel's loss meant the Gentiles' gain, Paul infers that Israel's future gain will bring mega-gain to the Gentiles (v. 12). The Gentiles will not lose out when Israel enters the Messiah's family; they will be richly blessed!

In verses 13-14 Paul adds to the point about gospel jealousy by talking about his own ministry. So then, Paul desires to make unbelieving Israel jealous. The spiritual riches of the Gentiles may serve to provoke the Jews to belief. And Paul wants to see them saved. That is the passion of Paul—to see people put saving faith in the Messiah (cf. 1 Cor 9:20-23).

Paul gets back to the main argument in verse 15, that is, the interlocking destinies of Israel and the Gentiles. Israel's rejection gives occasion

for the Gentiles to be reconciled to God—a blessing for the nations. That
has already been stated (v. 12), but what does this last phrase mean: "life
from the dead" (v. 15)? It is quite mysterious. Most likely, Paul is saying
that Israel's coming to faith in the future will be so dramatic that it will be
like a resurrection (Bird, *Romans*, 385). So hope for the future is held out.

Ponder this idea of gospel jealousy. There is a sinful form of jealousy. James calls it "demonic" envy (Jas 3:13-16). We must resist this,
obviously. But gospel jealousy is different. One might argue that prior
to conversion, Paul was "jealous" of Stephen. Did Stephen's faith create a sense of longing in Paul's heart? Whether or not it did, we know
that many unbelievers are drawn to Christ through the attractive witness of believers, who possess great joy in their relationship with Christ.
Many see the faith of others and say, "I want in on that!" This is one of
the goals of preaching—to portray Christ as being so lovely, satisfying,
and sufficient that unbelievers say, "I want to know this Christ!" We also
do this when we sing. Corporate singing not only edifies believers, but
it may also impact outsiders, creating in them a hunger to know this
Christ. The question we need to ask ourselves as Christians is whether
we are deriving so much pleasure in Christ that other people want what
we have. I am not talking about being boastful or showy—quite the
opposite. I mean genuinely adoring Christ, in good times and bad, so
that others are compelled to ask questions and seek answers, becoming
like the jailor who asked the persecuted-yet-singing Paul and Silas, "Sirs,
what must I do to be saved?" (Acts 16:30).

Redemptive History, the Olive Tree, and Gentile Arrogance (11:16-24)

In verses 16-24 Paul discusses God's purposes and Gentile arrogance.
He continues talking about Israel's future hope with an illustration of
an olive tree. The olive tree represents the people of God. The root represents the patriarchal promises. The natural branches refer to ethnic
Israel. The wild olive shoot refers to the Gentiles (Bird, *Romans*, 386).

In verse 16 the apostle begins with some language about botany
and bread to prove that what is true of part of something is true for the
whole. This is a transitional thought. It reflects back on verses 10-15,
where Paul links the destinies of Jew and Gentile together, and it looks
ahead to the upcoming olive tree illustration. The general point of verse
16 is that "the qualities associated with an item's germinal state extends
[sic] to its germane parts" (Bird, *Romans*, 387).

Paul then applies the olive tree illustration (vv. 17-18). So "some of the branches" (ethnic Israel) may have been "broken off" (due to their stumbling over the stumbling stone and their unbelief and hardness), but the "wild olive branch" (Gentile Christians) has been "grafted in" to share in its nutrients (salvation in Christ). But notice Paul's emphasis. He does not want the Gentiles to "boast" over the broken-off branches, that is, over unbelieving Israel. What they should see instead is their place in salvation history. Believing Gentiles stand on the shoulders of the Hebrew patriarchs.

As Christians, we love the patriarchs, the Old Testament, and most of all, the Jewish Messiah, Jesus! There should be no smugness toward unbelieving Jews. There should be brokenhearted evangelism that says, "My friend, we have found your Messiah. Will you trust him?"

The gospel should always produce humility in our hearts, as Paul has already stated in the letter (3:27; 4:2). It should lead us to boast in God alone, and it should lead us to a humble love (12:9-13).

In verses 19-20 Paul addresses a potential argument from a Gentile believer and restates his point about humility. He grants the claim that God made a place for Gentiles (v. 20a) but denies a replacement theology (v. 20b)—that is, the idea that the church has replaced Israel. There is only one olive tree, whose roots are planted in the Old Testament and whose branches include believing Jews and Gentiles. Therefore, there should be no smugness among Gentile believers but instead a healthy fear before God.

Why should the Gentiles fear the Lord? This is one of the most serious warnings in the New Testament about continuing in the faith. The Gentiles should appreciate the kindness and grace of God since he has grafted them into the people of God by his grace. And they should also tremble at the severity of God, for God did not spare Israel from the consequences of unbelief even though they belonged to the patriarchs (Bird, *Romans*, 389). Gentile believers should not be presumptuous or arrogant but should continue in faithfulness. Persevering faith walks in gratitude to God and in the fear of God. This attitude not only pleases the Lord, but it also is necessary for cultivating the unity that God requires among the saints.

Paul shifts to talk about the future of Israel (v. 23). Israel can be saved if they will not persist in unbelief. This is a possibility because of the power of God. Paul has already pointed out that God is *willing* to save them (10:21). Now he adds that God is *able* to save them. Our sovereign God can open blind eyes and soften hard hearts so that unbelievers may embrace the Messiah.

Paul defends verse 23 by pointing to the believing Gentiles' testimony (v. 24). If God can bring pagan Gentiles to faith, grafting them into the people of God, how much more can he incorporate the Jews, who possess such spiritual privileges (9:4-5)! The Gentiles are the "outsiders," the "unnatural ones" who have been grafted in. Israel's belief would simply be returning to "their own olive tree" (Bird, *Romans*, 390).

The Mystery of Israel's Future Salvation (11:25-32)

In verses 25-32 we find the center of the chapter: the future of Israel. Paul says, "All Israel will be saved" (11:26). Prior to this, in verse 25, Paul says that to avoid conceit the Gentiles should remember that Israel's hardening was *partial or temporary* until the fullness of Gentile salvation is complete. Across history, most of Israel has not believed on Jesus, while many Gentiles have been saved. This fact summarizes the olive tree illustration. Paul's readers should not be "ignorant" of God's redemptive work among Jews and Gentiles (v. 25). When the gospel goes to the Gentiles in fullness, then something will happen: "And in this way all Israel will be saved" (v. 26). We must be careful and charitable as we move forward analyzing Paul's words here. We should always exercise caution and humility when we explore texts that deal with the future! All of our questions will *only* be answered when the reality is revealed.

As we carefully analyze the phrase "All Israel will be saved," three main questions need to be answered: (1) *Who* is Israel? (2) *When* does Israel get saved? (3) *How* does Israel get saved (Bird, *Romans*, 391)?

Who is Israel? I do not think Paul has in mind the elect from within both Jews and Gentiles. He is talking about *ethnic* Israel. It would not be a "mystery" (v. 25) to say that God will save all elect Jews and Gentiles. We know God will do this because we embrace the doctrine of election. So Paul is talking about the future of ethnic Israel here. However, I do not think that "all Israel" means every single Israelite without exception (who has ever lived or is living at a particular time in history). I think it means Israel as a whole—ethnic Israel in a general sense—like the phrase does elsewhere (cf. 1 Sam 12:1; 2 Chron 12:1; Dan 9:11). There can be exceptions. So, while not every single Jew will be saved, Paul seems to be saying that a vast number of Israelites will be saved at a future time, joining the believing remnant (11:5; Bird, *Romans*, 391).

What is mysterious is this divine plot twist (Bird, *Romans*, 391). Something different in the future is being projected for ethnic Israel, something mysterious, a plan that no one would see coming. Israelites—a great number of them—will believe in the Messiah in the future! This is why Paul calls this a "mystery" and why he ends by praising God for his infinite wisdom. Most Jews and Gentiles would not have worked out such a plan. It is God's "boomerang" of salvation: Jewish rejection will lead to Gentile salvation and then will work back to the Jews for their salvation (ibid., 384). This is what was alluded to in this olive tree illustration. God in his power will bring life from the dead to the Jewish people. God has a remnant throughout history, and at some point in the future many more Jews will believe on Jesus. Please note that they will not be saved in some way other than faith in Jesus. There is one way of salvation, as the book of Romans clearly shows us.

When does Israel get saved? Paul does his thing again, quoting the Old Testament in verses 26b-27, this time from Isaiah 59:20-21. This citation provides a scriptural basis for his argument, and it helps us understand when Israel gets saved. Obviously, some will be saved across history as the gospel is preached. But this text also points to something else, an event or events in the future. The "Deliverer" refers to Christ, and the event *relates to the second coming*. Yet Paul does *not* seem to know of a mass conversion of Jews to Christ as a kind of *catalyst* for the second coming, as some interpreters contend (Bird, *Romans*, 384). Even so, there is definitely a future look toward the return of Christ and the Jews coming to faith in greater numbers.

Interestingly, Paul changes a word from Isaiah 59:20-21. The Deliverer is coming "from Zion" (Rom 11:26) rather than "to Zion" (Isa 59:20). The fact that the Deliverer (cf. 1 Thess 1:10) will come *from* Zion carries the idea that the Messiah's return from heaven (cf. Phil 3:20) will mean that Israel will finally experience salvation, entering into a new covenant and experiencing the forgiveness of sins (v. 27). So, Paul is talking about something around the time of the return of Christ. When, exactly? I am not sure, as Paul leaves it unspecified.

How does Israel get saved? Some have argued through the years that Israel will be saved without faith in the Messiah. This must be rejected (cf. Rom 1:16-17; 4:1-25; 9:30,33; 10:4-17; 11:20). How will this great number of Israelites be saved? *By faith in the Messiah.*

To summarize, then, when the gospel has penetrated to the ends of the earth—the Gentile world—and the fullness of the Gentiles has come into the family of God through faith in Christ, then in God's mysterious saving grace he will lift the veil on his ancient people, and multitudes of them will trust Jesus as their Savior, sometime around the return of Christ.

In verses 28-32 Paul wraps up the entire argument in chapters 9–11 by reminding us of some of the most basic points in this portion of the letter. Paul says that currently Israel refuses to believe the gospel and is thus understood as "enemies"; but due to God's electing grace, that is, due to God's redemptive purposes, Israel is "loved" because of the promise made to the patriarchs (v. 28). God will not withdraw his promises to the fathers, which is what he means by saying, "God's gracious gifts and calling are irrevocable" (v. 29).

Paul gives us the gospel boomerang again in verses 30-31. The Jews' rejection led to the Gentiles' experience of mercy; and the Gentiles' experience of mercy will eventually lead to the Jews' experience of mercy. One cannot miss the constant emphasis on salvation by God's grace and mercy in Romans 9 and 11. God will have a people for himself, from both Jews and Gentiles, who have been saved by God's grace and mercy.

Finally, Paul finishes the argument by saying, "For God has imprisoned all in disobedience so that he may have mercy on all" (v. 32). The "all" here refers to both Jew and Gentile. All of humanity, Jew and Gentile, have been condemned in Adam (1:18–3:20). But through the Messiah—the new Adam, the true Israelite—the curse will be reversed. One day more Israelites will be saved. They will join the remnant, and they will join a host of believing Gentiles, and they will all together rejoice in God's mercy. Here then is the grand aim of history: *that the nations glorify God for his mercy*. It makes sense for Paul to begin his list of exhortations in Romans 12 by recalling God's *mercy* ("in view of the mercies of God") as the proper incentive for a life wholly dedicated to God. What mercy it is!

God Deserves the Glory Forever
ROMANS 11:33-36

Paul has been wrestling with the burden of his Jewish kinsmen being lost, and when he gets to this point, he is marveling at the promises and purposes of God. He is in awe of God's plan. This is a stunning doxology and a fitting conclusion to such a section of Scripture, a conclusion that appropriately begins with "Oh." This gospel, this redemptive plan, this theology, leads Paul to doxology, a hymn that arises from the depths of his heart. The gospel should always give us an "Oh" as we react to it with greater amazement than one who has found a vast treasure. Let's meditate on these words with Paul, with such amazement. This hymn celebrates God's wisdom, God's self-sufficiency, and God as the Creator, Sustainer, and goal of creation.

We cannot plumb the depths of God's wisdom and knowledge (v. 33). The gospel magnifies these attributes of God. His grace is rich and his wisdom is unmatched. Further, his judgments are "unsearchable" and his ways "untraceable." You cannot track the ways of God.

Paul offers two biblical citations to emphasize God's self-sufficiency, from Isaiah 40:13 and Job 41:11. His point is that God's infinite wisdom means he does not need any help, and he has no need of counselors. He is self-sufficient.

The Isaiah reference is from a context where God's power to save Israel is being described, a second exodus—from Babylon. Israel is fearful because Babylon is so strong, but Yahweh assures them that he can accomplish his plans because the nations are nothing before him (Schreiner, *Romans*, 635). God's plans are not thwarted by the Babylonians or anyone else!

The Job reference is from a context where God asks Job more than sixty questions related to his sovereignty. Job previously doubted God's wisdom. He gets rebuked for doubting God's judgments and ways. God needs no advisors and has no creditors. He acts in his own wisdom and is obligated to no one (Bird, *Romans*, 408). Schreiner applies the Job passage to Paul's context:

> Just as Job doubted God's wisdom and ability in his suffering, so too the Roman Christians might be inclined to question God's wisdom in terms of his saving plan for world history. Job's vision of God's greatness was too circumscribed. God accomplished his plan with respect to Job in wisdom and justice, and so too his plan to save some Jews and Gentiles is wise and just. He is debtor to no one's wisdom, strength, or goodness, and he has accomplished his purposes by his own initiative. (*Romans*, 637)

Indeed, and these truths should cause us to sing God's praise!

Paul closes the doxology by praising God as *the source* of all things ("from him"), as *the agent* by which all things are created and sustained ("through him," cf. Col 1:15-20), and as *the ultimate end* for which he made all things ("to him"). Therefore, "To him be the glory forever. Amen" (v. 36). We are called to align ourselves with this great purpose: to glorify God in all things.

So let's glorify God in evangelism as we share Paul's burden for the salvation of people. Let's glorify God in unity as we live lives marked by humility, gratitude, and the fear of God. Let's glorify God as we live in the hope of our coming Deliverer. And let's glorify God in worship, praising him for his infinite wisdom, his matchless mercy, his astonishing sovereignty, his self-sufficiency, and his saving purposes in Jesus our Messiah.

Reflect and Discuss

1. Why is this chapter *practically relevant* for believers?
2. How does this chapter lay the groundwork for upcoming chapters on *unity*?
3. Go back and read 1 Kings 18–19. How does God reassure Elijah by speaking of a remnant? How can this story inspire believers today?
4. Explain the positive type of "jealousy" Paul describes in this chapter (v. 11).
5. Why should the Gentiles not be arrogant in regard to their relationship to the Jews?
6. Explain the "gospel boomerang" in this chapter.
7. How does God motivate the Gentiles to perseverance in verses 17-22?
8. To whom do you think "all Israel" refers?
9. When do you think "all Israel" will be saved?
10. What does Paul's move from theology (vv. 1-32) to doxology (vv. 33-36) teach us about studying theology?

Living in View of God's Mercy

ROMANS 12:1-16

Main Idea: In view of God's mercy, Paul exhorts believers to dedicate themselves to God in worshipful obedience and to serve others in the church.

I. **Offer Yourself to God (12:1-2).**
  A. Give your body to God (12:1).
  B. Give your mind to God (12:2).
    1. Do not let the world squeeze you into its mold (12:2a).
    2. Be transformed by the renewing of your mind (12:2b).
II. **Offer Yourself to the Church (12:3-16).**
  A. Think rightly about yourself (12:3).
  B. Use your spiritual gifts (12:4-8).
  C. Allow the gospel to shape your relationships and ethics (12:9-16).

Romans 12:1 marks a new section in the letter to the Romans. Paul's "Therefore" signals the shift and causes us to look back to the previous section in chapters 9–11, where Paul discussed God's gracious and merciful display of salvation in the Messiah (9:15-18; 10:32); it also causes us to reflect on the larger section that led up to Romans 9–11 (1:16–8:39). Believers are exhorted to live in view of these "mercies" (12:1)—that is, to build their lives on the mercies of God, to be motivated by God's saving provision in Christ (3:21-26; 5:1-11; 8:32,34), and to recognize the power and hope they now enjoy (7:6; 8:1-39), enabling them to live committed to God in worship and obedience (12:1-2).

The primary ways Romans 12:1-2 will be lived out is by giving ourselves to God's church through the use of our spiritual gifts (vv. 3-8) and through gospel-centered acts of love (vv. 9-16). In the following portions of the letter (12:17–15:13), Paul cites more attitudes and actions of love that should mark the Christian who is living out Romans 12:1-2: relating rightly to our enemies (12:17-21), viewing the government properly (13:1-7), living in light and love (13:11-14), and cultivating unity amid our diversity (14:1–15:13).

Beginning here in Romans 12, interpreters often discuss the shift between the "indicatives" of the gospel (the grammar of certainty and actuality) and the "imperatives" of the gospel (the grammar of command). Romans 1–11 includes a host of indicatives where believers are told what God has done for them in Christ. Romans 12:1–15:13 includes a host of imperatives where believers are commanded to now live in a certain way. The indicatives underlie and empower the imperatives: "Carrying out the imperatives would be an impossibility without the indicative" (Schreiner, *Romans*, 640). Let's rejoice in the glorious indicatives of the gospel! The facts of the gospel have caused us to soar in worship throughout Romans, and now they give the proper basis for practical obedience. God's grace should not make us lazy or passive but passionate and devoted to God, and this passion is "rooted in faith and energized by the power of the Holy Spirit" (ibid.).

Offer Yourself to God
ROMANS 12:1-2

In these two verses we are introduced to a call to offer ourselves to God in total surrender and dedication. For the Christian, all of life is to be lived as an act of worship unto God. It reminds us that sin problems stem from a worship problem. If a Christian is living selfishly and independently of the body of Christ, not obeying 12:3-16, then the problem is with the heart; the problem is a lack of surrender to God in worship. If a Christian cannot follow Paul's commands in 12:17–15:13, then the fundamental issue is a failure of living under Christ's lordship; it is a worship problem.

Give Your Body to God (12:1)

This first charge to present our bodies to God echoes the following two verses in Romans 6:

> And do not offer any parts of it to sin as weapons for unrighteousness.
> But as those who are alive from the dead, offer yourselves to God,
> and all the parts of yourselves to God as weapons for righteousness.
> (v. 13; emphasis added)

> For just as you offered the parts of yourselves as slaves to impurity,
> and to greater and greater lawlessness, so now offer them as

slaves to righteousness, *which results in sanctification.* (v. 19; emphasis added)

What Paul is saying here is "give your whole self to God" (Schreiner, *Romans*, 642). Paul underscores the seriousness of the charge by saying, "I urge you," or "I appeal to you" (ESV), or "I plead with you" (NLT). This is an authoritative and urgent call to give ourselves to God wholeheartedly. The basis for this, again, is the mercies of God (cf. 9:18; 15:9). We who are alive in Christ (6:11,13; 8:13) are now called to be living sacrifices.

The idea of a "living sacrifice" highlights an important aspect of Christian teaching. Other religions in Paul's day made sacrifices as a sign of dedication, and the same is true in our day. But Mike Bird points out,

> Christianity looked strange to Greeks and Romans because it was hard to conceive of a "religion" apart from temple, priesthood, and sacrifice. What we find in Romans 12:1 is part of the wider phenomenon in the New Testament where the language of temple, priesthood, and sacrifice is used without the actual physical apparatus associated with them. . . . "sacrifice" (*thysia*) is metaphorically applied to Christian service. (*Romans*, 413; cf. Phil 2:17; Heb 13:15; 1 Pet 2:5)

So then, the concept is clear: in light of God's mercy, offer yourself to God.

We do not somehow surrender our spirits and not our bodies. We are to be wholly consecrated worshipers, being committed to God in every realm of life, in every aspect of our being (cf. 1 Cor 6:19-20; Gal 2:20). This death to self is considered to be "holy and pleasing to God" (12:1). Our lives are to be a fragrant offering of worship to God (cf. Rom 15:16).

God is worthy of our singing. He is worthy of our corporate assemblies that magnify his grace. But Paul is calling for something more than this here. He is calling for a life of worship in everyday life. Do you want to worship God? Then live a holy life to his glory. The prophets, like Amos and Micah, rebuked those who had religious ceremonies but neglected a life of faithful obedience (Amos 5:21-24; Micah 6:6-8). We need the constant reminder of Romans 12:1 to be in our minds and hearts to avoid such hypocrisy. Paul is making this point when he says this is "your true worship," "your spiritual worship" (ESV), "your reasonable service" (KJV), "your spiritual service of worship" (NASB), or "your true and proper worship" (NIV). The total offering of ourselves in service to God is an act of worship, and this is the most sensible response to the mercies of God.

Give Your Mind to God (12:2)

The division between body and mind is helpful for sermonic divisions, but we should remember that Paul is not dividing them. Part of what it means to offer our bodies to God is explained here in verse 2; Paul views humans holistically, and there is always a relationship between what we think and what we do (Schreiner, *Romans*, 646).

How is it that you offer your mind to God so that you may offer yourself to God? There are two commands in verse 2: "Do not be conformed" and "Be transformed." So, first, *do not allow the world to squeeze you into its mold* (as the Phillips paraphrase puts it). The Christians in Rome are being summoned not to think like the outside world. Christians think differently about life because we have a different worldview than those in our age. In Paul's day the Roman way of thinking was radically out of step with a biblical vision of life. Because we have been redeemed from the mindset described in Romans 1:18-32, we must not let the world's messages and customs shape our way of thinking.

Second, Paul says "*be transformed by the renewing of your mind*" (emphasis added). Christians are urged to make a break from the "mindset of the flesh" (8:7), which typifies humanity, and the debased mind of pagans (1:28). Our minds are to be renewed by the Spirit (7:6; 8:27). This involves giving our minds to that which is good, right, and beautiful (Phil 4:8), not to what once marked our old way of thinking (Eph 4:22-32; Col 3:9). It involves filling our minds with the truth of Scripture (Ps 119:37; Eph 6:17; Col 3:16). It involves meditating on the glory of God in Christ (2 Cor 3:17).

This is important as we consider the influence of film and music, which have a powerful way of shaping modern minds. There is much to be enjoyed in these realms but also much that must be rejected. A polluted mind will lead to a polluted life; but a mind filled with gospel truth and eschatological hope will lead to a life dedicated to God in worship.

The purpose of this transformed self and renewed mind is "that you may discern what is the good, pleasing, and perfect will of God." This means we will be able to recognize and appreciate what honors God, and we can then set ourselves to obey his will.

Offer Yourself to the Church
ROMANS 12:3-16

Following those two important verses (vv. 1-2), Paul shifts to more specific application, first by renouncing an arrogant way of thinking (v. 3) and then by talking about using one's spiritual gifts for the good of the church body (vv. 4-8). These verses are followed by a series of exhortations on the importance of love within the body (vv. 9-16).

Think Rightly about Yourself (12:3)

Paul tells the church not to be full of themselves. The word "for" is important because it connects back to verse 2. The first thing Paul says after exhorting believers to have a renewed mind is not to think too highly of oneself. This does not mean to be self-loathing but rather to think with "sober judgment" (ESV). So this is what a renewed mind looks like.

Paul gives this exhortation with authority ("by the grace given to me"; cf. 1:5), and it includes everyone ("I tell everyone"). Everyone must think rightly about himself or herself within the church. There were tensions in the church, so this command should not surprise us. The path to unity always comes through humility and service (cf. Phil 2:1-11).

The meaning of the phrase "as God has distributed a measure of faith to each one" is debated. The best option in my judgment is to read it in light of the upcoming verses on spiritual gifts (vv. 4-8) and in view of the parallel texts on spiritual gifts (1 Cor 12:11; Eph 4:7). Read this way, the phrase "measure of faith" refers to different spiritual capacities that God apportions to each person and is thus equivalent to God's distribution of "spiritual gifts" (Bird, *Romans*, 424). Regarding Paul's use of the "measure of *faith*" (emphasis added), Mike Bird points out that the word for "faith" (Gk *pistis*) has enough range that it can mean "position of trust" or "trusteeship" (ibid.). He adds,

> Not only that, but in 12:6 Paul uses similar language when he says that prophecy should be performed in according with the "proportion of stewardship [faith]." Paul is referring to the behavior that befits prophecy in the sense of prophesying in a manner appropriate to what has been granted to them. (Ibid., 424–25)

So, God had given a measure of grace and faith to each member of the church. Each believer has thus been gifted. But we should not think too highly of ourselves when it comes to these gifts; rather, we should be humble and faithful stewards of them. Gifts should not breed arrogance. After all, God sovereignly provides them! We have not earned them or received them because of our good deeds or superior value (1 Cor 4:7). God drew us to faith by his grace and has given us spiritual gifts; therefore, he gets the glory (1 Pet 4:10-11). We need to have our minds transformed by this grace in order to keep us from self-promotion and self-exaltation. We should assess ourselves soberly and use our gifts to serve and bless others, not as a means of building our own names and platforms.

Use Your Spiritual Gifts (12:4-8)

In the 1 Corinthians 12–14 passage on the gifts, Paul sandwiches a section on love in the middle. Here Paul follows his passage on spiritual gifts with a section on love (Rom 12:9-16). Paul also combines "the body" metaphor with the use of gifts in both passages (1 Cor 12:12-31). Thus, in both texts we see how *corporate* Christianity is. Our faith is personal, but it is not individualistic. We have been called to love one another, and we have been called to use our gifts for the good of the body (cf. 1 Cor 12:7).

In Romans 12:4-5 Paul emphasizes the "one another" nature of Christianity. The body of Christ is a common metaphor for the church in the New Testament (cf. Eph 2:16; 3:6; 4:4,25; 5:29; Col 3:15). Paul obviously loved this picture of the church, and for good reason. Just as a body has many members that carry out important functions, so does the body of Christ. This speaks to our diversity and our unity. Regarding diversity, each member is unique and important in the body. As to our unity, we are one body in Christ. Our unity is not based on uniformity but is a spiritual unity established by our union with Christ.

Further developing the point of the diversity within the church, Paul mentions seven particular spiritual gifts (vv. 6-8). We should not read this as an exhaustive list, since Paul mentions other gifts elsewhere (1 Cor 12:7-10,28-30; Eph 4:11; cf. 1 Pet 4:10). Rather, this list is meant to summarize the types of gifts the church possesses (Bird, *Romans*, 425). What we should not miss in this particular list is how Paul calls believers to use their gifts *with excellence and passion* (vv. 6-8).

We might group these gifts into two categories: teaching gifts and serving gifts (cf. 1 Pet 4:10-11), or verbal and nonverbal gifts. The teaching gifts include "prophecy," "teaching," "exhortation," and "leading"

(I recognize that "leading" also involves a lot of nonverbal serving, but if "leading" here speaks of formal leadership in the church, it usually involves teaching; 1 Tim 3:1-7; 5:17; Heb 13:7). The serving gifts include "service," "giving," and "showing mercy." This does not mean that those who speak never serve, nor does it mean that those who serve never speak. But rather, it is simply to say that these functions of *word-and-deed ministry* are worked out in the body through the proper exercise of individual gifts. When we use these word-and-deed gifts, we build up the body of Christ and bring glory to God.

The most disputed of these gifts is clearly "prophecy" (v. 6). It is set apart here from "teaching" and "exhortation," so it should not be equated with preaching or teaching. Schreiner says, "It seems that prophecy is not only spontaneous in nature but it is also directed to concrete situations, giving practical guidance in particular circumstances" (*Romans*, 655). These prophecies must be "according to the proportion of one's faith." Some take this to mean according to a body of doctrine ("the faith," "the standard," or "the rule"). So those who prophesy must not deviate from apostolic teaching (ibid., 656). This is an attractive view because such a gift would otherwise open the door for fanaticism, but it does not seem to be the best interpretation. If "measure of faith" in verse 3 carries the idea of "according to the grace/faith sovereignly distributed to the believer," then Paul's point here is that if you have the gift of prophecy, you should use it in proportion to your faith and gifting. Schreiner notes,

> Prophets might be tempted to prophesy beyond the faith given by God, perhaps to impress others with their charismatic ability. They are exhorted, therefore, to prophesy in accordance with the faith that has been given to them. (*Romans*, 655)

"Service" carries the idea of practical help for those in need (v. 7; cf. Acts 6:1-2; 2 Cor 8:4). "Teaching" probably involves instruction in both formal and informal settings (cf. Acts 13:1; Eph 4:11; 1 Cor 12:28-29; 14:26; Col 3:15; Heb 5:12; Jas 3:1), for the building up of other believers. "Exhortation" has a range of meanings (comforting, encouraging, pleading) and may also be done in both formal and informal settings (v. 8; cf. 1 Thess 2:3-4; 1 Tim 4:13; 6:2; 2 Tim 4:2; Titus 1:9; 2:1-2,15; 1 Cor 14:3,31; 2 Cor 1:4; Col 4:8; 1 Thess 4:18; 5:11; Heb 3:13; 10:25).

Those with the gift of leadership are to lead "with diligence" (v. 8). Regarding formal leaders in the church (cf. 1 Thess 5:12; 1 Tim 3:5;

5:17), there is a temptation to laziness if one does not have any over-sight, so we must lead with zeal. Those with the gift of "giving" their pos-sessions and resources are called to generosity and sacrifice (cf. 1 Cor 9:10-11; 2 Cor 8–9; Phil 4:15), the kind of generosity that reflects God's generosity (2 Cor 8:9). Those with the gift of "showing mercy," who min-ister on behalf of the poor, weak, and hurting, are to be cheerful in their display of mercy (v. 8; cf. Acts 20:35; 2 Cor 9:7) instead of serving with a begrudging spirit. Generosity, zeal, and cheerfulness get at the attitude underneath these actions, for God cares about our hearts and motives and not just our external actions.

So in all the detailed discussion and debate about spiritual gifts, let me just underscore the obvious point here: *use your gifts for the good of the body*. You need to be in a local church to be edified by the gifts of others, and you need to be in a local church because others need to be edified by your gifts. Gifts are not given for one's own enjoyment, for self-exaltation, or to build one's platform. A Christian has no right to withhold his or her gifts from the church. God gave us these gifts because he loves the church, and we are to use our gifts for the good of our brothers and sisters.

Allow the Gospel to Shape Your Relationships and Ethics (12:9-16)

Various headings have been given for these verses, such as "Marks of the True Christian," "Love in Action," or "Christian Ethics." Whatever we title them, it is clear that Paul gives a string of exhortations that were and are countercultural. It is a list of attitudes and actions that come as a result of the Christian allowing the gospel to shape his or her rela-tionships and ethics. We see here how the gospel is to be worked out in the daily life of God's people. These verses (for the most part) are not difficult to understand, but they are difficult to apply. This is why we need to let the gospel permeate every aspect of our daily lives, having our minds renewed by the Spirit. A *renewed mind* leads to a new way of living; it involves attitudes and actions that are *not conformed* to this age. In Paul's day the hierarchical culture made these instructions radically countercultural, and they also go against the grain of our culture and our flesh as well.

If you think about it, the old mind, or the mind conformed to this age, wants to do the *opposite* of these instructions, leading one to fake love (v. 9a); to support and do that which is evil (v. 9b); to show no affection (v. 10a); not to honor others (v. 10b); to be lazy (v. 11a) or to be cold and apathetic to the things of God (v. 11b); to serve self, not the Lord (v. 11c); to get mad in trials, to turn inward in self-pity, not to rejoice, not to pray (v. 12); to be greedy and inhospitable (v. 13); to want to retaliate when persecuted (v. 14); to ignore the hurting and to get jealous when others succeed (v. 15); to live in disharmony with other brothers and sisters, complaining, criticizing, gossiping, and creating division (v. 16a); and to be arrogant toward others (v. 16b). This is why we need the gospel. This is why each of us needs a renewed mind. This is why we need the Holy Spirit to make us different (cf. 5:5). We need hearts that are saturated in grace to live out these instructions.

Several factors make this list challenging in my context. For starters, this picture is not a vision of a privatized Christian life. It is life lived in community. Further, the modern media culture has produced a loss of empathy in many, along with a lot of counterfeit community through social media, not to mention causing people to lose the art of life-on-life conversation with others. Moreover, our culture is impatient. We want high-speed everything. How then can we be patient in tribulation? And how can we love one another as well as our enemies in this age of anger?

Good news: we are not powerless. What's more, we should view these challenges as opportunities for powerful gospel witness. What would happen if others saw us living out these principles from Romans 12:9-16? Christians in the first century turned the world upside down by living out a gospel-centered, countercultural love, and who knows what may happen if we follow their example?

To do this, we need a gospel-centered *love* to permeate our churches. While not every verse addresses the subject of love to the same degree, I think it is fair to say that love is the primary motif of the whole section in verses 9-21 (and extends into the next two chapters; Moo, *Letter*, 772–74). Let's just linger over each one and ask God to make these instructions living realities in our lives.

"Let love be without hypocrisy" (v. 9a). Real love is sincere. It is marked by a compassion that leads to action (1 John 3:11-18). Christian love is not marked by mere platitudes. In the original context, life was structured around formal relationships that included the expectation to act in accordance with one's role in society. One's heart did not always align with those actions. Love was often ritualized, not sincere, not from the heart (Oakes, *Reading Romans*, 107–8). So this command was (and still is!) countercultural. So, do not be a fake. Be quick to forgive, apologize, and show mercy and grace.

"Detest evil; cling to what is good" (v. 9b). Love does not allow evil to persist in the name of "love." Love actually hates certain things. These are strong words: "detest" (hate it exceedingly) and "cling" (as in marriage). Love is not genuine when it leads a person to do something evil, allows a person to do evil, or avoids doing that which is good. Love knows the difference between right and wrong. The church must hate what God hates and love what God loves.

"Love one another deeply as brothers and sisters" (v. 10a). Let there be tenderness and warmth in the church. Affection can be expressed in a variety of ways, but the idea is that we are family. This too was a radical command in the Roman context. The church provided a radically new kind of family and was a massive encouragement to those without families, such as migrant workers, servants, the oppressed, and those rejected by their biological families when they became Christians. The church is a family, so let's love one another with affection.

"Take the lead in honoring one another" (v. 10b). Here is another radical command in the first-century hierarchical world. Oakes says,

> If, at church, I hold a door open for someone, it is not revolutionary, whoever it may be. In a first-century house church, if a slave held a door open for their master, no one would notice. If a master held a door open for a slave, this would be very radical. . . . Paul's call implies giving each person honour individually. . . . In first-century terms this is outrageous. (*Reading Romans*, 110)

Many of us live in a culture of dishonor. When we honor one another, we too are going against the grain of society. Let me encourage you to find ways this week to honor someone—surprise them with an act of honor. It can be a leader, but it does not have to be. This text says we must honor "one another."

"Do not lack diligence in zeal; be fervent in the Spirit; serve the Lord" (v. 11). Look at the intensity in this verse. The Christian life is neither cold nor indifferent (cf. v. 8). Wrongly directed zeal is dangerous (10:2), but rightly ordered zeal glorifies God and blesses people. In the Roman context, certain classes of people were exhorted to work hard. What made this command countercultural is that it is targeted at everyone—even the wealthier households are called to work hard.

We face many temptations to be passive or lazy today. So let's heed this word: live on fire for Christ! And let's see that God is gracious in giving us such a command. He knows our frames. He knows our passions can cool. So he exhorts us in love. I believe every Christian in a privileged part of the world must always ask, "Do I love comfort too much? Has it become an idol? Has it caused me to shrink back from passionate service to the Lord Jesus?" Allow the gospel to shape your mind and inflame your heart for passionate service to Christ, who loved you and gave himself for you (Gal 2:20).

"Rejoice in hope; be patient in affliction; be persistent in prayer" (v. 12). There is not a day in the Christian life in which we do not need to hear this verse. *Perseverance* is the unifying theme of these three phrases. It was a relevant exhortation in the Roman context for several reasons. Persecution was a real threat (v. 14). Further, the general way of life was hard. It was a world with far fewer provisions and less medical care, not to mention the fact that oppression was built into society.

To be "patient in affliction" implies that believers can expect tribulation in this life. How might believers endure trials? By applying the surrounding exhortations: "Rejoice in hope" and "Be persistent in prayer." To persevere we need to live with an undercurrent of joy (cf. 5:2-5; 8:18-30), and we must be persistent in prayer and making our petitions to the Father (cf. 8:26-27).

"Share with the saints in their needs; pursue hospitality" (v. 13). Here are two practical ways to show love: generosity and hospitality. The Greek word for "share" is often associated with financial support (see Acts 2:44; 4:32; Rom 15:26-27; 2 Cor 8:4; 9:13; Gal 6:6; Phil 1:5; 4:15; 1 Tim 6:18; Heb 13:16). This is a gift of some in the church (Rom 12:8), but it is also a responsibility for everyone.

Hospitality was important in Paul's day—Christians lacked accommodations for various reasons. We know Paul enjoyed the hospitality of many. Throughout Scripture we read of the gracious hospitality of our God, as he who welcomes weak and weary sinners (Isa 25:6-7; 55:1-3; Matt 11:28; Luke 14:12-24; Rev 21:3). This should motivate our hospitality (cf. Rom 15:7), and Peter urges us to do it without grumbling (1 Pet 4:9). Here in Romans 12 Paul speaks of the intentionality of it: *pursue it.* Be intentional about inviting others into your home and into your life. Use your home to bless others, to bless those in the church, and to bless people in need outside of your church, with wisdom and compassion.

"Bless those who persecute you; bless and do not curse" (v. 14). This verse seems more related to our attitudes and actions toward enemies, which Paul develops in verses 17-21. It also carries the line of thought from

Jesus's teaching on loving and praying for one's enemies (Matt 5:44; Luke 6:27-28). Throughout the centuries, believers have experienced a wide range of opposition, so this concept is relevant as well as challenging. We have to be gospel-shaped, mind-renewed, Spirit-empowered followers of Christ to live it out.

"Rejoice with those who rejoice; weep with those who weep" (v. 15). This often-quoted verse reminds us to come alongside other believers in the highs and lows of life. And do not limit that to funerals and weddings! Sometimes it is harder for us to rejoice with others than to weep with them, if they have obtained that which we want to obtain. Envy and jealousy and competition make it difficult to rejoice. But this is why we need the gospel. A sign of growing in grace is that we are able to rejoice in the success of other brothers and sisters. This is a wonderful way to love others: rejoice when they rejoice.

What about weeping? How do we do this? Showing up is most of the job, right? You do not need a great speech. Just be present with the hurting. This would have been a radical idea in a hierarchical Roman culture: the elite weeping with the poor migrant worker. But that is what brothers and sisters in Christ do—regardless of background or class.

"Live in harmony with one another. Do not be proud; instead associate with the humble. Do not be wise in your own estimation" (v. 16). This too was radical in Paul's context. The homeless, the migrant worker, the cabinetmaker, the household servants, the elite, and the Jew and Gentile are called to live in harmony (Oakes, *Reading Romans*, 96). This was a powerful witness of the kingdom of God in the empire of Rome! It is a unity that reflects the unity of the Father, Son, and Spirit.

To live in harmony means working through conflict, misunderstanding, miscommunication, and wounds. Through those awkward conversations, gracious interactions, and repentance, reconciliation and harmony are experienced. Harmony takes hard work, humble work, and heart work.

A Christian should never say, "This task is beneath me," or "This person is beneath me." Jesus did not consider our condition as beneath him. One of the signs that the gospel is transforming us is that we will associate with all kinds of people. Phillips puts it this way: "Don't become snobbish but take a real interest in ordinary people." To do this we need the mind of Christ, not the mind that is "wise in [our] own sight " (ESV). The humble saint with a renewed mind thinks this way and associates with the lowly, reflecting the character of Christ.

Paul's portrait of service and of love in these sixteen verses is remarkable. And it is really a portrait of Jesus.

- Jesus offered himself as the ultimate sacrifice dedicated to the Father's will.
- Jesus gave himself for the church (Eph 5:25).
- Jesus loved us with a genuine love, with words and actions, not with religious pretense.
- Jesus hates what is evil, loves what's good, and died for evil people to make them good.
- Jesus loved the brothers and sisters with brotherly affection, as revealed in the Gospels.
- Jesus was dishonored that we may be honored.
- Jesus was a man of zeal. He took up the psalm, "Zeal for [God's] house will consume me" (John 2:17).
- Jesus rejoiced in hope, endured tribulation, and was constant in prayer.
- Jesus was generous; he became poor that we might be rich in him (2 Cor 8:9).
- Jesus has shown us hospitality; the friend of sinners dines with us and welcomes us.
- Jesus loved his enemies; he did not have a sword in his hand but nails in his hands, as he said, "Father, forgive them, because they do not know what they are doing" (Luke 23:34).
- Jesus rejoiced with those who rejoiced (Luke 10:17-24), and he wept with those who wept (John 11:35).
- Jesus unites people in harmony from every tribe and tongue (Rev 5:9).
- Jesus associates with the lowly. He even took a repentant thief to paradise with him (Luke 23:43)! And he has associated with us.

As the body of Christ, in view of the mercies of God, let's offer ourselves to God and one another for the good of the church and the glory of our triune God.

Reflect and Discuss

1. Explain the importance of the word "Therefore" in verse 1.
2. Why do you think Paul chose the word "mercies" in verse 1? Why should the mercies of God cause us to worship and serve one another?

3. What is a "living sacrifice"?
4. What does it look like not to be "conformed to this age" in your context?
5. What are some practical ways to renew our minds?
6. How is verse 3 connected to verse 2, regarding the renewed mind?
7. What strikes you most about Paul's gift list (vv. 4-8)? What do you find surprising, challenging, or encouraging?
8. What makes verses 9-16 so challenging in your context?
9. What would it look like for those in your church to "outdo one another in showing honor" (ESV)? How might you put this into practice now?
10. How can you pursue hospitality?

Living in View of That Day

ROMANS 12:17–13:14

Main Idea: In view of God's mercy displayed in Christ and in view of the coming day of Christ, believers' ethical lives should be driven and shaped by the realities of the gospel.

I. **Leave Vengeance to God (12:17-21).**
II. **Look at the State Rightly (13:1-7).**
    A. What (13:1a)?
    B. Why (13:1b-5)?
    C. How (13:6-7)?
III. **Love Your Neighbor (13:8-10).**
IV. **Live in the Light (13:11-14).**

Paul wants the gospel to saturate every aspect of the Roman believers' thinking and living. For Paul the gospel not only brings the dead to life, but it shapes the way believers interact with one another and how they live out their faith in the wider culture. You see this reflected especially in this latter part of Romans (12:1–15:13).

Here in Romans 12:17–13:14 Paul tackles a number of subjects related to the outside world, and it is interesting to see how the gospel should shape our thoughts regarding our enemies, the government, our neighbors, and the temptations of this world. Paul essentially views these things in light of the already-not yet dynamic of the gospel. Since believers are already in Christ but still await the final consummation, they can leave vengeance to God; they should see the divine purpose but limited role of the state; they can love their neighbor; and they should live in the light (not submitting to the darkness of this present age).

Several scholars have pointed out how these paragraphs carry an eschatological (end-time) emphasis. David Peterson notes that all the exhortations in chapters 12–13 are firmly in an "eschatological framework" (*Commentary*, 470). Additionally, commenting on Romans 13:11, Schreiner states, "The first part of the verse can then be paraphrased, 'Put into practice all the exhortations in Romans 12:1–13:10' *in light of the imminence of the end*" (*Romans*, 697; emphasis added).

These paragraphs remind me of the famous quip attributed to Martin Luther: "I have two days on my calendar, *this day* and *that day*." Indeed, the Christian lives in view of God's great mercy in Christ Jesus today, and he or she also looks ahead to *that day* in which judgment will be executed perfectly and our salvation will be experienced gloriously. Because *that day* will come, we can leave vengeance to God (for he will have the last word); we should look at the government rightly (letting go of political extremism); we should love our neighbor (as the basic Christian ethic in this life); and we should live in the light (resisting the temptations of the world and the flesh). We could spend four sections on these four subjects, but due to space constraints, let's briefly look at each one and consider them in light of *that day*, which will surely come.

Leave Vengeance to God
ROMANS 12:17-21

Beginning in verse 17 Paul shifts subjects to address how the Christian relates to the outside world; however, we should not make too hard a division between Romans 12:9-16 and verses 17 and following. Paul is in the same flow of thought, and he already mentioned persecution (the outside world) in verse 14. But now Paul begins to develop this issue of the Christian and the world more fully.

His first subject is *retaliation* (vv. 17-19a). Paul clearly prohibits believers from responding with retaliation toward their enemies. Paul's exposition is rooted in Old Testament teachings, which are clear about not seeking revenge (Lev 19:18; Prov 20:22; 24:29). Believers are to leave vengeance to God. Bird says, "The spiral of pain and loss would only be amplified if everyone attempted to exact revenge on their adversaries" (*Romans*, 435).

Notice the emphasis on honor again in verse 17. Believers are to be marked by this trait (cf. v. 10b). It is a big theme in the next passage as well, when Paul talks about the governing authorities (13:1-7). Instead of responding with dishonorable retaliation—that is, repaying evil for evil—believers are to live honorable lives in the sight of everyone (cf. 1 Thess 5:15; 1 Pet 3:9).

In verse 18 Paul states his desire for the church to "live at peace with everyone." To live out an ethic of *honor* and *peace*, Christians need to live with renewed minds (Rom 12:1-2). In this age of rage and dishonor, here is a real challenge for believers as they seek to "not be conformed to this age" (Rom 12:2).

Next, Paul returns to the issue of revenge stated in verse 17 as he quotes Deuteronomy 32:35 and Proverbs 25:21 (vv. 19b-20). An important principle to keep in mind here is that if you do not believe in *the wrath of God*, you can never do this! You will always want to take vengeance into your own hands.

We need to see how practical the doctrine of the wrath of God is for everyday life. If you really understand God's wrath in a biblical sense, you know that those who oppose Christ and his people will get something far worse than your puny little effort at retaliation. Believing this, you can say, "I'll leave vengeance to God." You do not have to become a vigilante; you can be a saint who humbly trusts in the God of justice and who actually blesses those who persecute you (v. 14). You can give your thirsty enemies "something to drink" (v. 20) in hopes that such an act of grace may cause them to change.

To summarize, Paul says, "Do not be conquered by evil, but conquer evil with good" (v. 21). The way you overcome the enemy is not by vengeance and vitriol but by grace and goodness. This kind of life is motivated by Christ's work for us on the cross in the past, and it is motivated by our belief about the coming day in the future. At the cross Christ loved his enemies. He has made us, former enemies, his friends (5:10). And one day he will have the final word on all those who oppose him and his people. So we can focus on blessing, not vengeance, now. We can be people of grace, peace, and honor until the final day. So let's live this way and humbly trust our God.

Faith in the judgment of God is how you abstain from joining this culture of hate and violence. Of course, on a civil level, we need courts and law enforcement, and that is what Paul addresses next.

Look at the State Rightly
ROMANS 13:1-7

The reason we can avoid vengeance is not only because God will execute perfect justice in the future but also because God has appointed government as the institution to carry out judgment in the present age.

The main point of 13:1-7 is clear: *submit to the governing authorities* (13:1,5). Such an idea is not popular!

Why is civil obedience and respecting officials so disliked? For starters, it is because we are sons and daughters of Adam. Rebelling against authority is as old as the garden. We do not even want God to tell us what to do! Further, in some countries (like America), free speech tends to foster rebellion against authority. Free speech is a wonderful freedom, but some use this freedom to talk about every leader as if he or she is a total buffoon. Trashing the authorities is a source of entertainment for some. It is how many talk radio hosts and entertainers make a living. This kind of thing does not happen in many other countries. (And can you imagine the Romans speaking this way about Nero?) Further, many people have had some bad experience with those in authority. So the natural inclination is to respond negatively to a passage like this.

We must remember that Paul was *not* writing in a perfect political climate. Nero was reigning. Nero was somewhat sane early in his career, but he grew progressively more maniacal. Still, Paul wrote Romans 13.

The fact is, this is God's Word. All of God's Word is profitable for shaping us into the image of Jesus. God's Word is more important than any other word.

Now, this text does not answer all of our questions related to the state. It is only seven verses. But it gives us some general truths that are important, particularly when it comes to how God has instituted the governing authorities for our good and how we should relate to the government in this present age.

Paul is writing to Christians in the epicenter of Roman rule; therefore, this topic really needs to be addressed. In these seven verses Paul stresses the need to avoid political extremism. The apostle Paul corrects two extremes: an *overrealized eschatology*, which says, "The kingdom is here, so ignore Caesar," and an *underrealized eschatology*, which says, "The kingdom is not here, so pick up your sword against Caesar and let's bring it!" Paul is trying to avoid the "ignore Caesar" or "fight Caesar" positions (Bird, *Romans*, 442–43).

So, how do citizens of heaven live as citizens on earth? How do those "in Christ" and those "in Rome" live faithful Christian lives? *We must submit to the governing authorities.* Let's consider the *what*, the *why*, and the *how* of this exhortation.

What? (13:1a)

Paul says, "Let everyone submit to the governing authorities" (v. 1a). Paul includes "everyone" in this command. Paul is not making a distinction between Christian and non-Christian citizens; nor is he making a distinction between Christian and non-Christian *rulers*. Everyone is called to submit to governing authorities. "Authorities" refers to any person that represents the authority of the state: from local bureaucrats all the way up (e.g., emperor, prime minister, president).

To "submit" (or "be subject," ESV) is broader than "obey." It conveys the idea of standing under the government in recognition that this is how God has ordered the world. The authorities exist under the authority of God. This is not an isolated reference to submitting to the authorities; we see it stated throughout the New Testament (1 Tim 2:1-3; Titus 3:1; 1 Pet 2:13-17). But we are to obey the civil authorities ultimately out of reverence for and submission to *the Lord*, or "for the Lord's sake" as Peter says (1 Pet 2:13 NIV). Schreiner comments on 1 Peter 2:13:

> We have an implication here that the ruling powers should be resisted if commands were issued that violated the Lord's will. It is impossible to imagine that one would obey commands that [broke] God's [commands] "for the Lord's sake." (*1 Peter*, 128)

Realize, then, that this passage reflects basic biblical teaching elsewhere. Government is one expression of God's common grace; it is here for our good. It is designed to provide justice, order, and civility. It is like the gifts of marriage and family in the sense that it is given to preserve and enrich humanity. We should submit to the state for the Lord's sake.

This passage is troubling to people for a few reasons. Some argue that Paul's sweeping, unqualified demand to submit to governing authorities justifies the actions of evil rulers and demands obedience to such rulers at all times. However, the New Testament clearly teaches that we must ultimately "obey God rather than people" (Acts 5:29). The reference in 1 Peter 2:13 also points to the ultimate authority: "for the Lord's sake" (NIV). We are to engage in civil disobedience when the government prohibits us from doing what the Lord commands or when it commands us to do what the Lord prohibits. This is implicit in every exhortation to "submit." Throughout Scripture we have various ways in which we are to submit *as unto the Lord* (e.g., Eph 5:21,22,24; Col 3:22).

The parallel to marriage is helpful. A wife is to recognize God's design for marriage, as we recognize God's design for government. The husband is the leader, the guide. But that does not mean the wife is to do whatever the husband demands. If he is promoting sin, is leading her into sin, or is abusing her and not caring for her, then she should not follow him; she then should not submit to him. In the same way, there will be times in which we cannot submit to the authorities. Sometimes the grievousness of a demand and the extent of it requires civil disobedience. With that said, Paul is not dealing with exceptions in this passage. He does not address when it is right to rebel against unjust rulers. His concern is with authority and order.

Others protest, claiming that Paul was naïve. They think, *Paul should avoid politics and stick to propitiation.* But Paul is drawing on personal history and redemptive history. He was not naïve about the government's role and its relationship to God. Paul had a somewhat mixed experience with Roman authorities. At times he was protected and helped by Roman officials (Acts 16:35-40; 18:12-17; 21:39; 22:23-29; 25:10-11). His bold, gospel speeches show respect and thoughtfulness. Yet he knew the state could be unjust. He knew this from the life of Jesus, who suffered the ultimate injustice. Further, Paul himself experienced various afflictions and imprisonments in the Roman Empire (2 Cor 11:23). What is more, Paul himself had been an unjust leader prior to his conversion. Paul clearly knew that rulers could be unjust, and at the time of writing, Nero was in charge. Paul knew Nero was no saint.

Paul also knew redemptive (biblical) history. The Bible clearly teaches that God is sovereign over the authorities (Ps 75:7; Isa 40:23-24; 45:1-7; Dan 2:21; John 19:11). Paul's heritage also taught him that evil rulers must be resisted at times (Exod 1:17,21; Dan 3:12-18; Heb 11:23). Yet he still penned these words about submitting to the governing authorities. So Paul is not speaking naïvely.

Why? (13:1b-5)

The reason is clear: "Since there is no authority except from God, and the authorities that exist are instituted by God" (v. 1b). We submit to the state because God has instituted governing authorities. God sets up kings and removes them. Piper says,

> This means that the Roman Christians and we today should learn that it is God's will to govern the world of mankind through human civil authorities. This is God's plan. Man did not create government. God did. Man does not sustain it. God does. Civil authority is God's idea in this age. ("Subjection to God and Subjection to the State, Part 1")

Sometimes God gives authorities as a blessing to a people, and sometimes he institutes them as a means of a trial of judgment. God has his own purposes.

Unfortunately, many Christians cannot see past the earthly government to the government of God. They do not trust in the providence of God. Many professing Christians essentially lose their minds when it comes to politics. They fail to see the God who is over the government. Should we engage in the political process? Yes, of course. Speak truth to power? Yes, when possible. But freak out or make an idol out of a party or a system? No way.

So Paul points out that the authorities are working out some of the purposes of God (Moo, *Letter*, 809). Consequently, if we rebel against the authorities, we are rebelling against God's order, and it will bring judgment as a result (v. 2).

Further, the authorities act as "God's servant," punishing evil and rewarding good (vv. 3-4). If believers want to be free from fear of the authorities, then they should be people who do "good." Again, this is the way it is supposed to work. We are all aware of horrific events in which authorities have abused their power and punished or killed innocent civilians. But when it comes to citizens and authorities, both are to serve the common good.

Often, Christians complain about their current situations but spend no time trying to bless their towns, cities, and nation. Jeremiah's word to Israelites living in Babylon is instructive for Christians living in a pagan world: they were to serve the king of Babylon and work for "the well-being of the city" (Jer 29:4-7). Similarly, Paul did not say, "Go fight Nero," but, "Go do good."

In verse 4 Paul dignifies the civil office but also puts the leader under God. Usually "servant" (*diakanos*) refers to someone ministering consciously on God's behalf, but occasionally it denotes a public official (Esth 1:10; Jer 25:9). Many civil leaders unconsciously serve the purposes of God in the world (Moo, *Letter*, 801). Again, Paul is describing how the officials are supposed to rule. He is aware of exceptions but does not mention them here. These civil servants are intended for our "good" (v. 4a). This is what our officials should be doing: promoting that which leads to human flourishing (cf. 1 Tim 2:1-4).

Paul adds that the authorities have the right to punish wrongdoers (v. 4b). They do not bear the sword in vain. The government has the right to punish those who violate its laws (Moo, *Letter*, 802).

In verse 5 Paul summarizes the argument. Since we know God ordains the government, we should submit and do good and avoid God's judgment. The idea of "wrath" here is linked to verses 2-4, referring to the wrath and judgment of civil authorities. However, Schreiner points out,

> The distinction between the two should not be pressed too far, however, since the judgment and wrath of the government upon evildoers anticipates and foreshadows God's judgment and wrath on the day of the Lord. (*Romans*, 685)

The phrase "for the sake of [your] conscience" (ESV) refers to our moral responsibility to do what is required (ibid.). It is right and good to submit to the state. Our consciences confirm that God has established it, and we should walk in alignment with his good design for his glory.

How? (13:6-7)

Paul gives some practical ways to live out this ethic. The phrase "for this reason" links to the previous section. We see here two ways to keep a good conscience and to submit to the authorities.

"Pay taxes" (vv. 6-7a). Nero's taxes were highly unpopular, but Paul says Christians should not get tangled up in the backlash against them (Bird, *Romans*, 446). Paul states generally, "pay your obligations," but then moves to the more specific: "taxes to those you owe taxes" and "tolls to those you owe tolls," referring to both direct and indirect taxes. Recall Jesus's words: "Give to Caesar the things that are Caesar's, and to God the things that are God's" (Mark 12:17). Jesus legitimized government but put it in proper perspective. It is not ultimate. Give your coin to Caesar. Give to God what he deserves. The coin bears Caesar's image; give it to him. You bear God's image; give your life to him.

In case we missed it already, Paul reminds us, "[They] are God's servants." The word is different this time (*leitourgos*); it is a word for the people who served in the temple and in the New Testament as "ministers of the Lord" (Moo, *Letter*, 804; e.g., Rom 15:16). It is strong language; civic leaders are serving God's purposes.

Honor leaders (v. 7b). Respect the office, even when you disagree with leaders. Honor them for the Lord's sake. Paul preached the gospel to Felix and Agrippa, but he respected them as leaders (Acts 24–26). In Rome the way to stay under the radar as a marginalized group (which Christians were) was to live honorably, not rebelliously. We should have a respectful attitude toward leaders, not because the world esteems them or we like their policies but because they are fulfilling God's design. So then, how do citizens of heaven live as resident aliens in Rome? Allow me to list some action steps:

- Submit to governing authorities, acknowledging God's design for them, and thank God for all the good that is done through them.
- Pray for those in leadership (1 Tim 2:1-4). Avoid being the kind of Christian who spends more time criticizing than praying.
- Be a good citizen. Pay taxes. Obey the law. Be respectful. Pour yourself out for the needy. Live with a clear conscience before God. Serve your city and country for the common good.
- Engage the political process with truth and justice and the common good in mind. If you are a civil leader, lead with biblical values (Prov 8:15; 16:10,12; 29:4; 31:8-9) and bring your convictions into the public arena (Prov 14:34).
- Rest in the providence of God. Calm down. God is sovereign. No matter the circumstances, our testimony is "Our God reigns."
- Make your ultimate allegiance to King Jesus. Danny Akin says it well: "So, as a devoted follower of Jesus, I will say 'yes' to obeying the government and paying taxes to Caesar, but I will say 'no' to disobeying the Word of God and worshiping a man or institution. Independence Day for the Christian is not marked by a flag. No, our independence day is Easter, marked by a cross and an empty tomb" (*Mark*, 279).

Soon Jesus will establish a one-party kingdom, in which he will rule with perfect peace and justice forever. Kings and kingdoms fade away, but the kingdom of Christ endures.

Love Your Neighbor
ROMANS 13:8-10

The next daily action of the eschatologically minded saint is love for one's neighbor. The most frequented theme in Romans 12–14 is *love*. Jesus boiled down the whole law to "love God" and "love neighbor" (Matt 22:34-40). Here in Romans 13 Paul shows the relationship between love and law. I will just make a few comments on this paragraph.

We should point out that love is *not sentimentalism*; it has objective content found in God's law. So love and law are *not* enemies; they are "in-laws," united by their relationship to Jesus (Sinclair Ferguson, "A Single Debt and Some Essential Clothing"). Without Christ the law is powerless; without the law love is directionless. Because of Christ, the Holy Spirit has been poured into believers' hearts, enabling us to love (Rom 5:5); and Spirit-empowered love involves keeping God's commands (13:8-10; cf. John 14:15). The law is like the train tracks, and the Spirit like the engine.

In verse 8 Paul says that the only thing we should "owe" is "to love one another." Pay what is owed, fulfilling your agreements. This is not a proof text for never taking out a loan. (That is an issue of wisdom and integrity; it is an issue that is related to contentment, stewardship, simplicity, and self-control—important considerations for the modern world, to be sure!) The point here is that there is a debt that will never be settled: the debt of love for others. We do not have a choice in this; we are obligated to love. The debt of love is permanent.

Paul adds, "For the one who loves another has fulfilled the law" (v. 8). What does he have in mind? In the next verse Paul quotes four *horizontal* commands (regarding adultery, murder, stealing, and coveting) and then quotes Leviticus 19:18 about neighbor love. Adultery is not love because it violates God's commandments. It is an expression of rebellion, lust, and selfishness, not love. Regarding murder, you obviously are not showing love if you murder a person! Likewise, you do not love a person if you steal from him! In contrast, love is about faithfulness (not adultery), about wanting to see others flourish (not murdering them), and about blessing others (not stealing from them).

Regarding coveting, Paul moves from actions to a "desire." Coveting is not an expression of love for neighbor. Coveting is wanting what God has not chosen to give you. It is wanting what someone else has and not being content with what God has given you. If you want another person's wife, life, car, house, reputation, gifts, or anything else, that is not love. Paul adds the phrase "and any other commandment" (v. 9) to say that all of God's commands reveal what love is. God's law reflects God's own character.

Paul's citation (in v. 9) of Leviticus 19:18 shows that love is also more than *not* violating God's commands. Love involves *looking for ways to bless your neighbor*. For the husband, it means not only refusing to cheat on his spouse but also looking for ways to serve her, to care for her as himself. For the church member, it means not only avoiding sinning against one's brothers and sisters through the violation of God's commandments but looking for ways to bless them. Look for ways to love. Listen. Care. Give. Encourage. Do Romans 12:9-21 kinds of things.

In verse 10 Paul says that love fulfills the moral norms of the law, norms that transcend time and are fulfilled in Christ. When we love, we fulfill the law of Christ (Gal 6:2); we can do this by the enablement of the Spirit.

How do we live *this day* in light of *that day*? Every day, love your neighbor as yourself. It is *that day* that Paul now focuses on more clearly.

Live in the Light
ROMANS 13:11-14

"Besides this" heightens what has just been said. In other words, "Add the following to the list of exhortations in 12:1–13:10—in light of the imminence of the end."

Paul urges the Romans to wake up. He does not want the church to be spiritually asleep but rather wide awake, ready for action, awake to what matters because the end is near. (For a striking parallel to this text, see 1 Thess 5:5-8.) He then speaks of the consummation of our salvation. As Christians, we *are* saved (Eph 2:8), we are *being* saved (1 Cor 1:18), and we *will be* saved (Rom 5:9). Final salvation and judgment are coming, so we should not be asleep to these realities (cf. Matt 24:42-44; Luke 12:35-36; 1 Thess 5:1-2).

Paul goes on to use darkness and night as metaphors for sin (v. 12). For the believer, living in the already–not yet, he or she will reject the temptation to live in the darkness. He or she lives with the awareness that "the day is near." The world around us may not believe this, and certainly they do not live in view of it, but it is true. Currently it is the nighttime, but soon the morning will dawn for the saints. Every day we live, that day is getting closer, so let us live to glorify Christ, the "morning star" (Rev 22:16). Our Savior will soon dispel the darkness, and a new age will dawn. Let us live this day in light of that glorious day!

The "armor of light" is what we must put on (v. 12b). We are to wake up and get dressed with battle gear. In verse 14 he adds, "Put on the Lord Jesus Christ." We must put on the armor of light and live with an awareness of our identity in Christ because the darkness still threatens us. There is a war on! The desires of the flesh still attract us (v. 14). We are still tempted to do evil. So Christian, know that you are in a battle. Throw off the darkness and pursue light (cf. Eph 5:11).

The saint living in view of the end must "discard" some works of darkness (v. 12; cf. Eph 4:22-24; Col 3:8-10; Jam 1:21; 1 Pet 2:1). Paul mentions some of them here in Romans (v. 13). Many of these Christians were saved from these lifestyles, so Paul warns them about relapsing. He urges them to avoid the sins that characterized the outside world: wild partying and sexual sin. But he also highlights the sins that are often more acceptable to professing Christians: "quarreling and jealousy" (cf. Gal 5:19-21).

Paul tells us to put on the character of the Lord Jesus instead of engaging in sins of the flesh and of this age (v. 14). Let Christ be the clothes, or the armor, you wear (cf. Eph 6:11-12; 1 Thess 5:8). We realize that all who are baptized have already put on Christ (Gal 3:27), but Romans 13:14 exhorts us to continually "put on . . . Christ." We are clothed in Christ, and we need to put him on. Not only should we put on his character, but we should also live in personal fellowship with him. Live in the power and hope and joy of your new identity. Living in light is not just about being a *good* person; it is also about living as a *Christ-centered* person. Out of our identity in Christ, through communion with Christ, we pursue lives of holiness.

This reminds us that we have *power* to say no to sin and yes to God. To "make no provision for the flesh" means to say no to any thought that may lead you to sin; avoid even the desire for it. Do not plan to sin. Do not daydream about sin. Do not seek comfort in sin. Do not flirt with sin. Specifically, in light of this passage, do not entertain the idea that a wild night of drunkenness and partying will cure your loneliness, sadness, or boredom. As a married person, do not entertain the idea that committing adultery will satisfy your unfulfilled romantic desires. As a person frustrated with your current situation, do not entertain the thought of growing jealous of others. As a bitter person, do not begin quarreling with others.

Make no provision for the flesh. Instead, direct your mind to the promises of God in Scripture. Direct your mind to the beauty of Christ! Follow the lifestyle of the Savior in this present age. Direct your mind to the glory that is to come. We have a wonderful Savior who satisfies our human longings and empowers us for this kind of obedience. Jesus is better than sin—the sin of retaliation, the sin of dishonoring the government, the sin of failing to love our neighbors, and the sins of the flesh. One day soon he will come and eradicate the world of sin once and for all, and we will no longer wrestle in these bodies of flesh. Live *this day* in view of *that day*!

Reflect and Discuss

1. Why is it important for us to live in light of the coming day of the Lord? What practical difference could it make in your day-to-day life (in view of this passage)?
2. What does Paul say about retaliation (12:17-21)? How is his teaching countercultural today? How can a belief in God's final judgment help you leave vengeance to God?
3. What would it look like for your life to be marked by grace and goodness, not vengeance and vitriol?
4. How can you overcome evil with good today?
5. Why should we submit to the governing authorities?
6. How can we submit to the governing authorities?
7. Is your first instinct to criticize civil leaders or to pray for them? Stop and pray for some of your governmental leaders now.
8. How are love and law related (13:8-10)? Why is it important to keep these two things together?
9. Why is it important for Christians to remember that we are in a spiritual war right now (13:11-14)?
10. What kind of temptations are you encountering regularly? How can Paul's teaching in Romans 13:11-14 help you win these battles?

Gospel Unity

ROMANS 14:1–15:13

Main Idea: Paul shows us the way of unity in the church: gospel central-ity, liberty in the nonessentials, love for one another, and the imitation of our Lord's example.

I. **Liberty (14:1-12)**
   A. Do not criticize one another (14:3).
   B. Honor the Lord (14:4-12).
II. **Love (14:13-23)**
   A. Do not impede fellow believers (14:13-15a).
   B. Christ died for them (14:15b-16).
   C. The kingdom is more important than food (14:17-23).
III. **The Lord's Example (15:1-13)**
   A. Put others first (15:1-6).
   B. Welcome one another as Christ welcomed you (15:7-13).

Essential oils are all the rage today. I love them. I love the smells. Our family uses the diffusers. I use them in my homemade beard balm. Recently, my youngest daughter told me that I smelled like mosquito repellent! I thought it was glorious. However, I do think the "essential" name is a bit overstated. Are these oils really *essential*? Can you not live without them? Maybe these names would be more appropriate: helpful oils, special oils, or not-quite-essential-but-wonderful oils.

In Romans we read about something we cannot live without: the gospel. It is not an overstatement to say that it is truly *essential*. But at times churches can lose sight of what is essential and begin majoring on the minors. A gospel-centered church makes the *major thing* the *main thing*—in everything.

This text teaches us how people from different backgrounds can stay united in the gospel. It is not hard to follow Paul's argument, but it is hard to practice. It requires believers giving freedom to one another in nonessentials, and it requires them to walk in love toward those who have different cultural practices, preferences, and customs. This text is one long discussion on *love, liberty,* and *the Lord Jesus Christ.* Paul spends so much time on this issue because unity in Christ is so important—not uniformity but a unity with rich diversity centered on Jesus.

Remember Romans 12:16: "Live in harmony with one another." The passage under consideration gives us a challenge for practicing Romans 12:16. Can we live in harmony with fellow believers who practice nonessentials differently from us?

Christians have always had a hard time with this matter. It is easy to fall into the trap of criticizing and rejecting fellow believers because they do not take on our cultural practices. A mark of Christ-centered love and unity is that we welcome and build up other believers despite their differences of opinions on nonessentials.

Weak and Strong

In the first two verses of chapter 14, Paul introduces his specific burden and gives the main thrust of the argument. Believers must welcome/accept/receive one another. Here the emphasis is on accepting the person "weak in faith," but later in 15:7 the call is for everyone to welcome "one another."

The community is divided into two groups: *weak* and *strong.* The weaker brother or sister has trusted Jesus for salvation. But the weaker Christian is overly conscientious about issues not addressed specifically in biblical revelation. The weaker brother is thus more easily offended than the stronger Christian (cf. 1 Cor 8:1-13). The stronger Christian feels more freedom regarding certain cultural practices.

In this text it seems that the weaker Christians were trying to enforce particular customs and practices that are not required. It mainly had to do with Torah observance. It appears that the weaker Christians kept the Old Testament food laws and observed the Sabbath strictly, and they probably observed other Jewish holidays. Further, some of them apparently did not eat meat or drink wine for various reasons (see 14:17,21). Regarding meat, Paul says the weaker person "eats only vegetables" due to concern about the food's uncleanness or because of its association with pagan idolatry (14:2; cf. See Lev 11:1-47; Deut 14:1-21).

While it may be fair to say that the majority of the "weak" were probably Jewish Christians (many of whom relocated back to Rome after Claudius's edict) and the majority of the "strong" were probably Gentile Christians (Bird, *Romans,* 466), we should remember that some of the "weak" probably included some Gentiles who had first become God fearers accustomed to Jewish practices. And some Jewish Christians (like Paul) were not in the weaker brother category (see 15:1).

This is an important text for many reasons today, and it is not hard to find a similar situation in churches around the world. For instance, those who convert to Christianity from Islam or Hinduism or another religion may have a history with certain dietary practices that makes it difficult to handle certain cultural practices by Christians. Through the years theologians have called matters that tend to divide Christians *adiaphora*, that is, "things indifferent" (cf. "disputed matters" in 14:1). These are matters not essential to the faith that sincere Christians may disagree on, but sadly "things indifferent" become "things too important." Without compromising the gospel, Christians need to hear Paul's word here and accept those whom Christ accepts (cf. 15:7).

Now, the "weak" did not believe that by abstaining from certain foods and by observing the Sabbath one would obtain salvation, but it does appear that they believed you would be a better, more dynamic Christian. If they had believed a different gospel, Paul wouldn't have been so accepting. Just read Galatians! Paul gives liberty on the nonessentials but gives no ground on the purity of the gospel.

Regarding the "strong," they seem to be the larger group in the church, and they celebrated Christian freedom. Notice verse 2 again. Paul says they eat "anything." Further, every *day* was equally important to the stronger Christian (v. 5).

We must remember that a "stronger conscience" does not mean you can do whatever you want in the name of "I have a stronger conscience"! It means an "informed conscience." It is a conscience informed by the Scriptures.

The problem with the weaker brother or sister is the inability to accept certain new covenant teachings. His or her conscience needs strengthening. Remember Peter in Acts 10? The Lord said, "Get up, Peter; kill and eat" (Acts 10:13). He says, "No, Lord!" Peter knew Jesus's teaching, but he struggled to accept it. Certain things take a while for one to embrace. So we must be patient and charitable. The Jews had been taught to view their calendars in certain ways, and abstain from certain foods, for centuries. These habits and attitudes were hard to change.

Both the strong and the weak believed in moral norms—stealing is a sin, sexual immorality is sin, murder is a sin, adultery is a sin, drunkenness and gluttony are sins, and so on. They simply disagreed on certain cultural and social practices.

Paul thinks both groups should be tolerated, but he is *not* neutral. He is a stronger brother (see 15:1). He clearly thinks the stronger brother is in the correct position, but there is liberty and charity here for the weaker brother and sister, giving time for growth and making an effort to maintain unity (Stott, *Message*, 357). Paul does not hold to the food laws. "Everything is clean," he says (14:14,20). He believes the Old Testament regulations on foods are no longer binding on us (Gal 4:10; Col 2:16-17). Requiring things the Bible does not require and having greater strictness in nonessential matters does not show that a person is a stronger Christian but a weaker one.

Paul is subtle about this critique, but you can catch his drift. He is likely subtle for a number of reasons, one of which is that he is mainly concerned about the stronger Christian's lack of love more so than the weaker Christian's practices. This is a good word for the "freedom in Christ" crowd. Paul does not kick the weak to the curb. He wants unity in the church, and to see this happen: *liberty must be given, love must be displayed,* and *the Lord's example must be followed.*

Liberty
ROMANS 14:1-12

Paul urges Christians not to "argue about disputed matters" (14:1). This is key for liberty to be practiced in the church. Some Christians love to argue. While it is good to be passionate about the truth, we must beware of thinking that everything is equally important. We can end up being legalistic, divisive, cranky, and argumentative. Let's heed Paul's word: Do not break fellowship over debatable nonessentials. Paul wants the strong to welcome the weak into fellowship, and the weak to welcome the strong, and no one to disrupt the unity of the church over disputable matters.

Mike Bird gives three levels of importance: (1) matters essential for salvation; (2) matters that are important to the faith and the church but not essential for salvation; and (3) matters of indifference—debatable nonessentials/preferences (*Romans*, 493). Verse 2 is an example of a level-three debatable issue: *eating meat.* The weak were concerned about eating "unclean" things, but the strong were not. Further, in Rome, the vast majority of meat available would have been pork and meat associated with ritual meals and pagan idolatry (ibid., 469).

Do Not Criticize One Another (14:3)

In verse 3 Paul's word to the church is clear: **do not criticize or condemn
one another.** He highlights the temptations of the strong and the weak.
The strong are tempted to criticize and be condescending toward the
weak; and the weak are tempted to condemn the strong for their more
flexible conscience. In my context, I can imagine the stronger calling
the weaker Christians "fundies" and the weaker Christians calling the
stronger "worldly."

Paul says in verse 3 that God has accepted the stronger brother; that
is, he or she is a Christian. So he appeals to the weaker brother, How
can you not fellowship with someone that God is in fellowship with? By
not welcoming the other, the weaker Christian is implying that God's
acceptance of the strong Christian is misguided.

Therefore, stronger brothers, do not criticize the person whose
conscience is easily offended. Weaker brothers, do not condemn the
person with the stronger conscience.

Honor the Lord (14:4-12)

In verses 4-12 Paul adds that whatever position you take on debatable
issues in general, the concern should be the same for both: **honor the
Lord.** In verse 4 Paul says to leave judgment to the Lord. It is like Paul
is asking (speaking mainly to the weaker Christian): "Who do you think
you are, claiming to be the stronger Christian's master?" The Christian
has only one master: the Lord Jesus (Moo, *Romans*, 449). Christ is the
final Judge of one's salvation.

The stronger Christian "stands or falls" before his Master. This is
salvific language. Paul adds that the Lord will keep the strong Christian;
the Lord will enable him or her to stand. Both the weak and the strong
are recipients of the Lord's favor; therefore, they should not judge one
another since the Lord has accepted them.

The apostle brings up the issue of *days* in verse 5. This probably
refers to the Sabbath but may also include certain Jewish holy days.
Whatever position one takes, Paul says each should be "fully convinced
in his own mind"; that is, obey your conscience on this matter.

To clarify the point about judging others, it is not wrong to be concerned about the well-being of a brother or sister who has fallen into grievous sin. We must restore fallen believers (Gal 6:1). What Paul is saying here in Romans is different from this important restorative ministry. Here, the weaker are not judging the strong because of grievous sin but because the stronger—we might say today—does not take Saturday off from work or because she likes bacon! But these are not sins! So Paul essentially says, "How dare you?"

In verse 6 Paul underscores the proper Christian motivation: to honor the Lord. Every Christian should live in such a way that everyone knows the lordship of Jesus has preeminence over his or her choices. This is the key. If both the weak and the strong are seeking to honor the Lord, they should not be criticizing or condemning one another.

Paul elaborates on what it means to live under Christ's lordship in verses 7-9. He says that it means you do not live for your own self-interests but for the interests of Christ, the One who died and rose that he may be Lord of all. Whether in life or death, Christ owns us. Therefore, the Lord expects our conduct to please him. The Roman Christians were trying to dictate to one another how one should treat the other in debatable matters, but Paul calls for liberty and for both groups to live under the lordship of Jesus and allow the Lord alone to judge.

Paul reminds the readers that we will all "stand before the judgment seat of God" (v. 10). We are ultimately accountable to God, not to one another's faulty bar of judgment. In verse 11 Paul quotes Isaiah 45:23 to highlight the judgment of God at the end of history, and then he reiterates the point in verse 12. So when you choose a position on a debatable issue, do so with the sovereign Lord in mind. God will judge; live your life accordingly.

For there to be real gospel unity in the church, there must be Christian liberty—a kind of liberty that avoids criticizing and condemning one another and that stays focused on the lordship of Christ and the essentials of the faith.

Love
ROMANS 14:13-23

A second component of gospel-centered unity is the need to display love to one another. Paul begins this section with an exhortation against judging one another directed at both the weak and the strong, but the strong are primarily in view in the verses that follow.

Do Not Impede Fellow Believers (14:13-15a)

The call not to "put a stumbling block" in the way of another Christian is an exhortation to the strong. Paul means, **do not do something that will impede a fellow believer's spiritual progress.** Love never does something that will seriously damage a fellow Christian's discipleship.

In verse 14 Paul tells the strong that they are actually right about food (cf. Mark 7:19; Acts 10:14). Saying all food is "kosher" follows Jesus's teaching. The old food laws have been fulfilled. You can eat anything. But while the strong are correct, Paul tells the strong to consider the unity of the fellowship and the consciences of others. They are to give the weak room—to respect their opinions. A stronger Christian must never flaunt his or her freedom but must seek to build up everyone.

The apostle adds that when the stronger Christian eats what he or she is free to eat in front of the weak, the strong are hurting, distressing, or causing pain to the weaker brother. Peer pressure and flaunting one's freedom in front of the weak may lead the weak to violate their consciences or perhaps even walk away from the fellowship.

So, what should the strong do? They should *walk in love* (v. 15). Love has regard for the weaker conscience. Love limits its own liberty (Stott, *Message*, 365). It asks, "Am I loving my brother with this action?" The strong are not wrong in their view of food and drink, but they are wrong when they enjoy this freedom in a way that harms other Christians. They need to reorder their priorities. They need to ask whether they should put down their freedoms; after all, a freedom is something that can be taken up but *may also be put down!* If you cannot put a freedom down, you are *enslaved* to that thing rather than enjoying it rightly.

The gospel and the unity of the church must be the first priority. "No belief about food is worth throwing a wrecking ball through Christian fellowship," Bird quips (*Romans*, 479). To the Corinthians, Paul said he was free, but he was also a servant of all for the sake of the gospel (1 Cor 9:19-23). Martin Luther once said it like this: "A Christian man is a most free lord of all, subject to none. A Christian man is a most dutiful servant of all, subject to all" (in Bruce, *Romans*, 246).

Christ Died for Them (14:15b-16)

Paul goes on to tie love to the work of Christ and the kingdom of God. These glorious realities must be in view if we are to love well. So first, he says, **do not distress or destroy weaker Christians because Christ died for them** (14:15b-16). Paul takes us to the cross on this issue. The cross is the appropriate place to talk about unity and about love. John Stott comments here:

> Did Christ love him enough to die for him, and shall we not love him enough to refrain from wounding his conscience? Did Christ sacrifice himself for his well-being, and shall we assert ourselves to his harm? Did Christ die to save him, and shall we not care if we destroy him? (*Message*, 365)

Because Christ has redeemed your weaker brother or sister, walk in love toward him or her.

Paul adds in verse 16 not to allow the liberty you enjoy to be spoken of *as evil.* This may happen when the strong flaunts a freedom, causing the weak to make insults about a gift that God has given (Moo, *Letter*, 855; Bird, *Romans*, 477). Instead, keep the cross in mind. Do not overestimate the importance of certain freedoms, and do not underestimate the importance of the cross!

The Kingdom Is More Important Than Food (14:17-23)

Second, Paul adds, **do not distress or destroy weaker Christians because the kingdom of God is more important than food** (14:17-23). This is the only place in Romans where the phrase "kingdom of God" is used (Moo, *Letter*, 488). Do not overestimate the importance of food and drink, and *do not underestimate the importance of the kingdom of God.* The kingdom of God is about righteousness, peace, and the Holy Spirit. We are righteous in Christ Jesus and thus have peace with God, and the indwelling Spirit empowers us and gives us a foretaste of the future. These things are what really matter! Because we are righteous in Christ, we now live righteous lives, peaceful lives, and joyful lives. This is the kingdom of God at work. This is the King ruling in our midst.

Whoever seeks first the kingdom and acknowledges that food and drink are secondary matters pleases God and "receives human approval" (v. 18). This means the Christian community esteems this kind of person.

Verses 19-21 are a list of exhortations kingdom-minded people should follow. Paul says that Christians should prioritize building up, not tearing down, a brother or sister (v. 19). Prioritize peace and harmony, not insisting on your way. Many love the idea of unity until they are faced with the decision to practice this verse (along with the rest of Romans 14!).

Paul adds, "Do not tear down God's work because of food" (v. 20). I take this to be referring to *the work of building Christian community*. The Christian's responsibility is to build up the fellowship, not tear it down by insisting on one's views of nonessentials. You can do great damage to the church by living self-centeredly.

This point is pressed further. Objectively, you are free to eat meat (cf. 1 Tim 4:4); however, some believers might stumble by what a person eats. He adds wine to the list in 14:21. Meat and wine should be avoided when they might cause offense but not necessarily at other times. Jews did not think it was wrong to drink wine; they celebrated it as a gift to enjoy (Ps 104:15); however, some in Rome apparently feared that the wine was tainted with idolatry through pagan practices (Moo, *Letter*, 856). The point is, do not do something that will harm a brother or sister. At times, you should relinquish freedom to avoid division.

Paul finishes this section by drawing a distinction between belief and action, that is, between private conviction and communal behavior. There is no need to broadcast your views on disputable matters, trying to convince people that you are right. The strong Christian is blessed because his conscience approves of his eating everything, so he can follow his conscience without any feelings of guilt (v. 22). Those who still doubt should not eat meat because it is wrong to violate one's conscience (v. 23). Doing so would not be done "from faith," that is, with a sincere belief that it is OK to do so. Here Paul is using faith in the sense of personal conviction. Stott comments:

> Although, as we have seen, [conscience] is not infallible, it is nevertheless sacrosanct [sacred], so that to go against it (to act not from faith) is to sin. At the same time, alongside this explicit instruction not to violate our conscience, there is an implicit requirement to educate it. (*Message*, 368)

Throughout the history of the church, there have been unnecessary divisions over things like the theater, cosmetics, playing cards, clothing, food and drink, dancing, sports, and more. We all need a good dose of Romans 14! The often-quoted line (attributed to a number of people) is a good one to ponder and apply: "In essentials unity, in nonessentials liberty, but in all things charity." If we divide over nonessentials, tearing down the work of God, then we are no different from the world. Let's learn to differentiate between matters of biblical command and matters of personal preference, and in all things let's walk in love and build up our brothers and sisters for whom Christ died and whom Christ accepts. (For a great resource on the conscience, see Andrew Naselli and J. D. Crowley's book *Conscience: What It Is, How to Train It, and Loving Those Who Differ.*)

The Lord's Example
ROMANS 15:1-13

In this section Paul first summarizes how the strong should treat the weak (15:1-6). He then roots his teaching in the broader story line of Scripture, showing the global purposes of God in the Messiah (vv. 7-12). The Lord Jesus's example of serving others (and not himself) is stressed, and the Savior's work of redeeming and welcoming a people from all nations is celebrated. Paul has already emphasized the lordship of Christ in his instruction on liberty and love in Romans 14, and here again we are drawn to Christ's life, ministry, and saving purposes as motivation for Christian unity.

Put Others First (15:1-6)

What is the responsibility of the strong? The strong (that is, those who are free to eat meat and drink wine and who esteem all days alike) ought to bear with the failings of the weak (v. 1). They should modify their conduct for the good of the weak. Further, they should not live to please themselves. Paul's point is clear: it is selfish to trample on the consciences of the weak. That is not the way of a humble servant of Christ (cf. Phil 2:1-4).

The apostle adds a positive way to say what has been said: instead of causing a Christian to stumble (14:13,20-21), tearing a brother down (14:20), or damaging him (14:15), the strong should seek to build up the weaker brother.

Paul then gives a theological basis for such behavior (vv. 3-4). Why should we heed verses 1-2? It is because Christ did not please himself. If Jesus gave up the glory of heaven and his own life (Phil 2:5-11), then we can give up our liberties for the good of our neighbors when love requires it.

Paul also reminds the readers of Psalm 69 to show what kind of attitude the Lord Jesus had. This particular psalm is found throughout the New Testament as writers highlight the suffering of Jesus (Matt 27:34; John 2:17; 15:25; Acts 1:20; Rom 11:9-10). I think Moo is correct that Paul may have in mind the insults that the weak are hurling on the strong (*Romans*, 471). He comments, "Like Jesus, the strong in Rome should be willing to serve in love even those who are being nasty to them" (ibid.).

Paul then provides a basis for citing the Old Testament (v. 4). This is a parenthetical comment, but it is an important one regarding how we view Scripture. Paul says that the Old Testament was written for us— Christians. It is a gift to us because it reveals our Messiah, and this brings us hope. Christians can do hard things through the encouragement of the Holy Scriptures. So then, let's meditate on them day and night in order to see our Savior and follow his ways.

Paul then uses these words, "endurance and encouragement," in his prayer for the church in Rome (vv. 5-6). This is a wonderful prayer for unity that churches would do well to memorize today. It is a unity that is Christ centered ("according to Christ"), that follows the example of Jesus. Paul's prayer is that the church would be filled with Christ-centered harmony and love, instead of quarreling and division, so that God may be glorified. Paul knows this kind of unity requires prayer and the unifying work of the Spirit. In order for the church to have unity that transcends preferences and differences of opinions and disputed matters, we need more than a pep talk. We need God to intervene.

Welcome One Another as Christ Welcomed You (15:7-13)

Paul comes back to his opening appeal of accepting the person weak in faith (14:1) by urging the weak and the strong to "welcome one another" (15:7). This mutual acceptance reflects the nature of Christ's grace. He has "accepted" (NIV) or "welcomed" all believers. In this mutual acceptance, God is glorified.

In verses 8-13 Paul then puts the issue in light of the grand story of redemption. Through the Messiah, God's promise to the patriarchs has been fulfilled, bringing salvation not only for the Jews but also the Gentiles (vv. 8-9). God's faithfulness to the Jews with the inclusion of the Gentiles sums up a key theme in Romans, bringing closure not only to the weak and strong discussion but also to the whole letter (Moo, *Romans*, 477–78). God's Word has not failed, for Christ has confirmed it (cf. Rom 9:6)!

God's saving plan always included the Gentiles in God's people, just as Scripture foretold (v. 9). Rescuing the nations was not an afterthought but has always been part of God's saving purposes. The Messiah's work not only confirmed God's truthfulness, but it was also intended to lead the Gentiles to "glorify God for his mercy" (v. 9). What a glorious transformation! The Gentiles ("the nations," *ethna*) go from being idol worshipers to worshipers of the triune God, who has blessed them with saving mercy (cf. Rom 9:16,18,23; 11:30-32; 12:1-2).

It is important for believers to see petty squabbles in light of God's glorious plan of salvation. For the believers in Rome, this reminder about God's eternal plan of having a people for himself from among the nations should have made it inconceivable to divide over matters of indifference. The Messiah has come for the Jewish Christians as well as the Gentile Christians, for the weaker brother as well as the stronger brother. The appeal to unity, then, is not based on a thin foundation but on God's saving purposes.

To support this assertion about God's saving purposes for both Jew and Gentile, Paul cites a handful of verses from the three main sections of the Hebrew Scriptures (Law, Prophets, and Writings). Each quotation includes the Gentiles ("the nations"). Paul also uses several words for "praise" to underscore God's purpose of having the Gentiles praise him for his mercy. And two of the verses (15:10,12) make clear that their inclusion in the people of God depends on the Jews (Moo, *Romans*, 479).

The first citation (v. 9) is taken from Psalm 18:49 and is also found in 2 Samuel 22:50. Paul cites this royal victory psalm of David to highlight how God's plan included Gentiles through the Davidic line (of which Jesus is the ultimate heir). The second citation (v. 10) is taken from Deuteronomy 32:43. Moses is calling the Gentiles to join Israel in praise to God. The third citation (v. 11) is taken from Psalm 117, and it too calls the nations to praise God. The final citation (v. 12) is taken from Isaiah 11:10, where the Davidic King, the Messiah, is proclaimed as the hope for the nations.

Paul picks up the theme of "hope" in verse 13 with another prayer petition to the "God of hope." Paul asks God to fill the Christians in Rome with "all joy and peace in believing" (ESV) or "as you believe" (CSB), meaning that joy and peace only come through *believing* in the Messiah. The purpose of this filling is so that "you may overflow with hope by the power of the Holy Spirit." So once again the note of hope is struck, another major theme in Romans (cf. 4:18; 5:2-5; 8:20-25; 12:12;

15:4,12,24). If Christian hope permeates the lives of both the weak and the strong, it will transform their relationships.

To conclude this marvelous section of Scripture, it is clear that Paul's appeal to unity rests not on some modern view of tolerance, nor some vague sentimentalism, but on the fact that Jesus Christ has come for the nations, and if he has welcomed people from every background who trust in him, we must also welcome one another. Such mutual acceptance and upbuilding will require sacrifice and putting others first. It will happen when we make the gospel central, refusing to divide over disputable matters. It will happen when we are filled with hope, living in view of God's saving purposes revealed in Scripture. It will happen when we do what Romans 14:1–15:13 calls us to do: submit to our Lord and Savior Jesus Christ and walk in his ways. Some twelve times in this passage the word "Lord" (Gk *kyrios*) is used (Bird, *Romans*, 488). This is where we should begin in seeking unity, by fixing our eyes on our Lord, who lived, died, and rose again to have a people for himself from every tribe, tongue, people, and nation (Rev 5:9).

Reflect and Discuss

1. Who does Paul say is "weak in faith"?
2. What kind of attitude does Paul say the weak and the strong should have?
3. Why should the reality of the Lord's final judgment have an impact on how we relate to one another in the church?
4. What does Paul say about honoring the Lord?
5. What is Paul's own view of "unclean" food?
6. Explain why the reality of the kingdom of God should impact our relationships in the church.
7. Do you think Romans 14:19 would be a good verse for churches to cite before meetings or for Christians to read when dealing with conflict? Consider how you may read and apply this verse.
8. Regarding relationships in the church, why must we remember the way of Christ, that he "did not please himself" (15:3)?
9. Concerning Christian hospitality, why should we remember that Christ has welcomed both weak in faith and those strong in faith?
10. Regarding conflict, why should we see earthly squabbles in light of God's global purposes of salvation?

Great Commission Christians

ROMANS 15:14-33

Main Idea: As Paul describes his special calling, past travels, and future plans for ministry, we find several theological and practical directives for being Great Commission Christians.

I. Be Part of a Healthy, Gospel-Centered Church (15:14-15).
II. See Life and Mission through the Lens of Worship (15:16-18).
III. Remember that Fruitfulness Is the Result of Divine Enablement (15:15b-19).
IV. Have a Passion for the Gospel and a Heart for People (15:20-21).
V. Support the Work of Church Planting (15:19-24).
VI. Support the Work of Mercy Ministry (15:25-27).
VII. Refresh Those on the Front Lines (15:28-29,32).
VIII. Pray for Those on the Front Lines (15:30-33).

About every eighteen months, some of the pastors and elders at Imago Dei Church gather up all of our international missionaries in one location for a time of encouragement and care. These times of worship, prayer, counseling, and just sheer fun together have been a highlight of my pastoral ministry. In one of these gatherings, I had the privilege of leading the group through Romans 15:14-33. I saw it as being extremely fitting for the occasion since this text highlights the special bond between the church and the missionary—in this case, the greatest missionary ever, the apostle Paul.

Antioch had been Paul's original home base (Acts 13). It was his sending church. Now he wants to go to Spain, and he wants the church in Rome to be the new Antioch, supporting his work in pioneer regions. The first section (Rom 15:14-21) is about Paul's special calling and past travels. The second section (vv. 22-33) is about the apostle's future plans.

In this little glimpse into Paul's travels, we see the heart of the greatest missionary ever. We get a look at the mission of God, the mission of the apostle, and the mission of the church. Mike Bird says that this portion of the letter is "all about mission, mission, mission!" He writes, "Romans is theology written from the frantic frontline of the mission field, not in the serene surroundings of a seminary professor's office" (Bird, *Romans*, 502). Indeed, Romans is written from the missional trenches, and we should never think of it as purely containing doctrine devoid of mission.

In light of this missionally drenched portion of the letter, I would like to identify eight directives for being Great Commission people. Great Commission people make Jesus's final command their first priority. What is this command? It is to make disciples of all nations (Matt 28:18-20). While few Christians will cross continents and cultures to make the gospel known, all Christians should make the gospel known somewhere. For some this will merely involve crossing the street or the hallway or the gym. There is a need for Great Commission Christians everywhere because spiritual lostness exists all around us. Further, Great Commission people support one another. In this text we see the importance of the local church supporting Paul's work among the nations.

Of course, this text is not an end-all for missions, and we must be careful making application from it. These are *Paul's experiences and his travel plans*. But we can learn some important principles if we consider which principles are *timeless* and are *taught elsewhere* in Scripture. There is much here that qualifies.

Be Part of a Healthy, Gospel-Centered Church
ROMANS 15:14-15

Consider what Paul says about the maturity of the Roman Christians in verses 14. Some think Paul is flattering the church here for the sake of drawing support, but I disagree. He is sincerely affirming them. After writing rather "boldly" (v. 15) on some points to the Romans as an apostle ("because of the grace given me by God"), he pauses to encourage them. This affirmation had to mean a lot to the church. Encouragement and affirmation are important aspects of ministry to one another.

Paul identifies three marks of a healthy church: *goodness, knowledge,* and the *ability to instruct one another.* There seems to be a good collection of churches in Rome, made up of faithful saints. They were high-character people, as the word "goodness" speaks of moral excellence. Further, they were theologically discerning people ("filled with all knowledge"). He has alluded to various hymns and creeds they shared and the standard of teaching they embraced (1:3-5,8; 4:25; 6:17; 10:9-10). Paul could go into some of these deeper issues of theology with the

Romans because he was not starting from a blank slate (Bird, *Romans*, 504). Finally, they were marked by mutual edification, being able to "instruct one another" (v. 14). Ordinary Christians—not just the clergy, and especially those who are mature and wise in the faith—should counsel, warn, encourage, and challenge other Christians. Like Paul, faithful Christians will be about the ministry of instruction and reminding (v. 15). This ministry of reminding one another of the gospel is one of the primary ways a church becomes gospel centered.

No church is perfect, but churches that are pursuing goodness and knowledge and who are all about admonishing one another with the Word and reminding one another of the good news are churches Paul would commend. To this kind of church Paul appeals for missionary support. The Roman location was certainly strategic for getting to Spain, but Paul does not highlight geography here but rather the saints' spiritual maturity. It is those of a healthy, gospel-centered church who not only bless one another but also reach out to the world in mission.

See Life and Mission through the Lens of Worship
ROMANS 15:16-18

Paul says that he has been appointed as "a minister of Christ Jesus to the Gentiles, serving as a priest of the gospel of God" (v. 16). Notice this idea of priestly service. The language carries the idea of performing holy duties unto God as a priest. So, in one sense, Paul saw his ministry as that of a priest offering sacred worship to God. He was a worshiper/priest, as all Christians are (1 Pet 2:4-10). Paul was not a priest the way many people today may think of a priest, but his ministry was priestly, as it involved holy work done for the glory of God.

In what way? Doug Moo states, "[Paul] is a priest using 'the gospel' as the means by which he offers the Gentile converts as a sacrifice acceptable to God" (*Letter*, 890). Paul was not offering animals for sacrifice but offering the Gentiles to God; they were to live out their faith as living sacrifices to God (12:1-2). Paul's aim was to bring the Gentiles to the obedience of faith (1:5; 15:26). He says in the next two verses that in Christ Jesus he is proud of his work (recognizing it is empowered by Christ—my next point) and that his word-and-deed work is aimed at the obedience of the Gentiles. So then, Paul was a worshiper who sought to make more worshipers. He was a living sacrifice who sought to see more living sacrifices. We too should see our mission through this lens of worship.

Our lives are to be an offering of worship, and our work of mission is to be an offering of worship. We go and send to glorify God, and we long to see God's name magnified where it is not. When you see "Gentiles" in this passage, think "nations" and "people groups." The nations dominate this section (vv. 15-32; cf. vv. 9-12). Thousands of people among nations are not worshiping Christ, and that is why we go to every people group on the globe. One day Jesus will be exalted by those of every tribe and tongue (Rev 5:9), and the Father will give the Son the nations as an inheritance (Ps 2). Until that day we pour out our lives in sacrificial mission as an act of worship to our King who is worthy.

Remember that Fruitfulness Is the Result of Divine Enablement
ROMANS 15:15B-19

In these verses Paul says that the Father, Son, and Spirit are working through him. A beautiful, Trinitarian enablement is expressed here. This point is true for all Christians: our work is Trinitarian work.

The Father chose Paul and prepared him by "grace" (v. 15). Additionally, his work among the nations was effective because of the Holy Spirit's work (v. 16). How do you turn idolatrous pagans into Christ worshipers? Not by your own power! A missionary heart is a dependent heart. Further, Paul's work is Christocentric work, as it is "in Christ Jesus" that he is proud of his work (v. 17). That is, Paul cannot take credit for fruitfulness; he recognizes it is "in Christ" that he is able to be effective in ministry. He also speaks of "what Christ has accomplished through [him]" in verse 18.

We need to settle this in our hearts and minds. If we see any fruit in ministry, the glory goes to God. Pride says, "Look at me." But genuine Christian ministry says, "Look at what God is doing!" Doug Moo warns about this danger of pride:

> "Successful" ministers are prone to pride, one of the most
> basic of all sins. It is frighteningly easy to fall into a mode in
> which we begin taking credit for whatever positive spiritual
> impact we are having. . . . Moreover, pride is not only wrong in
> itself, it can lead to so many other sins. I am positive that many
> prominent ministers fall into sexual sin precisely because
> they begin to think that they are immune to such ordinary

temptations or, worse yet, they begin unconsciously thinking they are above the law. (Moo, *Romans*, 496)

This is a sober-minded and needed word. Stay low, stay dependent on God's power, and if any visible fruit comes from your ministry, be quick to give God the glory for it.

There is more to consider regarding the need for divine enablement. Paul says that Christ has accomplished things "by word and deed for the obedience of the Gentiles" (v. 18). I take "word and deed" to mean evangelism and compassionate service. Christ worked through him to do these ministries.

In verse 19 Paul says that he was God's point man for bringing the gospel to the Gentiles (Moo, *Romans*, 487) and that God worked mightily through the apostle "by the power of miraculous signs and wonders, and by the power of God's Spirit." As Paul carried out his word-and-deed ministry, God often did wonders through Paul, displaying his supremacy among the nations (cf. 14:8-18), from "Jerusalem" (Acts 9:26-28) all the way around to "Illyricum" (near present-day Albania). This geography highlights more than Paul's past travels; it also seems to indicate that a significant phase of ministry has been completed (ibid., 487). After working and establishing churches in these areas, Paul is ready to move on (v. 20; ibid.).

So, let's learn the importance of humble reliance on God. Ministry is not about us. It is not our word; it is not our power. We plant the seed and beg God for rain. Let's always assign glory to God alone for any fruitfulness we may see. And let's be encouraged that God uses ordinary people, by his power, to bring others to worshipful obedience.

Have a Passion for the Gospel and a Heart for People
ROMANS 15:20-21

In verses 20-21 Paul speaks of what John Piper calls "a holy ambition" ("Holy Ambition"). The apostle then grounds this ambition in a text from Isaiah 52:15.

What is this holy ambition? It is to proclaim the good news where people had not yet heard the name of Christ spoken. Paul was a pioneer missionary. Not everyone will have Paul's ambition. Some will build on someone else's foundation, and that is fine (cf. 1 Cor 3:3-11). We all have different gifts (cf. 1 Cor 7:7), and we must each individually account to our Master (Rom 14:4). Still, we should all share Paul's concern for the unreached peoples of the world who will perish apart from the gospel (1:18-25). We should do our part to reach the thousands of unreached people groups.

How can we help spread the gospel to every nook and cranny of the world? Some Christians love to debate the question, What happens to those who never hear of Jesus? But as my friend David Platt says, our primary concern should not be to resolve the issue but to remove the issue! We should pray for God to raise up more frontier evangelists, and we should support those who are doing such courageous work.

To have a holy ambition means to have a Christ-centered cause controlling your life, your decision making, and your interests. The right kind of ambition is one driven by the gospel and a heart for people; the Great Commission and the great commandment should drive believers' lives.

So, Christian, has your passion cooled? Will you allow Paul's passion to serve as an inspiration for you to "fan into flame" the gifts God has given you (2 Tim 1:6 ESV)? We should remember that when it comes to mission, the people who make much of their lives are not always the smartest or most gifted; they are those who are extremely devoted.

Paul shows us a holy ambition and the value of it. Most do not think Paul ever made it to Spain, despite the planning and dreams. But N. T. Wright reminds us that God still used Paul's ambition:

> Did Paul ever get to Spain? There is no evidence whatever
> that he did. But his desire to do so, and the fact that he wrote
> Romans as part of the preparation for such a trip, points
> out an extremely important lesson for us all. Perhaps God
> sometimes allows us to dream dreams of what he wants us
> to do, not necessarily so that we can fulfill all of them—that
> might just make us proud and self-satisfied—but so that we will
> take the first steps towards fulfilling them.
>
> And perhaps those first steps (as they appear to us) are in
> fact the key things that God actually wants us to do. Paul may
> not have got to Spain. That didn't matter; the gospel got there
> fairly soon anyway. What mattered then, and has mattered
> enormously in the whole history of the church, is that, as part
> of his plan to go to Spain, he wrote Romans. We should never
> underestimate what God will do through things which we see
> as small steps to a larger end. (*Romans, Part 2*, 125–26)

Indeed, often there are many unexpected turns and shifts with a holy ambition. Sometimes God gives us a passion for something that will bless people in ways we never dream. Great Commission Christians long to do something that aligns with the mission of God for the glory of God, and then they set out to do it, by the Spirit of God, leaving the results to God. In verse 21 we see where Paul got his ambition, as he roots it in this citation from Isaiah 52:15. Paul is not on some personal agenda; rather, he is driven by the biblical expectation that the nations will be greatly amazed by the Suffering Servant we read about in Isaiah. Paul longs to preach to people who had not been "told" nor had ever "heard" about the good news, being encouraged by the expectation that many would hear and believe in the message of Jesus.

It is interesting, as well as instructive, that Paul does not mention a personal, experiential calling here. He mentions a Scripture as his motivation. I am not discounting calling (Paul alludes to his calling in places like Acts 26:17-18) but just pointing out that here in Romans 15 Paul says that this all-consuming ambition is found in a text (Isa 52:15). Piper comments,

> When Jesus called Paul on the Damascus road to take the gospel to the Gentiles who had never heard, Paul went to the Old Testament and looked for a confirmation and explanation of this calling to see how it fit into God's overall plan. And he found it. And for our sake he speaks this way. He doesn't just refer to his experience on the Damascus road, which we will never have. He refers to God's written word that we do have. And he roots his ambition there. ("Holy Ambition")

So then, dear Christian, meditate on God's Word day and night, and ask him to ignite a passion within you. Let the Word of God inspire and shape your holy ambition. Let the Word of God give you a passion for this Suffering Servant who, Isaiah goes on to say, "willingly submitted to death, and was counted among the rebels; yet he bore the sin of many and interceded for the rebels" (Isa 53:12). For the Lord Jesus has completed his holy mission, has poured out his Spirit on us, and has made us his ambassadors on earth.

Some may find it surprising that, after all this doctrine in Romans, you come to chapter 15 and find that the apostle is consumed with world evangelization. If this does not happen to you, there is a sense in which you have missed the point of Romans.

Support the Work of Church Planting
ROMANS 15:19-24

In verse 19 Paul said something that may appear puzzling. We passed over it, and I want to highlight it now. He said that he had "fully proclaimed the gospel of Christ from Jerusalem . . . to Illyricum," or "fulfilled the ministry" (ESV) in these regions. How can there be no more work to do? After all, not every individual had been evangelized. The answer has to do with Paul's church-planting philosophy and practice. After evangelizing some unbelievers, Paul established churches made up of new disciples and moved on. His unique work was done, even though other people needed to be evangelized in these parts of the world. Paul's practice involved establishing churches in major areas and then moving on.

So it is important to see Paul's church-planting strategy. It involved frontier evangelism and church planting (vv. 19-21). He has preached from Jerusalem to Illyricum, preaching where the name of Christ had not been preached. And because Paul has been all about this work of frontier evangelism and church planting, he has not been able to get to Rome yet (v. 22). But now he has no more of his kind of work to do in these areas (v. 23). Of course, there was work to do there! Though Paul's work on the eastern Mediterranean was heroic and fruitful, still only a small number of congregations existed. Many more people were in need of the gospel. Paul told Timothy to "do the work of an evangelist" (2 Tim 4:5) in that same region. But we should remember Paul's unique strategy: preaching the gospel to unreached people and establishing churches in major, influential cities: Ephesus, Corinth, Philippi, Thessalonica, and Athens. Paul believed that by focusing on these influential cities, he would also reach the outlying areas (e.g., Acts 19–20).

Having followed this city-to-city pattern, Paul believes it is time to move to a new influential area: Spain (vv. 23-24). Schreiner comments on the passion of Paul, citing that Paul would have been about sixty years old when stating his ambition! He adds that Paul most likely would need to learn Latin in order to minster there ("Proclaiming the Gospel to the Ends of the Earth"). It is not common to hear of sixty-year-olds learning new languages and going to unreached people groups, but here is an example to inspire elderly saints! Paul desires to go to a remote part of the world, where they speak a different language and where there seems to have been virtually no Jewish presence (Bird, *Romans*, 508). But he is determined to go to this distant coastland, inspired most likely by Isaiah's vision of the "coasts and islands" hearing about the Lord (Isa 11:11; 41:1; 42:4,10; 49:1; 51:5; 60:9; 66:19-20).

Paul mentions church-planting support in verse 24. He wants to be "assisted" by the Romans on his journey to Spain. In verses 28-29 he says that he hopes to leave from there to go to Spain. This assistance or support would have certainly involved money, but it may have also included some Latin translators and a place to retreat if the trip went badly (Bird, *Romans*, 509). In one sense, then, Romans is a "missionary support letter" (Piper, "Joy + Debt").

This portion of Romans 15 underscores the importance of local churches supporting the work of world evangelization. It is a great privilege to be a part of the global work of God around the world through giving and resourcing missionaries and church planters today. Isaiah foresaw the gospel advancing around the world, Paul launched this work, and now we get to participate in it through our giving, praying, and going.

Support the Work of Mercy Ministry
ROMANS 15:25-27

Perhaps you have seen articles or books on wonderful "places to see before you die." Paul lists three places he plans to visit before he dies: first he wants to go to *Jerusalem*, then to *Rome*, and from Rome to *Spain*. But he is not on a vacation; he is on a mission. His travels required risk and resolve. In this instance he makes a long detour, going from Corinth to Jerusalem before heading for Rome. John Stott has calculated that, assuming Paul traveled by sea, the first leg of his journey from Corinth to Jerusalem would be around eight hundred miles. The second, from Jerusalem to Rome, would be fifteen hundred miles. And the third, from Rome to Spain, would be seven hundred miles, making a total of three thousand miles by ship! His travels reveal something of his missionary heart (*Message*, 384).

Paul has not been able to get to Rome because of his pioneer work in other regions, and now he adds another hindrance, in somewhat of a parenthesis; that is, he is going first to Jerusalem, taking aid to the poor saints there (vv. 25-26; cf. Acts 11:28-29). This act of mercy had been a great project for Paul. He had been organizing a collection for the saints in Jerusalem from the churches of Galatia, Macedonia, and Achaia (1 Cor 16:1-5; 2 Cor 8:1-24). So Paul is not asking the church in Rome to participate in this particular act of mercy, but he does highlight the example of these churches, which serves to highlight the importance of generosity and the unity of the Jew and Gentile in Christ. These churches are known for generosity and compassion, and perhaps Paul wants to spur the Romans on to the same kind of generosity and compassion for future ministry.

In verse 27 Paul teaches us that we should give and show mercy to magnify the fruit of the gospel in our lives. Paul says the Gentile churches owe it to the Jerusalem saints. The Gentiles have been grafted into the people of God, trusting in the promised Messiah, and therefore they should be happy to provide material aid to the saints in Jerusalem. The Gentiles' gift to the Jews was a sign that they were family; the Jewish Christians' acceptance of the gift was also a sign of family. This gift was a symbol of the long-awaited promises of Scripture of the Gentiles being part of the people of God—not just in right relationship to God but also in relationship to Jewish believers. We should do all we can to build bridges and show how the gospel brings us together across ethnic lines. To do this, we should look for opportunities to do good, especially toward those who are of the household of faith (Gal 6:10; cf. Gal 2:10).

Refresh Those on the Front Lines
ROMANS 15:28-29,32

This text is peppered with references about the refreshment derived from personal relationships. In verse 24 Paul speaks of enjoying the company of the Romans. Here Paul adds, "So when I have finished this and safely delivered the funds to them, I will visit you on the way to Spain. I know that when I come to you, I will come in the fullness of the blessing of Christ" (vv. 28-29). In verse 32, after requesting prayer Paul says, "And that, by God's will, I may come to you with joy and be refreshed together with you." Clearly Paul does not envision a sending church to be the kind to make a mechanical business deal. He is not using the Romans. He wants relational support (cf. 1:11-12). He hopes to be an encouragement to them and the Romans to him.

This is one way we can support those on the front lines: *relational refreshment*. Piper says, "God loves to refresh his people through his people" ("Resting and Wrestling for the Cause of Christ—Together"). We find this kind of refreshment throughout the New Testament (e.g., 2 Tim 1:16). We also know from experience how valuable the refreshing community of another believer can be. One of the greatest challenges of being a missionary is lacking community. Sometimes in the States I hear disgruntled Christians saying, "I don't have community." I sometimes want to say, "I'd like to take you to a few of our missionaries and show you what a lack of community looks like!"

Paul did get to Rome and was refreshed but not the way he anticipated. You can read Acts 20–28 and find out how Paul got to Rome—in chains! And it would take not months, but years, with many trials along the way.

Let's refresh one another. Let's refresh those in leadership. Let's refresh those overseas on the front lines of global mission. Let's make the ministry of refreshment part of our regular Christian lives, through personal visits, by communicating through available means, and by practicing hospitality, all with gospel-saturated words of encouragement.

Pray for Those on the Front Lines
ROMANS 15:30-33

Finally, Paul asks those in the church to strive together in prayer for him. I see six takeaways from this prayer.

First, see prayer as a privilege (15:30). It is a gift of grace to offer our prayers "to God." This glorious God of Romans, who is sovereign, wise, good, just, and merciful, invites us into his presence through prayer. We get to approach *Abba* Father regularly because of his work in Christ on our behalf and through the enablement of the Holy Spirit.

Second, love others through your prayers (15:30). Notice Paul's mention of the "love of the Spirit"—that is, the love that comes from the Spirit (cf. 5:5). He speaks of the bond the believers have with one another through this Spirit-produced love. By calling attention to love, Paul shows us the link between love and prayer. Genuine love should drive us to pray for one another. It is an expression of love for one another.

Third, pray passionately and persistently (15:30). Observe Paul's language: "Strive together with me in prayers." He asks the church to "agonize with him" (Gk *sunagonizomai*) in prayer on his behalf. Prayer requires time, effort, energy, and perseverance (cf. 12:12).

Fourth, pray for those on the front lines to be spared and for their work to be acceptable (15:31). Paul mentions two dangers: one from *without* and one from *within*. Regarding the former, he asks for prayers that he would be rescued from unbelieving Jews in Judea. Many hated Paul and considered him a traitor (Acts 23:12). Regarding the danger from within, Paul longed for the collection to be acceptable to the Jewish Christians. He did not assume this would be the case, given the antagonism that existed. These are still two important prayers for those in ministry leadership: (1) to be spared persecution from outsiders, and (2) for insiders to receive their ministry.

Fifth, pray with awareness that God may not answer your prayers the way you envision (15:31-32)! From the book of Acts we see that these requests were answered, but one of them was not how Paul imagined. Regarding the gift, according to Acts 24:17, it appears that it was received. Regarding the threat of persecution, Paul was kept safe . . . by being sent off to prison. Some say the prayer was not answered, but it was—just in an unusual providence. The Roman tribune rescued Paul from death. That is how Paul was kept safe. God often answers our prayers in ways we do not expect. Sometimes the journey is much different from what we imagine. Through it all, pour out your heart to God in prayer, knowing that you can trust his providential guidance and sovereign power.

Sixth, pray not just for the immediate needs but for long-term desires (15:32). Paul's prayer does not stop with the immediate need of going to Jerusalem. He prays with vision. In this case it includes the desire to go on to Rome and be refreshed. It is certainly good and right to pray for the immediate (the next worship service, sermon, meeting, and so on), but we may also expand our horizons to where these requests may lead. You do not have to limit your prayers to the narrow, immediate, or short-term. Jesus Christ is risen from the dead; he will build his church, so pray with vision and longing and holy ambition!

Paul completes this missionary support portion of Romans with a brief blessing appealing to the God of peace (v. 33). That is the refreshment we all need, the refreshment that comes from the God who gives peace (*shalom*) to all his people (cf. 5:1; 8:6), both Jew and Gentile.

There is a time to refresh those on the front lines and a time to wrestle in prayer for those on the front lines. Let's refresh one another, and let's pray for one another. Let's pray for those in leadership and engaged in mission, believing God answers prayer. Let's pray for the physical safety and well-being of those on the front lines. Let's pray that their ventures will be successful and that God may be glorified in their ministries.

Paul spends many chapters in Romans teasing out the gospel and its implications, but in Romans 15:14-33 we find the missional heartbeat of the letter. Paul's missionary heart is on display. It should not surprise us. When you have a gospel as big as the gospel presented in Romans, you will want to take it to the nations. It seems to me that many do not have a passion for the nations because they do not have a gospel worth preaching. But if you soak yourself in the good news presented in Romans, I cannot help but believe you too will want to be a Great Commission Christian, pouring your life out for the fame of Christ among the nations. Paul gives us a vision of what that looks like:

- Be part of a healthy, gospel-centered church.
- See life and mission through the lens of worship.
- Remember that ministry fruitfulness is the result of divine enablement.
- Have the right kind of ambition: driven by the gospel and a heart for people.
- Support the work of church planting.
- Support the work of mercy ministry.
- Refresh those on the front lines.
- Pray for those on the front lines.

Jesus Christ has fulfilled his mission, has forgiven us our sins and made us new creations, and has given us the Holy Spirit. Now, compelled by his grace, let's make his final charge our first priority.

Reflect and Discuss

1. What does it mean to be a "Great Commission Christian"?
2. What three marks of a healthy church does Paul mention in Romans 14? Why are they significant?
3. How are mission and worship related?
4. How does this passage show us our need for divine enablement in ministry?
5. What is "holy ambition"? What can we learn from Paul about a holy ambition?
6. What does this passage say about church planting?
7. If you are not a church planter, how can you be involved in church planting?

8. What might the ministry of refreshment look like? How can you practice it?
9. Which point on prayer strikes you the most in Romans 15:30-33? Why?
10. Are you praying for those on the "front lines" of ministry? Pause and do that now.

Christian Friendship

ROMANS 16

Main Idea: This final chapter of the letter emphasizes the importance of Christian friendship, shows how the gospel is at the heart of it, and gives some ways we can experience it.

I. **How Christian Friendship Is Emphasized (16:1-16,21-23)**
   A. Paul's Commendation of Phoebe (16:1-2)
   B. Greetings to More Friends and Churches (16:3-16)
   C. Greetings from Corinth to Rome (16:21-23)
II. **How Christian Friendship Is Established: The Gospel (16:1-16)**
III. **How Christian Friendship Is Experienced: Love (16:1-27)**
   A. Honoring one another (16:1-23)
   B. Showing hospitality to one another (16:1-23)
   C. Showing affection for one another (16:1-23)
   D. Doing ministry together (16:1-23)
   E. Staying focused on the gospel together (16:17-20,25-27)

At first glance this chapter does not look very significant, does it? After all the robust theology in Romans, we come to a list of names? After a passionate chapter on missions, we have what might as well be a list of Paul's Twitter followers? I doubt that you would direct a person new to the Bible to Romans 16 first. To the question, "Hey, I'm interested in reading the Bible, where should I start?" you probably would not respond with, "I think you should start with a lot of names that are hard to pronounce in Romans 16." Yet while you may not direct such a person to Romans 16 first, we should not think for a moment that this passage is insignificant. There is gold here.

I love this chapter. As a church planter, I used it during our core team meetings in order to express my appreciation to my colaborers. I continue to refer to it in order to emphasize the importance of biblical community. I have spoken on this text at conferences in different places around the world to talk about the value of meaningful relationships. And I have used it at events to talk about the importance of churches working together.

Leon Morris says this chapter reminds us that Romans was written to real, ordinary Christians, not professional theologians:

> The multiplicity of greetings to people of whom we know nothing apart from their being listed here roots the letter in a specific context. It was a letter to real people and, as far as we can see, to ordinary people; it was not written to professional theologians (though through the centuries scholars have found the epistle a happy hunting ground). As we consider the weighty matters Paul deals with, we are apt to overlook the fact that it was addressed to people like Ampliatus and Tryphena and Rufus. Clearly Paul expected this kind of person to be helped by what he wrote, a fact which modern experts sometimes overlook. And it is fitting that this letter, which has given us so much solid doctrinal teaching, should end with this emphasis on persons, on love, and on a reminder that humble servants of God perform all sorts of active ministry. (*Epistle*, 527)

You cannot miss the emphasis on relationships here. Whether you choose to use the word *fellowship* or *community* or *friendship*, the fact is, this text reminds us that so much of the Christian life revolves around *relationships*. One of the joys of the Christian life is being together, hanging together, laughing together, playing together, eating together, praying together, weeping together, thinking together, dreaming together, planning together, doing mission together, and worshiping together. This is what the community of saints does. This is what Christian friends do.

In Romans 16 Paul highlights the gift of Christian friendship/fellowship and provides a case study on it. Where do we go to find strength in the midst of stress and discouragement? We go to the gospel of grace, and we go to our Christian brothers and sisters. All of this is made possible through Jesus Christ, the friend of sinners.

Christian friendship is a gift of God's grace. Dietrich Bonhoeffer's line is true: "It is grace, nothing but grace, that we are allowed to live in community with Christian brothers and sisters" (*Life Together*, 20). Real Christian friends have your back when you are attacked, and real Christian friends lift you up when you are down. I am reminded of the western movie *Tombstone*. When Wyatt Earp is in danger, his friend Doc Holiday comes to his rescue, even though Doc is sick and dying. When asked why he is out of bed and fighting for Wyatt, Doc responds, "Wyatt Earp is my friend." To this, someone says, "I have lots of friends." Doc says, "I don't." It is a great gift of grace to have a friend, especially a Christian brother or sister who shares the same ambitions and interests in life—who lives on the same mission with you.

Saying goodbye to your friends is difficult and at times agonizing. Think about it. If someone offers you a job in Europe, what is one of your primary reactions? I cannot speak for everyone, but for many the first thought is, *What about all my friends here?* Saying hello to a friend is much sweeter than saying goodbye. And being hurt by a friend is painful, and that requires a chapter in itself.

In the book of Acts, it is amazing to see how often Paul spent time with his friends. It is remarkable how intentional Paul was in spending time with them. It took sacrifice to be with them. Romans 16 also shows us that Paul was not a one-man band. Paul swam in friends. He had ethnically diverse friends. He had Jewish and Gentile friends. He had weak brothers and strong brothers. He had friends who were slaves and friends who were free. He had friends who were male and friends who were female. Paul traveled with his friends. He stayed with his friends. He visited his friends. He worked alongside his friends. He got beaten alongside his friends! He was imprisoned with his friends. He sang in prison with his friends. He encouraged his friends and was encouraged by them. He, at times, disagreed with his friends. And he, at times, reconciled with them.

It is important for us to remember the theology of friendship and community in the Christian life. Paul's constant interaction with his co-laborers and partners in ministry was not due to some *weakness* in his life. It was not due to an *extroverted personality* either. It was a sign of his *being made in the image of God,* and it was a sign of *spiritual maturity.*

As image bearers of God, we are made for relationships. If you think back to Genesis 1–2, the only mention of something being "not good" was that Adam was "alone" (Gen 2:18). Why? It is because we cannot even enjoy a paradise without companionship (Keller, "Spiritual Friendship"). If you feel lonely when you are isolated, that is not weird; that is normal. It is because you are made in the *imago Dei.* You long for friendships because you are made in the image of our relational, triune God.

I have stood at the deathbeds of many individuals during my ministry. In dying moments no one is thinking about their diplomas, their trophies, or their accolades. They are thinking about people. They want to be with their loved ones. Children of dying parents will drive through the night to be with parents; friends will make every sacrifice to be with their dying friends. No one says before his or her final breath, "Can I hold my high school basketball trophy one more time?" But you will want to hold a person when you are about to die.

Further, we need to realize that when a person becomes a Christian, the desires and need for community and friendship do not disappear. Even the mighty apostle Paul needed friends. This is a sign of maturity. Paul was a justified sinner in need of strength, just as we are. He never got to some hypothetical level of maturity that enabled him to no longer need anyone. Christ's sufficiency and strength are often expressed through the love and support of other Christians. Remember what Paul said to the Corinthians regarding Titus:

> In fact, when we came into Macedonia, we had no rest. Instead, we were troubled in every way: conflicts on the outside, fears within. But God, who comforts the downcast, comforted us by the arrival of Titus, and not only by his arrival but also by the comfort he received from you. He told us about your deep longing, your sorrow, and your zeal for me, so that I rejoiced even more. (2 Cor 7:5-7)

Paul says when he was downcast, God sent Titus to lift him. And this "Titus touch" was the result of the church's lifting of Titus. God uses his people to bless and lift us up in our times of need. And even the most gifted and brightest need encouragement.

The fact is, we need to elevate the ministry of encouragement and see the importance of genuine Christian friendship. We need this not only to cheer our spirits, but because of what is at stake. The author of Hebrews writes,

> Watch out, brothers and sisters, so that there won't be in any of you an evil, unbelieving heart that turns away from the living God. But encourage each other daily, while it is still called today, so that none of you is hardened by sin's deception. (Heb 3:12-13)

Our hearts are prone to wander. Sin never sleeps. Satan rages because he knows his days are short. In light of this war, we need to come alongside fellow soldiers with gospel encouragement.

With this lengthy introduction in mind, let's now consider Romans 16. In verses 1-16 Paul sends greetings to his friends and coworkers in Rome. In verses 21-23 he sends personal greetings from his friends in

Corinth. In between (vv. 17-20) he gives a warning about false teaching and division. He concludes with a gospel-drenched doxology in verses 25-27. I would like to hover over this passage and point out three observations regarding Christian friendship: how it is *emphasized*, how it is *established*, and how it is *experienced*.

How Christian Friendship Is Emphasized

ROMANS 16:1-16

This one is easy to see. The importance of Christian friendship is emphasized in this chapter by *the number of greetings given—to and from diverse individuals and churches*. More greetings are found in this chapter than in every other letter of Paul combined (Bird, *Romans*, 519).

Paul is likely trying to strengthen the familial bonds between the saints as they form this partnership for his work in Spain. Paul probably does not know all of them directly, but he does know many of them, and he has labored alongside of many of them.

Consider the diversity of *terms* that Paul uses in this passage: *friend, coworkers, sister, brother, servant, saints, benefactor, church, countrymen, fellow prisoners, approved in Christ, chosen, mother,* and more. Consider also the various *ethnicities* involved. Most names are Greek, but some are Jewish, and a few appear to be Latin. Consider the diversity of *classes*. We read of slave names as well as prominent households and influential people.

Finally, consider the diversity of *gender*. A number of brothers are mentioned in the chapter, and that is not surprising based on Paul's pattern of ministry that we read of elsewhere. What is more striking is how many women are mentioned in Romans 16. But if we read through the New Testament carefully, it is obvious that Paul sought to equip and encourage women in the gospel and that he had many female gospel partners. In Philippians 4 Paul says that Euodia and Syntyche had "contended for the gospel at [his] side" (Phil 4:3). Paul mentions women in relationship to various house churches also, like Lydia (Acts 16:15,40) and Nympha (Col 4:15).

But the most extensive list of female gospel partners is found in Romans 16. We read of Phoebe first (v. 1). He refers to Priscilla, who is mentioned several times in the New Testament (v. 3; cf. Acts 18:2,26; 1 Cor 16:19; 2 Tim 4:19). Paul goes on to mention Mary, Tryphena, Tryphosa, and Persis—each person "worked hard in the Lord" (vv. 6,12). Paul also mentions Junia (v. 7). Paul speaks a sweet word about Rufus's mother, who had been like a mother to Paul (v. 13). In verse 15 Paul mentions Julia and the sister of Nereus. Of about twenty-eight people Paul wants to greet in Rome, ten of them were women.

That is a significant number in its own right, but when you consider the fact that it occurs in a male-dominated culture, it is unusual. When we consider not just Paul's ministry but also the whole sweep of the New Testament, along with significant women in the Old Testament, it is clear that the mission of God is not reserved for men. Missional women have always played a vital role in the advancement of the gospel. The church—as the bride for whom Christ bled, died, and was raised to life—ought to be a place where women are encouraged, loved, taught, respected, heard, and deployed for service. They should thrive as Christ's ambassadors to the world as they are built up in him.

This long list of names, then, and the diversity contained in this list, highlights the importance and uniqueness of Christian friendship. Romans 16 is an illustration of Galatians 3:28: "There is no Jew or Greek, slave or free, male and female; since you are all one in Christ Jesus" (cf. Col 3:11). Such relational diversity magnifies the gospel over all other unifying forces, which glorifies our Savior who died to give us such unity amid this beautiful diversity.

Christian friendship is also magnified in the mention of various churches. Many of the people mentioned represented entire churches. It appears that there are *at least* five household churches:

- The house of Priscilla and Aquila (v. 5)
- The house of Aristobulus (v. 10)
- The house of Narcissus (v. 11)
- Asyncritus and his brothers and sisters (v. 14)
- Philologus and Julia, Nereus and his sister, and Olympas, and all the saints who are with them (v. 15). (Bird, *Romans*, 519)

Paul sees these churches as partnering together in the gospel as a network of brothers and sisters on shared mission.

Paul's Commendation of Phoebe (16:1-2)

Paul's "sister Phoebe" heads the list. Phoebe is the first of a number of women mentioned. She probably carried the letter to Rome. Paul calls her a "benefactor" (v. 2). This means she was a person of means and maturity (Bird, *Romans*, 519). It seems that she had the necessary resources to travel to Rome. Phoebe is, then, a great example of how wealthy Christians should use their resources: for the good of the church and the expansion of the gospel.

There is considerable debate about whether Phoebe was a deacon in Cenchreae (the port city of Corinth), but I am not going to dive into that discussion, as it has many layers to it. The word *servant* (Gk *diakonon*) can be general or specific (the specific uses being in Phil 1:1; 1 Tim 3:8,12). So it is impossible to know for certain. But the addition of "of the church in Cenchreae" probably indicates some kind of position in the church, and it at least highlights the fact that *she is well known for her service in the church*. (For discussion, see Schreiner, *Romans*, 786–88.) She is an exemplary saint, and Paul wants the church to receive her warmly.

Greetings to More Friends and Churches (16:3-16)

In verses 3-4 we read of *Prisca* (aka Priscilla) *and Aquila*. They were a great team! Like Paul, they were tentmakers (Acts 18:1-3). The couple went with Paul to Ephesus (Acts 18:18) and remained there when he went on. They were able to instruct the mighty Apollos in the faith (Acts 18:26). They had a church in their house in more places than one (Rom 16:5; 1 Cor 16:19; Morris, *Epistle*, 532). Paul refers to them here as his "coworkers," noting their great labor in the gospel. He also speaks of their faith and sacrifice, saying they "risked their own necks" for him, and the apostle is grateful for their willingness to do so. Finally, he adds that "all the Gentile churches" share his gratitude. How exactly did they risk their lives? We are not told. We know on one occasion in Ephesus, Paul was in danger (1 Cor 15:32; cf. Acts 19:23,30-31); they may have done something for him then.

Epaenetus is called "the first convert to Christ from Asia" (v. 5). This probably refers to Paul's first convert in Ephesus. The Greek word for "first convert" is usually translated "firstfruits." It carries with it the thought of a greater harvest to come. If you have read missionary biographies, you know that first converts are important because of what their faith represents: God has broken through after a lot of sowing and plowing. It represents great hope.

Next, Paul sends greetings to *Mary* (v. 6). She is probably Jewish, and though we read of many Marys in the New Testament, there is no reason to identify her with any of these (Morris, *Epistle*, 533). Paul says she has "worked very hard for you." We do not know what all of this entailed, but Paul is aware of it and wants others to recognize her labor.

Next comes *Andronicus and Junia* (v. 7). Paul calls them his "fellow Jews" and "fellow prisoners." The fact that they were "fellow prisoners" may mean that they were in jail together, or more likely that they had shared the same kind of experience at some other time. The fact that they were "in Christ before" Paul testifies to their early conversion. Paul's conversion must have taken place within a few years after the crucifixion, so they would have been some of the first converts. They were probably converted Jews from Palestine.

The difficulty in verse 7 has to do with the gender of *Junia*. Bird argues that we should read Junia as a female, despite the attempts to think of her as a male:

> There are over 250 examples of the feminine version of "Junia" in Greek and Latin inscriptions from Rome alone and not a single instance of "Junias" [male] has been found. . . .
> [P]atristic commentators are virtually unanimous in identifying the person as a woman. (*Romans*, 522)

At any rate, the two (perhaps a couple; see Schreiner, *Romans*, 796) "are noteworthy in the eyes of the apostles." That is, the apostles held them in high esteem. It could also mean that they were "apostles" in a general sense ("messengers," "sent ones," "ambassadors").

Paul then greets *Ampliatus, Urbanas, Stachys, and Apelles* in verses 8-10. Paul has a relational knowledge of the first three, calling them either his "friend" or "coworker." Regarding Apelles, Paul says that he is "approved in Christ" (v. 9). He apparently was a servant of tested excellence. So even though Paul may have only indirect knowledge of him, he is aware of his character.

The next mention is *the household of Aristobulus* (v. 10). This is the name of a grandson of Herod the Great. Scholars, however, debate the likelihood of this identification. Bird mentions, "Aristobulus himself died in 48/49; however, his household probably continued and his name remained associated with it" (Bird, *Romans*, 524).

The name *Herodion* (v. 11) is also connected with Herod, and thus likely linked with the household of Aristobulus, perhaps being a member of it (Morris, *Epistle*, 535).

Paul then greets *the family of Narcissus* who are "in the Lord" (v. 11). The language seems to indicate that either this specific Narcissus is dead or that the head of the household is not a believer; those "in the Lord" are to be warmly greeted. There is some discussion as to whether this was the Narcissus who was a powerful freedman who had been prominent under Claudius and forced to commit suicide during Nero's reign (Morris, *Epistle*, 535; Bird, *Romans*, 524).

Paul then mentions three women who have "worked hard in the Lord" (v. 12): *Tryphaena and Tryphosa*, and *Persis*. These women are known for their labor in the ministry. Paul also mentions Persis as a "dear friend," illustrating the value of Christian friendship and partnership between male and female servants of the Lord.

Next, *Rufus and his mother* are noted (v. 13). Rufus is said to be "chosen in the Lord." This can be said of every true Christian (1:6-7; 8:33; 9:24), but it may also point to a special calling on his life. We wonder if the Rufus mentioned in Mark 15:21—that is, the son of Simon of Cyrene, who carried the cross—is the same Rufus (it was a common name). The sweet phrase regarding his mother, "his mother—and mine," indicates that Rufus's mother had provided maternal care to the apostle at some point in his life.

Paul completes his list with what appears to be two households. One household includes *Asyncritus, Phlegon, Hermes, Patrobas*, and *Hermas*, along with "the brothers and sisters who are with them" (v. 14). Even though Paul may not have been intimately acquainted with this group, he identified them as important individuals that probably met together as a house church, with at least some of these individuals being leaders. The other household includes *Philologus, Julia, Nereus and his sister*, and *Olympas*, "and all the saints who are with them" (v. 15). Philologus and Julia may have been husband and wife. The name *Olympas* points to someone from outside of Rome who moved to the capital. The mention of "all the saints" also probably indicates a house church.

Paul urges them all to use a holy kiss as a greeting (v. 16; cf. 1 Cor 16:20; 2 Cor 13:12; 1 Thess 5:26; 1 Pet 5:14). Commentators do a lot of squirming to explain away "kissing Christians." Phillips's paraphrase puts it like this: "Give each other a hearty handshake all round for my sake." That is very reserved! While for many Christians in various parts of the world a holy kiss is socially awkward, whatever the context, there should be warmth, love, enthusiasm, purity, and cheerfulness as we greet one another—whichever way we choose to physically display it.

Greetings from Corinth to Rome (16:21-23)

We will come back to verses 17-20 in a moment. In verses 21-23 Paul passes on to the Romans greetings from his friends in Corinth.

Timothy is described simply as Paul's "coworker" (v. 21). The relationship between Paul and Timothy is one of the most special in the New Testament. Elsewhere Paul calls him "my true son in the faith" (1 Tim 1:2) and "my dearly loved son" (2 Tim 1:2), who had served with Paul "in the gospel ministry like a son with a father" (Phil 2:22; cf. Acts 16:1-3).

Lucius, Jason, and *Sosipater* are mentioned next as "fellow countrymen" (v. 21). Jason was the name of Paul's host at Thessalonica in Acts 17:5-9. This may be the same person.

Tertius then speaks: "I, Tertius, who wrote this letter, greet you in the Lord" (v. 22). Here is one instance in which we hear from Paul's scribe. Morris writes, "It is a human little touch. That the apostle allows this to be done in connection with such a weighty letter as this sheds light on the relationship between the apostle and his helpers" (*Epistle,* 543).

Gaius is likely to be the Corinthian Gaius whom Paul baptized (1 Cor 1:14). He hosted Paul in Corinth (v. 23) and maybe hosted a church as well.

Finally, we read of *Erastus* and "our brother" *Quartus* (v. 23). Erastus is the "city treasurer." Remarkably, one can find an inscription bearing his name in ancient Corinth today. Erastus apparently was an important Corinthian leader who supported Paul's missionary efforts.

This is quite a list of names! It illustrates for us the great privilege of knowing other brothers and sisters who share the same Holy Spirit. It reminds us that many of the heroes of the church through the years have been unsung heroes. The church has been blessed, sustained, and built up throughout its history by ordinary saints who work hard in Christ. This list shows us that it takes an army of Christians to make an impact. Paul did not operate by himself. Finally, this list points to the idea of something of greater significance than being known by a famous Christian leader: we are known by the chief Shepherd, Jesus Christ. He knows us by name and is aware of our service to him. Paul is just a shadow of Jesus. To receive a commendation by a great leader is one thing, but to hear "Well done, good and faithful servant" from the Lord of glory is another! Faithful saint, know that Jesus cares about your service to the church.

How Christian Friendship Is Established: The Gospel
ROMANS 16:1-16

Notice the Christ-centered basis for these diverse relationships (emphasis added):

- "welcome her *in the Lord*" (v. 2)
- "my coworkers *in Christ Jesus*" (v. 3)
- "the first convert *to Christ*" (v. 5)
- "they were also *in Christ* before me" (v. 7)
- "my dear friend *in the Lord*" (v. 8)
- "our coworker *in Christ*" (v. 9)
- "who is *approved in Christ*" (v. 10)
- "who are *in the Lord*" (v. 11)
- "who have worked hard *in the Lord*" (v. 12)
- "who has worked very hard *in the Lord*" (v. 12)
- "chosen *in the Lord*" (v. 13)
- "brothers and sisters . . . all the saints. . . . All the churches *of Christ*" (vv. 14-16)

These are former unbelievers, from various backgrounds, but Jesus changed them. Jesus made them family. The gospel creates new spiritual friendships.

What on earth would unite these diverse people in these various towns? They were united by a common faith in Jesus. They called Jesus "Lord." C. S. Lewis said, "Friendship . . . is born at the moment when one man says to another 'What! You too? I thought that no one but myself . . .'" (*Four Loves*, 78). In other words, common interest creates friendships. Friendship is usually not born when you say to someone, "Will you be my friend?" It happens through a shared love. And Christians have the greatest commonality: *we are in Christ*.

Because Spirit-filled Christians share a common salvation and a shared passion for Christ and his kingdom, people who may have otherwise never spent time together can become great friends. They can share life together on mission, even though they may come from radically different backgrounds.

- Techies can become friends with retirees.
- Hip-hoppers can hang with farmers.
- Artists can be in an edifying small group with jocks.

- Older businessmen can be in a wonderful Bible study with hipsters.
- Valley girls can love and serve home girls.
- Duke students can pray with and for monster truck lovers.
- Alabama fans can even marry Auburn fans!

Jesus, the friend of sinners, creates remarkable spiritual friendships. The gospel not only changes one's personal identity; it also establishes a new community.

How Christian Friendship Is Experienced: Love
ROMANS 16:1-27

Let me list five ways, rooted in this chapter, that we can love one another in the community of faith.

Honoring One Another (16:1-23)

This sense of honor runs right through the chapter as Paul says things like "welcome [Phoebe] . . . in a manner worthy of the saints" (v. 2). He honors Prisca and Aquila by mentioning their labor and sacrifice (vv. 3-4). Some are honored for being older in the Lord (v. 7). Paul also commends those who worked hard (vv. 6,12). The entire chapter illustrates Paul's putting into practice Romans 12:10: "Take the lead in honoring one another."

Showing Hospitality to One Another (16:1-23)

Paul urges the church to "welcome" Phoebe (v. 2). He mentions a handful of house churches, which implies the practice of hospitality. He also mentions Gaius as being a host to Paul (v. 23). This entire chapter shows the practice of another exhortation in Romans 12: "pursue hospitality" (12:13).

Showing Affection for One Another (16:1-23)

Throughout the New Testament we read of warmth and affection (e.g., Acts 20:37; 21:5-6). Here in Romans 16 the church is exhorted to "greet one another with a holy kiss" (v. 16). I do not want to push this too far, and I certainly do not want to encourage any sort of strange or inappropriate behavior, but our greetings should be warm and sincere. Some people only receive happy greetings from their pet dogs! Let's practice this exhortation that we read about in Romans 12: "Love one another deeply as brothers and sisters" (Rom 12:10). Let's remember that short greetings and conversations are important, not unimportant. We should not think you have to have three-hour meetings with people for them to be significant. A warm greeting and a word of affirmation go a long way.

Doing Ministry Together (16:1-23)

This list in Romans 16 is not a social roster. It refers to a band of brothers and sisters serving the Lord together. Community is developed strongly in the trenches of loving service to the Lord *together.*

Staying Focused on the Gospel Together (16:17-20,25-27)

Allow me now to address verses 17-20 and 25-27, where I see three important reasons for staying focused on the gospel.

Staying focused on the gospel keeps us unified (16:17-19). In the middle of all these greetings, Paul drops a warning about divisive people. Paul wants the saints to be careful, not allowing false teachers to disrupt the unity of the believers. Unity can only happen around the truth of sound doctrine.

How may we detect false teaching? Simply put, false teaching is not consistent with the truth of the historic gospel—as Paul says, "Contrary to the teaching that you learned" (v. 17). Many false teachers will say some things that sound good ("love your neighbor," "honor people," "serve the poor"), but they may deny essential truths of the faith, like the atonement, the resurrection, justification by faith alone in Christ alone, and so on. Paul says this regarding smooth talking false teachers: "Watch out for" them and "avoid them" (v. 17)! Why? False teachers are not really serving Christ because they deceive and they divide.

In verse 19 Paul commends the church for their obedience and then urges them to be wise. He tells them to stay focused and obedient. He wants them (and all Christians) to be discerning enough to detect evil and to avoid it.

Staying focused on the gospel keeps us hopeful (16:20). Speaking of evil, Paul draws attention to Satan. You can hear the echo of Genesis 3:15 here. Jesus has won the ultimate victory over Satan already, but the evil one is still raging, for he knows his days are short (Rev 12:12). We still deal with false teachers. We still deal with Satan's attacks in various ways. We still deal with sin. But in the near future the God of peace will crush Satan under our feet, and we know this because our Messiah has already won the battle at the cross! Now we await his glorious return. Then we will live in total *shalom,* in perfect peace and harmony—without sin, death, and temptation. Until that day we live in dependence on the grace of Christ and the Spirit's power to be faithful to the end.

Staying focused on the gospel gives us strength to endure to the end (16:25-27). How do you end the greatest letter ever written? The same way you started it! Paul bookends the letter with a reference to the gospel according to the Scriptures (1:1-6; 16:25-27). Here it is in the form of a beautiful doxology that magnifies several important aspects of the gospel. This doxology is similar in some ways to the doxology in Romans 11:33-36, magnifying the wisdom of God and the glory of the gospel.

Observe how Paul says the gospel has power not only to save unbelievers *but to strengthen believers.* Here we are reminded of the sanctifying power of the gospel. Be thankful for friends who keep you focused on the gospel, thus bringing you strength.

This doxology also shows us that *the gospel is about Jesus.* The gospel involves "the proclamation about Jesus Christ" (v. 25). When you are discouraged, you need to listen to Christ-exalting preaching and teaching. You can find strength in so doing. You find strength in knowing that the ultimate victory comes through the work of Christ, not your own work. You find strength knowing that your hope is based on his perfect record, not your performance.

Paul also underscores that *this gospel is the grand message of the Bible!* Notice the phrase, "the mystery kept silent for long ages but now revealed and made known through the prophetic Scriptures." Many things were mysteries, but not anymore. The gospel fulfills what the prophets projected, and Paul played an important role in unfolding this mystery, in telling this glorious story of which Jesus is the hero. This was "according to the command of the eternal God" who determined when the mystery of the gospel was to be revealed.

This good news, Paul also says, is *for the nations* ("among all the Gentiles," v. 26). That is, for their "obedience of faith" (v. 26; cf. 1:5). We do not serve a mere tribal Savior but the Lord of the nations, who intends to have a people who worship the Messiah from among the nations.

All of this magnifies the infinite *wisdom* of God (v. 27; cf. 11:33-36). When you behold the gospel, you are not only beholding the love of God and the justice of God; you are also beholding the wisdom of God. God's wisdom is most revealed through the work of Jesus Christ, which we have the privilege of declaring (1 Cor 1:24,30). The final word, "To the only wise God, through Jesus Christ—to him be the glory forever!" (v. 27), inspires praise from the believers' hearts.

So give God praise, believer. Praise God for the gospel! Praise God for the victory we have through our union with the Lord Jesus! Praise God for the gift of community—for the gift of Christian friendship.

Let's pray for growth in Christian love—that we may honor one another, show hospitality to one another, and show affection to one another. Let's pray that we can do fruitful ministry together and that we will stay focused on the gospel together.

What a wise God! What a wonderful gospel! What a wonderful hope! To the only wise God, through Jesus Christ, be glory forever. Amen.

Reflect and Discuss

1. Why is it important to remember what Leon Morris says about Romans being written to ordinary Christians, not professional theologians?
2. What does our being made in the image of God have to do with friendships?
3. Consider how Paul knew and loved and worked with so many fellow Christians. What does this teach us about the Christian life?
4. What strikes you the most about all of these names and people? Why?
5. How does Paul show us the importance of females serving the body of Christ?
6. What is the basis for these friendships? What difference should this make in our cultivating and maintaining friendships in the church?
7. How does Paul honor these individuals?
8. How do we see the practice of hospitality emphasized?
9. What does Paul say about false teachers? Why is this significant?
10. What strikes you the most about Paul's doxology? Why?

WORKS CITED

Akin, Daniel. "The Epistle to Romans." Article available online at https://www.danielakin.com/wp-content/uploads/old/Resource_460/Romans.pdf. Accessed January 2, 2020.

———. *Exalting Jesus in Mark*. Christ-Centered Exposition Commentary. Nashville: B&H, 2014.

Augustine. *Confessions*. Translated with an Introduction and Notes by Henry Chadwick. New York: Oxford University Press, 1991.

Bird, Michael F. *Romans*. The Story of God Bible Commentary. Grand Rapids: Zondervan, 2016.

Bruce, F. F. *The Epistle of Paul to the Romans: An Introduction and Commentary*. Tyndale New Testament Commentaries. Grand Rapids: Eerdmans, 1963.

Burke, Trevor J. *Adopted into God's Family: Exploring a Pauline Metaphor*. Downers Grove, IL: InterVaristy Press, 2006.

Crowley, J. D., and Andy Naselli. *Conscience: What It Is, How to Train It, and Loving Those Who Differ*. Wheaton, IL: Crossway, 2016.

Ferguson, Sinclair. "Reality Check." Sermon available online at https://www.monergism.com/search?sort=created&order=asc&keywords=Sinclair%20ferguson%20Romans&format=25&f[0]=series%3A38954. Accessed 2019.

———. "A Single Debt and Some Essential Clothing." Sermon available online at https://www.monergism.com/series/exposition-romans-mp3-series-dr-sinclair-b-ferguson?page=2. Accessed October 12, 2020.

———. "His Transforming Spirit." Sermon available online at https://www.monergism.com/series/exposition-romans-mp3-series-dr-sinclair-b-ferguson?page=2. Accessed 2019.

———. "When God Gives Up." Sermon available online at https://www.monergism.com/search?sort=created&order=asc&keywords=Sinc

lair%20ferguson%20Romans&format=25&f[0]=series%3A38954. Accessed October 12, 2020.

———. "Without Excuse." Sermon available online at https://www .monergism.com/search?sort=created&order=asc&keywords =Sinclair%20ferguson%20Romans&format=25&f[0]=series%3A 38954. Accessed October 12, 2020.

Goswell, Gregory, and Peter Lau. *Unceasing Kindness: A Biblical Theology of Ruth.* Downers Grove, IL: InterVarsity Press, 2016.

Grudem, Wayne. *Systematic Theology: An Introduction to Biblical Theology.* Downers Grove, IL: InterVarsity Press, 1994.

Hughes, R. Kent. *Romans.* Preaching the Word. Wheaton, IL: Crossway, 1991.

Keller, Timothy. *Romans 1–7 for You.* Charlotte, NC: The Good Book Company, 2014.

———. "Spiritual Friendship." March 1, 1998. Gospel in Life. Sermon available online at https://gospelinlife.com/downloads/spiritual -friendship-6582. Accessed October 12, 2020.

Letham, Robert. *Union with Christ: In Scripture, History, and Theology.* Phillipsburg, NJ: P&R Publishing, 2011. Kindle.

Lewis, C. S. *The Four Loves.* In *The Inspirational Writings of C. S. Lewis.* New York: Harcourt, Brace and Company, 1994.

———. *Surprised by Joy.* New York: Harvest, 1955.

Longenecker, Richard N. *Romans.* The New International Greek Testament Commentary. Grand Rapids: Eerdmans, 2016.

Luther, Martin. *Romans.* Translated by J. Theodore Mueller. Grand Rapids: Kregel, 1954.

Moo, Douglas. *The Letter to the Romans.* The New International Commentary on the New Testament. Grand Rapids: Eerdmans, 1996.

———. *Romans.* NIV Application Commentary. Grand Rapids: Zondervan, 2000.

Morris, Leon. *The Epistle to the Romans.* The Pillar New Testament Commentary. Grand Rapids: Eerdmans, 1988.

Mounce, Robert H. *Romans.* New American Commentary. Nashville: B&H, 1995.

Oakes, Peter. *Reading Romans in Pompeii: Paul's Letter at Ground Level.* London: SPCK Publishing, 2009.

Owen, John. *A Commentary on Hebrews: A Classic Puritan.* An Exceptional Exposition. Kindle (No publisher noted, 2016).

————. *On the Mortification of Sin in Believers.* In *Overcoming Sin and Temptation,* edited by Justin Taylor and Kelly M. Kapic. Wheaton, IL: Crossway, 2015.

Packer, J. I. *Knowing God.* Downers Grove, IL: InterVarsity Press, 1993.

Peterson, David. *Commentary on Romans.* Biblical Theology for Christian Proclamation. Nashville: B&H, 2017.

Piper, John. "The Absolute Sovereignty of God: What Is Romans Nine About?" November 3, 2002. Desiring God. Sermon available online at https://www.desiringgod.org/messages/the-absolute -sovereignty-of-god. Accessed October 12, 2020.

————. "All Jews and Gentiles Are Under Sin." Desiring God. Sermon available online at https://www.desiringgod.org/messages/all-jews -and-gentiles-are-under-sin. Accessed October 12, 2020.

————. "A Holy Ambition." August 27, 2006. Desiring God. Sermon available online at https://www.desiringgod.org/messages/holy- ambition–2. Accessed October 12, 2020.

————. "John Newton: The Tough Roots of His Habitual Tenderness." January 30, 2001. Desiring God. Message available online at https:// www.desiringgod.org/messages/john-newton-the-tough-roots-of -his-habitual-tenderness. Accessed October 12, 2020.

————. "Joy + Debt = A Two-Thousand-Mile Detour to Jerusalem." September 10, 2006. Desiring God. Sermon available online at https://www.desiringgod.org/messages/joy-debt-a-two-thousand -mile-detour-to-jerusalem. Accessed October 12, 2020.

————. "Let God Be True though Every Man a Liar." March 7, 1999. Desiring God. Sermon available online at https://www.desiring- god.org/messages/let-god-be-true-though-every-man-a-liar. Desiring God. Accessed October 12, 2020.

————. "Resting and Wrestling for the Cause of Christ—Together." September 17, 2006. Desiring God. Sermon available online at https://www.desiringgod.org/messages/resting-and-wrestling-for -the-cause-of-christ-together. Accessed October 12, 2020.

————. "The Spirit Helps Us in Our Weakness, Part 1." May 26, 2002. Desiring God. Sermon available online at https://www.desiringgod .org/messages/the-spirit-helps-us-in-our-weakness-part-1. Accessed October 12, 2020.

————. "Subjection to God and Subjection to the State (Part 1)." June 12, 2005. Desiring God. Sermon available online at https://www

.desiringgod.org/messages/subjection-to-god-and-subjection-to
-the-state-part-1. Accessed October 12, 2020.

Ryken, Philip G. "C. S. Lewis the Evangelist." *Knowing and Doing*. Fall
2009. Article available online at http://www.cslewisinstitute.org
/CS_Lewis_the_Evangelist_page1. Accessed October 12, 2020.

Sailhamer, John H. *NIV Compact Bible Commentary*. Grand Rapids:
Zondervan, 1999.

Schreiner, Thomas R. *1 Peter*. New American Commentary. Nashville:
B&H, 2002.

———. "God Is for Us!" September 11, 2011. Clifton Baptist Church.
Sermon available online at https://www.cliftonbaptist.org/sermons
and-audio/sermon/2011-09-11/god-is-for-us. Accessed October 12,
2020.

———. "Grace That Conquers." October 31, 2010. Clifton Baptist
Church. Sermon available online at https://www.cliftonbaptist.org
/sermons-and-audio/sermon/2010-10-31/grace-that-conquers.
Accessed October 12, 2020.

———. "Proclaiming the Gospel to the Ends of the Earth." January 20,
2013. Clifton Baptist Church. Sermon available online at https://
www.cliftonbaptist.org/sermons-and-audio/sermon/2013-01-20
/proclaiming-the-gospel-to-the-ends-of-the-earth. Accessed October
12, 2020.

———. *Romans*. Baker Exegetical Commentary on the New Testament.
Grand Rapids: Baker, 1998.

———. "Romans 7 Does Not Describe Your Christian Experience."
The Gospel Coalition. January 13, 2016. Article available online
at https://www.thegospelcoalition.org/article/romans-7-does-not
-describe-your-christian-experience. Accessed October 12, 2020.

———. "The Saving and Judging Righteousness of God." July 11, 2010.
Clifton Baptist Church. Sermon available online at https://www
.cliftonbaptist.org/sermons-and-audio/sermon/2010-07-11/the
-saving-and-judging-righteousness-of-god. Accessed October 12,
2020.

Spurgeon, Charles. "High Doctrine and Broad Doctrine." January 1,
1970. The Spurgeon Center. Sermon available online at https://
www.spurgeon.org/resource-library/sermons/high-doctrine-and
-broad-doctrine#flipbook. Accessed October 12, 2020.

———. *Lectures to My Students*. Grand Rapids: Zondervan, 1954.

Stott, John. *The Message of Romans: God's Good News for the World.* Downers Grove, IL: InterVarsity Press, 1994.

Taylor, Justin. "Carson: What Is the Gospel?" Article available online at https://www.thegospelcoalition.org/blogs/justin-taylor/carson -what-is-gospel. Accessed October 12, 2020.

———. "Christ Is Praying for Those Who Are His." The Gospel Coalition. May 3, 2011. Article available online at https://www .thegospelcoalition.org/blogs/justin-taylor/christ-is-praying-for -those-who-are-his. Accessed January 2, 2020.

———. "5 Questions—5 Scholars: Paul's Letter to the Romans." The Gospel Coalition. March 19, 2019. Article available online at https:// www.thegospelcoalition.org/blogs/justin-taylor/5-questions-5 -scholars-pauls-letter-romans. Accessed October 12, 2020.

Vanhoozer, Kevin. *Hearers & Doers: A Pastor's Guide to Making Disciples Through Scripture and Doctrine.* Bellingham, WA: Lexham, 2019.

Whitney, Donald. "Think Much about Heaven." Biblical Spirituality. Article available online at https://biblicalspirituality.org/wp-content/uploads /2011/02/Think-Much-About-Heaven.pdf. Accessed October 12, 2020.

Wright, N. T. *Paul for Everyone: Romans, Part 1.* The New Testament for Everyone. Louisville: Westminster John Knox, 2011. Kindle.

———. *Paul for Everyone: Romans, Part 2.* The New Testament for Everyone. Louisville: Westminster John Knox, 2011. Kindle.

SCRIPTURE INDEX